D1180235

Reason and Faith in Modern Society

Reason and Faith
in
Modern Society

Liberalism, Marxism, and Democracy

By EDUARD HEIMANN

Wesleyan University Press · MIDDLETOWN, CONNECTICUT

HX
536
.H39

Copyright © 1961 by Wesleyan University

Although originally written in English, this book was first
published in German as *Vernunftglaube und Religion in
der Modernen Gesellschaft.*

Library of Congress Catalog Card Number: 61-6974
Manufactured in the United States of America
First Edition

Contents

78615

Preface

THIS BOOK was conceived, like two preceding ones, as a contribution to a "theology of society," in contrast to the conventional "sociology of religion." It is the latter in which the tendencies of today's social sciences culminate, because it subsumes religion under social phenomena and laws. A theory directed against the sociology of religion must then be, according to its very definition, a social theory too. This is true also of this book, in which methodological problems receive a fairly extensive treatment. (For a systematic presentation of this methodology, cf. the article "Christian Foundations of the Social Sciences," *Social Research,* Autumn 1959.) Some readers indeed, so soon as they see that the book takes religion as its starting point, will want to stop reading: if it is religious, then it plainly is not scientific. This book, however, is among those which argue that allegedly autonomous science rests on dogmatic—that is, unprovable—foundations, so that there is no difference in this respect, except that conventional science denies its dogmatic bond. A dogmatic bond, or in methodological language a dependence on fundamental hypotheses, is nothing but natural from our own point of view. Science cannot pull itself out of the dilemma of its own lack of presupposition by its own pigtail, like Munchausen. The question, dogma or no dogma, is erroneous.

We are far from denying that religion has fully deserved the disregard into which it has largely fallen in all Western countries. For generations its representatives have failed to shed the light of the faith upon the troubles of the times and to integrate the intellectual-spiritual discoveries of the times into the system of faith. It is only through such ever renewed "assimilation" (Henri de Lubac) of social and intellectual material that the unity of life can be preserved and the validity of faith demonstrated. As Christians fail in their task, contemporary society remains without guidance and runs into a blind alley; thereby it learns what it lacks. The description of this process fills large parts of our book. But the defect alone would not suffice for renewed insight if Christians themselves, put to shame by the poverty of their sermons, had not rediscovered and proclaimed the height and depth dimensions of their message. Deeply rooted in and committed to their time, steeled by constant wrestling with Marx, Nietzsche, and Freud, in a power of faith and wealth of ideas unknown for one hundred years, a generation of preachers and teachers after the First World War has disclosed new horizons. Will Christianity not preach again, however, an escape from the world into the Egyptian desert, or the erection of a Byzantine Empire or of a Puritan capitalism, or what else? But precisely because Christianity had been able, in unending metamorphoses, to achieve all this at its proper time, therefore it speaks to our time out of this time and its distress. This, too, our book tries to describe.

Hence Christian doctrine as a hypothesis of scientific thinking cannot curtly be rejected. Rather the decision between this hypothesis and the conventional one depends exclusively on the efficiency of either one in the analysis of the material problems. The proof of the pudding is in the eating. In this respect we contend that academic social science, because of its methodologically necessary narrowness, ignores the decisive events and problems of the present age, and that it discourages and must discourage the forces now active, since it must teach that all this is delusion. Unable to jump across the shadow of its own narrowness of method, it strives to cut the width of the social world down to its own reach. To sum it up in one sentence: Academic social science knows no theory of liberty. The wider scope of our own approach on the one hand permits and commands us to integrate into it the indispensable achievements of social science, but on the other hand our approach must be positively tested against the problems missed by social science, including e.g. the Marshall Plan and the emancipation of the colonial peoples. In other words, the truth of the Anselmian proposition "Credo ut intelligam" must be demonstrated.

The title of this book is a free adaptation of the title under which the German version appeared in 1955—*Vernunftglaube und Religion in der Modernen Gesellschaft.* This preface and some scattered passages throughout the book have been shortened by deletion of brief remarks which appear dated after six years. A few new additions are marked as such. The total of these changes is very small.

The German book of 1955 had been immediately preceded by another book, *Wirtschaftssysteme und Gesellschaftssysteme,* 1954 (*Economic Systems and Social Systems*), in whose preface the program of the theology of society was explicitly announced. The two books interlock insofar as "economic systems"—systems of life controlled by economic forces and objectives—are inspired by belief in reason; while "social systems"—which integrate and subordinate economic forces—feed upon religion. A rigorous *Social Theory of Economic Systems,* now in process of construction, is designed to replace the book of 1954 in its first and major parts.

An earlier book of 1947 had approached the same fundamental range of problems and had presented it as the ever renewed search for an equilibrium between *Freedom and Order.* In this light the disequilibria of the "economic systems"—individualism and collectivism—appeared as logically necessary, and so did their confrontation in history (p. 323). Most of the points which were made in that earlier book are not repeated in the present work.

I owe much gratitude to several friends. A good deal of what I learned from them is incorporated in the following pages. But I should like to record here that conversations with Werner Marx, Carl Mayer, and Reinhold Niebuhr in New York, and still more with Wilhelm Flitner in Hamburg, have helped me in the basic construction of the book.

Heinz-Dietrich Ortlieb in Hamburg, director of the Akademie fuer Gemeinwirtschaft, published the German book as one of the publications of the Akademie through the old and respected publishing house of J. C. B. Mohr, so that I could renew with the present head of the house, Mr. Hans-Georg Siebeck, the friendly relations which had connected me, twenty-five years

earlier, with his unforgotten father. Mr. Ortlieb's own critique
of gaps, overlappings, and obscurities has much benefited the
book.

Some pieces of the book had earlier appeared as articles. The
first part of the introduction is a new version of an article in
Christianity and Crisis, 1948. Chapter IV, except the newly
added last section, is an enlarged form of the article "The West
and the East," *Social Research,* March 1949. In Chapter V a few
pages are taken from a short article, "Marxism 1848–1948,"
Journal of Politics, August 1949. The first four sections of
Chapter VI had appeared under the same title, "Atheist Theocracy," in *Social Research,* Autumn 1953. Finally, in the first
four sections of Chapter VIII, the contribution "Rationalism,
Christianity, and Democracy" to *Synopsis, Festgabe fuer Alfred
Weber,* Edgar Salin ed., published by Lambert Schneider 1948,
has been used. I thank the editors and publishers of these publications for permission to reprint those articles. Their sum,
however, amounts to only a small fraction of the total volume
of the book.

The whole was rewritten from the first to the last line before
publication in German. The original manuscript was in English.

Reason and Faith in Modern Society

Introduction

The Vicious Circle of Faith in Reason

IN 1835 Alexis de Tocqueville, a young Frenchman who had recently returned from a study tour through the United States, completed the first volume of his report, which was to become the classic on American democracy. On the last page of the volume we find predicted that a hundred years later two giant states, based on the opposing political principles of liberty and force, would confront each other across the globe: the United States and Russia.

In 1850, from the extreme right of the political scene, came the voice of Donoso Cortes, the greatest theorist of the counter-revolution, predicting that liberal democracy would soon end in the deadlock of fruitless discussions between opposite interests and would give way to a terrible wave of revolutionary communism coming from Russia.[1] At the same time Karl Marx developed the same idea, although without reference to Russia.

These predictions, conceived in the framework of vastly different political philosophies, are not the only ones in the literature of the past on the approaching crisis of modern society. All such analyses were later summarized by Oswald Spengler, in words to which Karl Marx could have subscribed: "It is characteristic of the superficial way in which the whole white world thinks that Bolshevism is regarded as a Russian creation. Actually it was born in Western Europe, and born indeed of logical necessity as the last phase of the liberal democracy of 1770." [2] Those selected examples will suffice to make the point that there

1. Donoso Cortes, *The General Situation in Europe*, pp. 159–182 of his *Works* in the Spanish edition (Orti-Lara ed.). Available in French and German translations; no English translation.
2. Oswald Spengler, *The Hour of Decision*, 1934.

has been in modern history, within limits, a predictable logic of
events at work; that, in other words, history has generally obeyed
regularities.

Within limits: there always has been, and there is, ample
room for what we may call the contingencies of history, which
justify and require pragmatic piecemeal discussion. Such a discussion, however, unless qualified by and contained in the
framework of a more profound and comprehensive vision, is
misleading, because it suggests that the crisis is an accident, to
be attributed to our poor statesmanship and the wickedness of
our adversaries. The truth is less comfortable; it is that the Russians essentially are the negative replica of what we are. There
is little sense in blaming the Russians for their collectivism
unless it is first of all realized that it is we Western nations who
produced it. There is little sense indeed in blaming one's
shadow for being black. It is our corruption which drives people,
with the inexorable logic of history, to the opposite corruption.
If this had not happened in Russia, it would have happened
somewhere else in somewhat different form.

It is obvious that our corruption is the corruption of our
freedom. We place freedom supreme among the social values
and pride ourselves on defining by it our social and political
system.

There is much to justify our pride. Liberty, the inviolate
dignity of man created in the image of God, is the unique
achievement of the Western world, not matched anywhere else
at any time. It released rivers of creative forces that had been
lying dormant and ignorant of themselves; it thus transformed
deserts of the soul into fertile lands. It unfettered the power of
the human mind to cure the sick, save the mothers and their
little ones, and clean up squalor and misery. It gave the humble
a voice and made the rulers wary of their criticism. It permits a
new truth, whenever it pleases, to invade and conquer the body
politic and to demonstrate that human life continues to be
creative. If our freedom is to be criticized, this must be done
with a view to purifying and augmenting it.

If we could be sure that our freedom were the freedom of
the Christian conscience, everything would be all right. But

Christians know that man, far from being a pure incorporation of the Christian conscience, is liable to the seductions of greed and lust. This is particularly so in secular society, which disavows the Christian direction of brotherliness as its guide in the use of its freedom, and which interprets freedom as the freedom of private interest.

A secularized society, estranged from religion, is permeated by faith in rationality: people do not believe in the commandments of a higher power but assume that man can find the answers to the questions of his personal and social life in his own autonomous thinking. In its modern development this idea leads to the conviction that a thinking person will by and large act correctly, and he does act according to what he understands to be his interest. Freedom alone, not directed by Christian conscience, then becomes the freedom of the strong at the expense of the weak; in a commercial civilization, the freedom of property rather than of man. As a result we have social injustice, economic disorder, and, to clinch the superior freedom of the strong, the outrage of racialism. Economic freedom makes the strongest dominant in the world, and the white race rounds it out by racial discrimination against the colored, thus keeping them weak. This is the perversion of our freedom.

It is possible, then, to define our defense of freedom as a defense of the things we have come to understand by freedom: our privileges. This statement is not quite fair, and it will be qualified immediately. And it is decidedly unfriendly; but there is no reason why in the discussion of moral principles we should be friendly rather than unfriendly to ourselves. If we then define Western democracy as freedom with the implication of social and racial inequality, it follows that our shadow, the Soviet Union, is to be defined as social and racial equality minus freedom or plus tyranny. The Soviet Union is worse than we are, to be sure; but it is our product. This is how the terrible logic of history works, and the shadow gets stronger as a more glaring light is shed on us.

Now the two opposite systems are connected in historical logic because they rest on a common foundation, the belief in the autonomy and self-sufficiency of the human mind. It is this supreme tribunal to which both appeal in their dispute. But precisely because this common foundation is so much a matter of course for both, as if it were pure nature, the consciousness of the two concentrates on the things by which they are separated: free pursuit of private interests on the one side, egalitarian solidarity on the other. These indeed are mutually exclusive opposites. But it is the identical belief in reason which recommends to the strong the free pursuit of their private interests and to the many weak their interest in egalitarian solidarity. The one conclusion is as logical as the other; the two are irreconcilable brothers. A war between brothers is the worst war. The cleavage in a world united by the belief in reason is the tragedy of our time. It is the problem of our book.

It is not fair to say that all our freedom is perverted into privilege. Because it is not, it is possible for us to have much genuine freedom preserved. Tired as the people are, they normally leave the field to the lords of the party machines, of the press, and of the radio, who do their thinking for them. But when the people awaken, as they did in the emergency of crisis and war in the 1930's, they can and do assert their will. The years of crisis and war will go down in history as the heroic age of recent democracy, with the people forcing on the lords of public opinion the leadership of Franklin Roosevelt, Wendell Willkie, and Fiorello LaGuardia in the United States, of Winston Churchill and Stafford Cripps in England.

The Soviet regime, on the other hand, cannot be simply put down as pure Marxism, a reaction to Western shortcomings which happens to be located in Russia. What gives Marxism its power is Holy Russia, a vast and populous country with a colorful historical tradition, just as it is Marxism which gives that enormous power and vitality a specific direction. The two are by no means identical, but they are not distinct either; there is a natural convergence of Russian authoritarian and anti-Western anti-individualism as proclaimed by Dostoevski and Western anti-individualism of the Marxist variety. That Marxism came to power in Russia is among the contingencies of history, although even this coincidence has been in the making long enough to be predicted by Cortes.

Within this combination, however, the Russians developed even more lawlessness and cruelty than would be required for them to realize the (dialectical) program of tyrannical equality. They shot and hanged their critics and invariably slandered their memory as Fascists. Or even worse, they made them disappear in all countries under their control. Even children disappeared, never to be heard from again.

Equality under despotism does not have in itself that self-regenerating, self-correcting power with which a system of liberty, even of unequal liberty, makes us free to reorganize and perfect our freedom. (This crucial aspect of freedom will be discussed at some length later in this book.) In the system of equality under despotism there is much grave inequality, the inequality between the common people and the millions of functionaries in the hierarchy of despotism itself. The more glaring this deviation from original utopian expectations becomes, the more it is officially explained as required by the soundness of the structure itself—that is, by the interests of the governed. This makes the inequality only more rigid and more humiliating, in contrast to the inequalities in our system of liberty, which are at least unofficial and are considered more or less fortuitous. Nevertheless it would be dangerously misleading to infer that there is no equality in Russia, or no appeal in it. The vast majority of mankind has never known either liberty or equality, and Soviet Russia promises to them the destruction of discrimination, the equality of opportunity which brings even the highest position in the hierarchy of despotism within reach of anybody, regardless of ethnic, racial, religious, or social background.

The Russians are fanatics of their utopia. We are utopians too, but without fanaticism. We believe that individual freedom and its incorporation in political democracy is capable of solving all problems. The Russians believe that the stern rule of social and racial equality under dictatorship will in the end solve all problems. Reinhold Niebuhr is right indeed in saying that ours is the soft utopia and theirs the hard one.

But important as it is to see this, it is even more important to see it only as a qualification of the fundamental fact that the

two utopias are connected causally, that the Russians live on
our perversion by perverting it a second time. If Western democracy had not tended to pervert freedom into privilege, the
Russians could never dare to offer their equality under tyranny
as a higher form of democracy.

Soviet equality is not higher in any sense than Western freedom. The Marxist form of the dialectic, which is the Soviet
creed, believes that proletarian dictatorship is higher because it
emerges later and is the very product of liberal freedom. In a
strictly progressive development, that which is later must be
higher on this sole ground. Now the goal which Marx had in
mind—although he was far from understanding it—was the
community of the free, a synthesis of individualism and collectivism, which indeed must be something higher than either
one.[3] The Russians, however, following Marx's own lead, merely
substitute collectivism for individualism, equality for liberty as
the opposite on the same plane; a later but not in human terms
a higher form.

The previous principle of personal liberty arose with small
property, which in the Jeffersonian vision of democracy was not
at all designed to serve as a vehicle of commercial and industrial
progress but as a vessel of social equality and stability. The
transformation of property, which made possible and which
organized the tremendous rise of industry, is not favorable to
the principle of personal liberty. Big property is a form of
domination and stands side by side with personal and social serfdom of the masses in many countries of the world—the liberty
of the strong side by side with the serfdom of the weak. But just
as private property is far from guaranteeing the personal liberty
of nonowners, so the class interest of the nonowners may perhaps aim at their collective class property but certainly not at
personal liberty. It is not permitted to believe in automatic
progress.

The dialectic of recent history, hence, is something totally

3. Marx went so far as to define socialism as "restoring individual
property on the basis of . . . cooperation and the common possession of
the earth and . . . the means of production" (*Kapital,* I, p. 834 of the
Modern Library Giant edition). See Chapter VI of this book.

different from the Marxist dialectic. If progress is presupposed, as in Marxism, the later step must resolve the conflict of the preceding step; that is, the community of the free must result from and must resolve the conflict between bourgeois liberty and proletarian equality. If, however, one perversion merely engenders the opposite perversion on the same plane, the two reinforcing each other and hardening in the conflict, then we are caught in a vicious circle without outlet. Instead of a dialectic of progress, we have a dialectic of doom.

Liberty and equality, individualism and socialism, the person and the community, must not be torn apart. Between them they determine the world of man. Their union is something higher than either one and can be achieved only on a higher plane, from which both are derived. In Occidental history both are derived from, because they are contained in, Christianity. If so united, liberty and equality, individualism and socialism, the person and the community, protect each other from corruption.

But if torn apart and located at opposite poles, between them they still continue to determine the world. In the belief in rationality and the resulting calculation of interests, either the strong individual or the egalitarian solidarity of the weak is the supreme principle: the belief in rationality tears the world asunder instead of uniting it. Their conflict—for which there is no solution on their own plane, the plane of organization—drives the world to its doom. It is in this conflict that their essential unity manifests itself to those who tear them apart.

It is we who have torn them apart. Collectivist tyranny may be worse than the perversion of liberty into social and racial privileges. But collectivist tyranny is only the response, the effect. It is liberal democracy which, oblivious of man's temptations, proclaimed the sovereign freedom of private interest, sacrificed Jeffersonian equality, and enhanced the individual over the community, thus perverting both. Now the judgment is at hand.

It is necessary to contain the tyranny. It is necessary to preserve freedom in order that it can be developed. On these pragmatic points there is agreement.

But there is no fundamental agreement. It makes all the dif-

ference whether one does those things with a good and elated
conscience—such as can be derived even from the argument that
we are bad but the Russians are worse, so that the right is on
our side—or whether one realizes that, however bad the Russians
may be, they are the harvest of what our badness has sown; they
are the whirlwind but we have sown the wind. Never was there
more reason for contrition, for fear and trembling in our every
step. This is what the dialectic teaches us. It teaches us that our
perversion of freedom, the sundering of freedom from equal
justice and of the individual from the community, is not inci-
dental to the present tension but is the very hub around which
everything rotates. And that this tension and mortal danger are
essentially the punishment for, as they are the result of, our sins.

But by the same token, they also are our opportunity. We are
indeed free to ignore the opportunity and drift toward the doom
in which alone the vicious circle can find its logical resolution.
But we also are free to rise to a new level of thought and action
which would permit us to resolve the conflict in a new creation.
For our freedom, however much misunderstood and abused,
always includes the freedom to perfect our freedom. This is the
essence of liberty: that man can rise above himself and can build
a new life on a higher plane with a new outlook. The fatal circle
in which we are caught cannot be broken through on its own
level, but it can be resolved on a higher plane.

Are we still capable of the spiritual and moral strength required to lift ourselves above the plane of the conflict? The
question is fraught with destiny: not only the ethical judgment
but also the historical result of the present crisis will depend
on the answer. There is indeed nothing to justify a hope for an
early and easy solution of a crisis which has been smoldering for
one hundred years. But nevertheless there now is, after years of
despair, some ground for the hope that the Western world still
possesses the freedom from itself, the strength for self-renewal,
and has begun to prove it by historical achievements. Such
achievements appear in concrete technical form and must assert
themselves by virtue of this form; but they change the perspective.

We must know where we stand and where we should go. In

these perplexing times orientation and perspective are not easily gained. We must try to understand how we got caught in the pernicious circle, and which creative resources we still find at our disposal. It is these two questions which our book is designed to help clarify.

Problem and Terminology

The thesis which this book is designed to corroborate is simple. Society is constituted and held together by religion; the belief in reason splits society and is incapable of healing it. We aver, and shall attempt to prove, that the two conflicts—the one between religious faith and the belief in reason, the other inherent in the belief in reason itself—have dominated the life of modern society, that is, the life of white mankind, during the last three or four centuries; and that without an understanding of this dual conflict even its most massive phenomena of power politics and economic interests remain ultimately unintelligible.

But more accurately: we believe that the life of society is history; that is, it consists in change and cannot properly be understood by the scientific ascertaining of regularities because the framework in which these regularities proceed is itself subject to change and changes them too. This fundamental change is, according to our thesis, the gradual supersession of religion by the belief in reason—in other words, the gradual secularization of society. Modern society, according to a universally accepted definition, is secularized society, as opposed to religious society; we prefer, however, the expression "belief in reason" despite certain inherent difficulties, because "secularization" denotes the consequence and "belief in reason" the cause.

But belief in rationality obviously is not in exclusive contrast to religion, because it still is belief, not unbelief. Complete unbelief hardly exists at all, except perhaps in a few scattered individual cases without historical significance. Much more important, however, is the fact that the belief in reason originally arises from the religion which it then gradually supersedes, and that it takes over from its religious origin many more elements of thinking and faith than it likes to acknowledge in its later emancipated form. The thesis which we mean to prove is that these religious elements constitute and preserve society; that their retention permits the belief in rationality, as a real faith, to serve as the foundation of a living society, at least provisionally. V. A. Demant says correctly that the secularists consider and respect as the nature of man what in reality is the product of religious tradition.[4] It follows immediately, however, that, if the secularists have treated as nature what was tradition, tradition really petered out because it was not explicitly cultivated and renewed. In the end, then, secular society presents itself purified of religious residues and hence without the spiritual power to secure the further cohesion between people. Thus white society finds itself in a world civil war,[5] which splits all nations because there is no longer a faith binding upon all.

Hence our later discussion will proceed in two parts. If we want to know whether society can live with a belief in reason purged of traditional religious elements, this is apparently as unrealistic, hypothetical, and abstract an enterprise as the "purge" itself; the reality which is subjected to this theoretical purge is obviously permeated by religious elements. But the purged presentation is the mirror of what our secularists hope for programmatically, and it is becoming more realistic every day through the success of these aspirations to the extent that the religious inheritance is really consumed or expelled. Therefore the abstraction worked out in the first three chapters of this book is by no means of purely academic interest. On the other hand, the more complete presentation explores the traditional admixture to the program of rationality and tries to ascertain how much in historical reality is due to those admixtures and threatens progressively to vanish in the progressive purge. Our contention then is that white mankind, to a far higher degree than it realizes and would like to think, lives on its Christian inheritance and would become extinct with it.[6]

4. V. A. Demant, *Religion and the Decline of Capitalism,* 1952.
5. This striking expression was coined by Max Ascoli, who has used it repeatedly in the magazine *The Reporter.*
6. At this point originates our conflict with the Humanists, to whom we owe so much in other respects. For their most sublime minds are in-

The complexity of the element "belief" in the term "belief in reason" is not thereby exhausted. Not only does the old faith live a fairly long and vigorous life in the new form of rationality, but precisely by wrestling with the old religion reason rises to the dignity of a kind of counterreligion, with the claim to give a comprehensively valid explanation of the world and the place of man in it. "Belief in reason," hence, in the earlier case seems to suggest the dragging along of the old religious ballast in the new rational thinking; in the more recent case, however, it suggests the religious sanction of rational thought itself as it sets out to give the death blow to the old religion. The main example of this latter case would then be Marxism. But it is precisely Marxism which shows—and must be presented to show—that that distinction does not hold. For in the first place, the enhancement of rational thinking into counterreligion transcends the limits of mere rational thinking and revalidates the ancient forms of religious thought, however grossly distorted. From our point of view this is logical because of the narrowness of mere rational thinking, and it is what happens in reality. And in the second place, Marxism does not penetrate a vacuum in Russia but invades a space full of an ancient and colorful Christian tradition; that is, the official Marxist counterreligion lives in a kind of symbiosis with the Christian religion, fighting it or using it or bending it—and this once more is our point of view.

Hence problems of the religious element of faith in the concept "belief in reason" are problems of substance and must be carefully analyzed in this book. It is far more difficult, however, to account in a brief introduction for the terms "reason" and "rationality" in the concepts "belief in reason," "belief in rationality."

capable of understanding their own spiritual existence as the fruit of the Christian struggle for the enhancement of spiritual over political life. It is striking that the great Burckhardt, son of a Reformed minister and professor of a venerable humanist university, in his treatise on "Historical Greatness" (*Force and Freedom,* Chapter V) accords this honorary title, among all Christian "hierarchs," only to the first Gregory, with special reference to the fact that in his dealings with other bishops he did not act as their superior, while even the tragic giant figure of Gregory VII is excluded from the list of honor, nay, is characterized as "pert." Cf. on the latter Eugen Rosenstock-Huessy, *Out of Revolution,* 1938.

For we designate by these concepts a fairly well-marked attitude which opposes itself to the Jewish-Christian faith in a living God, despite those transitions and admixtures, and tends to oppose that faith more violently, the more it purifies itself of the admixtures. We mean by those names the attitude of a secularized society; we mean that which we can correctly call "rational autonomy." The great difficulty now is that "rational autonomy" or "the attitude of a secularized society" on the one hand, and "belief in reason" on the other hand, do not necessarily coincide and are therefore not unequivocally opposed to religion as the historical alternative which is our problem. We do not blame those to whom the alternative between religion and belief in reason appears unequivocal and complete; to such readers, what follows in this introduction is irrelevant and they may skip it. It is merely intended to avoid misunderstandings which might arise from the interlacing of philosophical terms, for our use of terms is not guided by the history of philosophy but by everyday language in its use of the words "reason" and "rationality." But then there is indeed the danger of misunderstanding.

In the history of philosophy and under its influence in the terminology especially of non-German countries, "belief in reason" means on the one hand something much more narrow than "rational autonomy," but reaches on the other hand into the religious sphere to which it is meant to be the opposite and alternative. This latter point becomes obvious as soon as we replace the phrase "belief in reason" by the word "rationalism." For Catholic doctrine in its more or less official Thomistic form claims to be rational, since God, as in Aristotle, appears as supreme reason, transcending indeed man's reason but standing in continuity with it. A concept of reason thus extended beyond human limits to include the suprarational is not what we mean.

On the other hand, however, what we call belief in rationality—the attitude of "rational autonomy" characteristic of secularized society—includes many things opposed to rationalism in the history of philosophy: naturalism, empiricism, sensualism, materialism, pragmatism, etc. For in the history of philosophy, rationalism is the name of the doctrine which holds

that the forms of human reason constitute reality, so that thinking man appears as the master or despot of reality, while all
those other accesses to the problem of the human mind have this
in common—that the active force is supposed to act upon the
human mind from outside. We are far from denying the importance of this distinction and of all the more special differences
between the schools of thought; but we do say that they are
irrelevant in comparison with the historically fundamental
distinction between a society intentionally Christian and one
consciously unreligious. For all of them, not just the rationalism
of philosophical terminology, have in common a faith in the
self-sufficient mind of man, and they all are thus arrayed in a
common front vis-à-vis the religious principle that man's mind
is not self-sufficient.

The fact that this unity far outweighs the philosophical differences within the group can be seen, among other things, from
the premise common to empiricism and pragmatism with rationalism in presupposing the active and self-sufficient nature of
man's mind, which not only receives impressions but works
upon them positively and answers them positively. The animal
receives the same impressions but does not work upon them
scientifically or technically, while the religious mind takes things
as God's and understands itself as in God's hand.

More particularly, pragmatism presents things and problems
to confront man without preconceived ideas and deals with them
piecemeal according to the merits of the case; but this procedure
presupposes that difficulties can always be solved by reorganizing
things piecemeal. Never does it occur to a pragmatist that experimenting reason might be incapable of solving the problem,
if e.g. the problem is one of failing social morality rather than of
social engineering. The self-sufficiency of the human mind, its
rational autonomy, is here presupposed exactly as in rationalism.
Hence our program demands no distinction between the different schools of thought. What here matters is the "modernity" of
them all; i.e. their unity in the thus defined belief in the self-
sufficiency of the human mind through its reason.

In the 1920's Paul Tillich in a religious booklet [7] spoke of a

7. Paul Tillich, *The Religious Situation*, 1931; German original, 1926.

self-sufficient finitude as opposed to a finitude transparent so as to point beyond itself. In a treatise on social science we cannot use this term. But it accurately designates what we circumscribe as the attitude of a secularized society, or what we term correctly but without symbolic power "rational autonomy"; or what, with a vigorous phrase from which we hope to have removed possible misunderstandings, we call "belief in reason."

PART ONE

Individualism Frustrated

* I *

Individualism and Individuality

Individualism and Liberty

THE starting point of this book, as suggested in the introduction, is a double relationship between liberty and equality in the modern understanding of these words, or between the two giant states which incorporate them. On the one hand, the two systems have a common ground, a common root; they do not find themselves in the same world by sheer historical accident. But on the other hand, they interpret and apply that which basically unites them in different and opposite ways. Their relationship, thus, is not simply one of conflict, but of conflict within the basic unity of modern society. Thoughtful and educated outsiders, such as East Indians, are quite prone to consider the entire problem a family quarrel in which they themselves have no direct stake, however much they realize that they will be affected by the outcome.

The fundamental concept of modern white society is that of reason. By making reason and the sciences created by reason the guides in the building of society, the modern age is distinguished from preceding ages as well as from contemporary non-Western society. And it is the recognition of scientific reason as the guide in social life which fundamentally unites West and East, the libertarian and equalitarian wings of modern society. The criteria of reason as the guide, and of public earthly welfare as the objective, which are accepted by both wings, would be acceptable to an East Indian only with strong qualifications. Without in any way belittling the frightful nature of the conflict, one may say that to the Eastern wing of rationalist society the rationality of the Western wing simply does not go far enough, while to the latter the former goes too far. The difference is that liberal democracy is to the Marxist only the first tentative step in the career of social reason, while to the democrat it is the one all-important and final achievement, however incomplete for the time being and however in need of further perfection in the light of the criteria. The criterion of scientific reason is in principle accepted by both. In sum, modern society claims to find in human nature, which includes human reason, a purely immanent basis for its life. The enlightened pursuit of enlightened interests—differently interpreted by the successive phases of modern history but underlying them all—is supposed to be sufficient for the life of society and to make any conscious relation of man to the supreme moral power superfluous. This is what we define as "social rationalism."

Reason and its scientific condensation and elaboration have been made the foundation of man's life because they were trusted to give life that unambiguous, unquestionable direction which religion had signally failed to produce. The acrimony of religious dissension, rooted in opposite dogmatic interpretations and culminating in religious persecutions and wars, had naturally made people suspicious of religion as their guide in life. For whatever the power of the appeal to religious dogma or speculation, it lacked the logically compelling nature which seemed to distinguish undogmatic scientific reason, and the still greater intellectual security which the mind gains from scientific methods of verifying experience. Science has to do with the tangible and palpable, religion with the spiritual, the "things unseen," the religious commandment or the Aristotelian speculation; that is why there was originally between them a shift of emphasis rather than antagonism and exclusiveness. Religion was not disputed but left alone as attention concentrated on science. But a truly scientific foundation of the life of man and society had to be couched in tangible and measurable terms, for the sake of the mental security which here directly constitutes social peace.

In quest of the palpable and measurable from which to build a scientific understanding of society—rather than of the Christian love of neighbor or the Aristotelian friendship between citizens—we are led to the massive interests which motivate people's actions. It is a trivial and certainly indisputable fact that man uses his intellect to serve his welfare. The power of material interests in society is anything but a new discovery; Greek political philosophy always speaks of the conflict of interest between the rich and the poor, and Biblical prophets and preachers from Amos to James use unmistakably sociological categories. What is new in the modern scientific approach is the exclusiveness of the emphasis on these interests of individuals and groups, the claim that they are not merely a powerful element but the very essence of social life. If this radical doctrine emerged only gradually, it was nonetheless the logical outcome of the new emphasis on the tangible and verifiable. Scientific criticism became more and more aggressive against spiritual claims and ended by disputing any spiritual, irreducible reality altogether, on the ground that only that on which science can put its fingers is real.

No doubt, life in society satisfies many vital needs. Following the ancient Epicureans, Hobbes and Rousseau go so far as to trace the very existence of society to a "social contract" between free isolated individuals for the promotion of those massive interests. It is true that only relatively few interpreters make society the product of as deliberate an action as a contract; but practically all explain society as a community of interests even though spontaneously grown. This, then, is the scientific approach to social life, the self-understanding of modern society; the society is reduced to its underlying tangible and measurable interests.

It is in such terms of material interest that the two antagonistic principles of liberty and equality, the programmatic values of the two antagonistic systems of state today, must be understood. Liberty can in principle and did in history mean many different, more or less related things. In a Christian understanding of life, e.g., it is generally understood to mean the liberty of the Christian conscience. But the modern world interprets itself as a world of interests, and its liberty as a man's freedom to pursue his interests as best he can. In other words, the libertarian system is a system in which the individual is supreme in the pursuit of his interests—the system called individualism. Likewise equality could mean various though related things. In the world of interests it must mean the suppression of that liberty which

could produce inequality because of differences in people's
physical or intellectual or financial strength. Then, however,
the separate spheres of responsibility of the individuals must be
merged into one collective sphere, with inequalities reduced to
that which the collective interest seems to require for the operation of its system. Individualism and collectivism are the two
systems in which the principles of liberty and equality are incorporated. The modern world, then, is one which uses scientific
reason as its guide and material welfare as its objective. In this
framework, it is divided between individualism and collectivism.

There are essentially two areas in which the spiritual significance of a social system is to be tested. What does that system do
to man himself? What does it do to the relationship between
man and man and to the relationship between man and the
whole of the community? In addressing ourselves to the first of
these two questions we can anticipate the answer: Whosoever
will save his life shall lose it (Matt. 16:25). In other words, individualism, the search of the self-realization of the individual,
ruins individuality.

Individualism and Technology

Nothing is more significant to the life of man than the work
he does. This is not an economic interpretation of life, in which
work would be the means to the end of living. Work is here
understood as an end in itself, as that which claims most of man's
waking time and must be human if his life is to be human. For
he lives on the goods he makes, but he lives in making them.

That he does so is largely forgotten in this age. Man tries to
escape from work by shortening the workday; and the general
attitude is that life begins where work ends. This attitude ignores the real meaning of work, which is man's creative activity,
that in which his essential nature as creator, as spirit, reveals itself. No other animal creates new things of kinds which were
not there before; man alone does that. Yet this creative urge,
this instinct of workmanship, man's pride through thousands of
years, seems to have evaporated from the life of the individual
in this very age of individualism, and to be more and more con-

centrated in collective work, or in more concrete terms, in the inventors, engineers, and technical and financial organizers. The tight discipline of the machine leaves no margin of creative freedom to the working individual. No wonder that people try to escape a work which is not theirs.

Werner Sombart, the historian of capitalism, has defined the precapitalist medieval setup as keeping man in the center of the process of production, while in modern technology the central position is occupied by the machine. That is, man's tools in the age of craftsmanship served him and were used by him, while the machine is not the worker's tool but all too frequently his rival and conqueror and, in regard to productive operations, his master, to whose motion and pace he has to accommodate himself. The craftsman's tools are designed to increase the stength and reach of his arm in making the product; the machine is substituted for man's arm in making the product, but it requires the service of man's arm for its operation. The roles are clearly reversed.

Medieval technique was man-centered not simply for lack of technical knowledge; it was deliberately kept man-centered when alternatives began to offer themselves. Not all technical improvements were rejected; within craftsmanship, vast progress in refinement and efficiency was achieved, as witnessed by the tremendous upsurge of economic and cultural life during the last centuries of the Middle Ages. Yet man's position in the center of the process was jealously guarded, not only against primitive machines but also against their forerunner and pathbreaker, a too narrow specialization of skills. Men knew, of course, that specialization increased productivity, both by saving time between different operations with different equipment and by perfecting the skill in performing any one operation. Tanning and shoemaking were regarded as naturally different trades. But the suggestion that the quantity of shoes could be increased by a specialization where one trade might make uppers, another might make soles, and a third might fit the two together into a shoe, would have been indignantly rejected. It was to remain a man's right to produce a whole well-shaped shoe, to which he could point in modest pride as the work of his personal art and industry. No division of labor, however productive, could be allowed to break up this human unity of work.

In order for a piece of work to be human, it must provide the worker with certain opportunities. Only romanticists can dream of a state where drudgery is completely banished from work and pure joy remains; the Biblical injunction precludes that. Life is not simply joy, nor can work be so if work is to be a legitimate part of life. In life there are aspiration, suspense, and success; but there is success only against the background of possible defeat and at the cost of sweat. Personal failure must be of consequence, otherwise victory is not. There are in life association, comradeship, and rivalry. There are the respect of the community and the self-respect which goes with it, but they reward only achievement and shun failure. Work is human if it makes these experiences accessible to the worker. A craftsman's trade may be a modest one; but his mastership in it gives him dignity.

No failure of this age is more serious than that it has emptied the worker's life of its meaning, in which lies that dignity. Mechanization does precisely this; it precludes aspiration, failure, and success. It does so in the interest of productivity, of efficiency in the process of production, and with the most spectacular success in raising the standard of living and, still more, the standard of health. The benefits of all this are by no means withheld from the worker. As a consumer he benefits by his degradation as a producer. And that he does so benefit as a consumer is the stock justification of the process in the judgment of our time.

Far be it from us to disparage the technical point of view and the consumer's interest in it. It, too, is indispensable to a full understanding of man's dignity; the Bible itself enjoins man to subject the earth and make it subservient to his needs. No spiritual dignity can be preserved or developed where wretched misery and disease break the body. One of the greatest contributions of American democracy, least understood by European intellectual and cultural conceit, is precisely the mass-production industries, whose productivity enables the common man to rise above hunger, cold, and disease and to partake of the things which make external life easier and healthier.

Moreover, there is no reason to assume that the problem of the machine should be insoluble in itself. From the havoc which, like an untamed river, an unregulated overriding technological development has wrought, one cannot conclude that this development cannot be regulated. The one thing which such regulation would require is a society aware of the problem and of its own power in principle to solve it. That the problem is soluble can be seen from the fact that we have begun to solve it. No one who has ever seen a modern power plant can doubt that this is the perfection of the machine, where both man and the machine come into their own, with the workers walking around in white aprons like surgeons, reading meters and turning switches whenever necessary, but doing something indispensable and of high qualification and responsibility even when they turn no switches. They clearly are the machine's lords, supervisors, guardians, if necessary its understanding friends and doctors. No one can complain that these workers are degraded, even though their new type of work is worlds apart from the medieval type; it is specifically modern.

This possible perfection of the machine being a reality, however limited in scope, the question why it has been so woefully missing and thrust aside in most of industrial history only becomes more urgent. The answer lies in the connection between productivity and profit. A technological improvement which increases productivity by increasing output per unit of labor or by reducing cost per unit of output does add to profit. The saved margin of cost either accrues to profit directly if the sales price is approximately unchanged, or it improves the position of the pioneering firm in the competitive race by permitting it to underbid its rivals and expand its market at their expense. Contrariwise, the workers are assumed to work as hard as possible anyway, in the interest of their wages; so no rise in productivity and no profit are expected from a rearrangement of production which might increase the satisfaction experienced in their jobs by the workers. The consumers' interest in productivity—more and cheaper goods—thus wins out over the workers' interest in satisfaction, because the former can and the latter supposedly cannot serve as a vehicle to profit.

The rise in living and health standards is the extraordinary achievement of the system of free enterprise. There may be other ways to such progress; in the country of free enterprise itself, huge construction projects of world fame have been realized under public management. But it remains true that the way of higher productivity had not been found before free enterprise in search of profit discovered it. On the other hand, there are other and often more dubious avenues to profit than progress in productivity, and the history of capitalism as a whole is not too savory. It remains true, however, that the spectacular rise of private wealth in the age of capitalism is only a minor concomitant of a far more spectacular rise in productivity—that is, in living and health standards.

This appears as the most impressive confirmation of the theory of preordained harmony between private profit and public good, the theory underlying the system of free enterprise. But there is here some reasoning in a circle. Private profit and public good coincide to the extent that the things on which they do not coincide—the cost in nonmaterial human values—are excluded from consideration; they are made to coincide by way of amputation. In the end, only quantity is counted—quantity of goods for the consumers including the workers, and quantity of profit for the entrepreneur. The workers as workers do not count. Nonquantitative considerations are branded as irrational—that is, as unworthy of thinking persons. The modern idea of progress disregards a grave loss in life and happiness.

Now the startling thing is that it would be utterly misleading to present the workers as victims and to blame the process on capitalist greed. While the active incentive for technological and organizational change is indeed provided by the profit motive, the effect is emphatically accepted and approved by the workers; it is the very prototype of what they praise as progress. For, whatever this progress may do to them as workers, as consumers they benefit alongside of everybody else in individualist society, and their standards of living and health appear fantastic to members of other societies and are the objects of admiration and envy.

Moreover, the Marxist interpretation of the workers' "real," "correctly understood" class interest teaches that this type of progress makes the collective rule of the working class ultimately imperative and inevitable because the monopoly phase, the old age of capitalism, stifles progress by suppressing competition and securing profit from the sheltered position of monopoly. This is altogether erroneous; if anything, progress accelerates under monopoly capitalism, as all statistics of the growth of the American national income confirm. But the erroneous Marxist criticism of monopoly leaves no doubt as to the ideological identification of labor with technical progress. And like the Marxist theory, so the Soviet practice would never admit the logical possibility of conflict between the consumers' interest in more goods and the dignity of work. The collectivist point of view is simply in the worker's service to the rising standard of living and the growth of Soviet power.

At the same time the reality of the laborer's life increasingly demonstrates the threat to the stability of man's mind through emptiness, and the threat to the stability of society through the restlessness of those rooted nowhere. That these facts are not even known to labor itself—they were to Karl Marx— clinches the argument on the degradation of man.

Individualism and the Market

If labor becomes a tool to efficiency, what about the bourgeoisie? After all, it is their rise of which the degradation of labor is the reverse side. It is independent individual action on the part of owners and managers which introduces the new type of work and the concomitant type of man. It is profit which should enable the recipients to build their lives more independently, more fully, more personally. Collectivism at the bottom of society would thus justify and reinforce the individualism at the top which organizes it and is its first beneficiary. The free person, independent through property, proud of his productive achievement, open to ideas and values, hopeful for broader welfare through greater productivity, a strict disciplinarian but a tremendous worker himself, modest in livelihood because devoting his growing wealth to the expansion of production rather than to luxury consumption—this is the type of man which individualism has in mind. But it has not worked out that way because of the exigencies of efficiency.

That formidable effort such as this should require much concentration of time and mental energy cannot be held against the system; efficiency naturally is a stern master. What is surprising is the fact that the very institution which makes this stern rule all-pervasive and compulsory—the market—should be presented as a specific form and unique guarantee of personal liberty. The famous argument of F. A. Hayek (in his *The Road to Serfdom*) runs that the free market is like a system of roads which every passenger uses to travel to his own personal goal, while every public intervention tends to lead to a planned economy which is like telling people where to go. Any non-market organization of economic life requires agreement on or submission to objectives and valuations—we must approve, or must be made to accept, that these bricks be used to build a church or a factory or an apartment house—while in the market organization people need agree only on means, not on ends: they must divide the available supply of bricks between themselves and their respective aims, but they owe each other no statement as to whether they want to build a church or a factory or an apartment house. Life in society always requires some consensus and conformity; conformity on ends is the mark of centralized rule, agreement on mere means of the social process leaves the ends undetermined and abandons the choice of them to the free decisions of the individuals within the means at their disposal.

This argument mistakes the logical distinction between means and ends for a psychological fact. It ignores that means sought at great effort and peril become psychological ends and push the original ends into the background. It ignores that science may be substituted for truth, church organization for religion, and war for peace in the minds of those in charge of means. It ignores that the intensity of the quest for money, goods, or power may ruin any sense of ultimate values or personal happiness which those means are supposed to serve. For the quest of efficiency and expediency is forced on all participants by the intensity of the modern dynamic market. Everybody has to comply if he is to survive; the ubiquity of the market struggle produces a new, efficiency-minded, and thereby standardized type of man—a man interested only in quantities because he is interested only in means. The transformation of society into one big market, the control even of cultural, literary, and scholarly activities and publications by commercial considerations, perverts spiritual life and dehumanizes and collectivizes the man of modern society who is supposed to seek in the market nothing but material means for his spiritual self-realization—how absurd. Individualism ruins individuality.[1]

Technology and the market do their work and achieve their goals, in Hegel's phrase, "behind the backs" of the people engaged in them; people are instruments of that "ruse of reason" which uses their freedom and motives for the attainment of ends altogether invisible to them and outside their intentions and reach. People are given the illusion of acting in freedom and spontaneity and are in reality harnessed into a strictly preordained objective process whose anonymous majesty dwarfs them into insignificance and destroys their sense of responsibility. For a man can be responsible only for things he controls, he is free only to the extent that he at least approximately controls his own actions and their probable consequences. He is responsible, e.g., for his unemployment if he has proved unreliable in his job; but his sense of responsibility gives way to cynical apathy if his best efforts to feed his wife and children are frustrated by the mass unemployment which the anonymous market produces for mysterious reasons beyond anybody's control. What is true of the workingman is true of the businessman who falls prey to fluctuations that sweep the community and make him defenseless. Conversely, when the anony-

1. To the psychological argument we add the economic one which has been developed by Adolph Lowe, *Economics and Sociology*, 1935, Chapter III: the market cannot technically function with purely psychological satisfactions as objectives; it requires for its operation the struggle for highest efficiency and highest material returns. Cf. *Wirtschaftssysteme und Gesellschaftssysteme*, p. 10.

mous processes do achieve beneficent results, as no doubt they have done on the largest scale for any long-range consideration, it is not man as free spirit who must be credited with the result but the anonymous process whose tool he is. The despotism of the process may be benevolent, but it certainly destroys freedom and responsibility and swallows up the individual into itself.

Individualism and Bureaucracy

There is a third area in modern life which develops and reinforces the power of anonymous social processes: bureaucratization. It is by definition a process in applied logic, where all lower positions are derived from the highest by appointment, and their functions serve the purpose of the highest by assignment. The entire body is altogether anonymous; hence a criticism from without of any one function is never accepted by the functionary because responsibility can never be fixed and is always passed on to somebody else who is just as elusive. In British parliamentary custom this aspect of modern bureaucratic government is given perfect expression, in that the Speaker never permits a member of the Commons to criticize an official by name or even by allusion; and the responsible member of the Cabinet always steps in in defense of his subordinate and assumes the full responsibility for the criticized action and person; if there was a mistake, it was the mistake of the minister, ultimately by appointing the official and assigning him to his task. Bureaucracy is a direct outcome of the increasing specialization of science, each bureaucratic function being vested in an expert who knows everything in his own field and is too modest and skeptical to claim any knowledge outside that field. So the synthesis which fails in academic education must be provided in practical policy by weighing the various expert judgments against one another and drawing them together in a final decision. Bureaucracy is the sociological parallel to technology, and it is made inescapable and all-pervading by the techniques of control which the technology of communication puts at the disposal of bureaucratic government. The member of the bureaucracy acts as a mere tool of his superior, not as a responsible man.

Hence the citizen who cannot avoid business with the bureaucracy—and who can?—confronts not a man but an anonymous apparatus with laws of motion of its own in which he is caught up unwittingly and without resistance or appeal. Fourteen years before seizing power Lenin organized the Communist Party "along bureaucratic lines"—that is, like an army —and later proclaimed that "society must be run like the big machine that it is"—that is, anonymously; all this in deference to the rule of efficiency in government; and in Lenin's Russia, of course, the government had a monopoly on will and action.[2] The perfect symbol of the anonymity and detached inhuman logic of bureaucratic efficiency is presented in Menotti's *The Consul* as a glass door which is rarely lighted from inside and is never opened; the decisions are supposed to be made behind the door in strict compliance with mysterious rules which spell life and hope to some applicants and despair and death to others, with nobody responsible for the result and everybody a potential victim. The perfect rationality of the bureaucratic process comes close to the perfect irrationality of a game of dice, which also obeys its mathematical rule but is inscrutable fate to man.

Since Aristotle's time the rule of law and the citizens' equality before the law have been praised as the foundation of freedom. Subjecting man to impersonal rules exempts him from subjection to persons; teaching him in advance the legal effects of any action he may take enables him to make a free and responsible decision between the various alternatives open to him. To the law St. Paul appealed when the imperial police, unaware of his Roman citizenship, arrested him; to the law Socrates submitted in sublime serenity when it spelled his death. Wherever

2. Stalin, in talking with Eric Johnston, President of the United States Chamber of Commerce (*Reader's Digest,* October 1944): "I like to do business with American businessmen. You fellows know what you want; your word is good, and, most important of all, you stay in office a long time, just like we do over here. But a politician is here today and gone tomorrow, and then you have to start all over with a new set."

the Roman legions marched—they did not march in Russia—
the rule of law was planted, however feebly, and the way was
open for liberalism and democracy when the time was ripe for
them. But *summum ius, summa inuria*—this again is what
Hayek's undialectical, unhistorical, unsociological mind ignores.
If the law is to make man free, it must be accessible and intelligible to him and he must be in a position to argue it out with
the interpreter of the law. The more complex the life of society,
the economic process, the administrative apparatus, the legal
casuistry, the techniques of regulation and control, the more
impenetrable does the rule of law in the form of a strictly law-
abiding bureaucracy become; the more it assumes the character
of a gamble, the more is its anonymity transformed from a
guarantee of freedom to an obscure, enigmatic, unidentifiable
despotism.[3]

Individualism and the Means of Communication

Technology, the market, and the bureaucracy are not the
only great standardizers and collectivizers. The means of propaganda, products of technology, stand out as the greatest of
standardizers, because they directly attack the integrity and
spontaneity of man's soul by confiscating his leisure time; telling
him what goods he should want although he does not need

3. There is no full parallelism between the three areas, here discussed,
of individualism frustrated. The free market is directly and by definition
an institution of individualism; but it is not by definition dynamic, controlled by increasing efficiency and thus standardizing the participants. A
static market is possible in logic and history; it has been shown in preceding publications of mine that it is modern technology which makes the
market the dynamic and standardizing institution as which we know it.
Technology in turn is not an institution of individualism; it is, however,
a discovery of individualism, introduced by individualism for its own ends
although outgrowing and perverting it. Bureaucracy can similarly be construed as linked to individualism historically although not essentially. The
common denominator of all these developments is modern science as the
science of control and manipulation. This aspect will be discussed in a
special chapter below. Max Weber uses "rationalization" as common
denominator. By understanding itself as "rational," individualism created
the forces which overwhelmed it.

them, what opinions he should hold on things beyond his own and the propagandist's judgment; and drowning his poise in an ocean of information, sensation, and noise. This process has often been described and needs no further comment.

Concentrating on that aspect of propaganda which appears least harmful, commercial advertising is rightly credited with a major contribution toward American economic stability in recent years, contrary to many gloomy forecasts and prophecies of doom. It had appeared perfectly sound to argue (with Keynes) that, as there was a minimum of income beneath which people were too poor to put a penny aside by way of saving, so with increasing income people would save more in proportion; or, to put it another way, the gap between their rising income and their more slowly rising consumption would widen. Saving, thus being defined as abstention from present consumption for the sake of some more or less distant future, reduces the present demand for goods. Thereby, however, it implies a growing threat to the stability of production and employment. The explosive development of productivity and income during and after the Second World War became paradoxically a cause for anxiety and foreboding. Would we not save too much to keep our economy and labor force fully employed?

All this proved totally erroneous. The demand for goods— new kinds of goods such as television—did not slacken in the least; it grew in proportion to growing income, restricted saving to proportional growth, and thus permitted full employment to continue even before the war in Korea again multiplied the demand for arms. Poverty, insofar as it persists in the United States, is not traceable to economic inadequacy but to social barriers, notably the color bar—although that too is gradually conquered. The gross national product in 1959 was $480 billions; that is, after $85 billions of taxes had been subtracted, the average income per each of the almost 180 million inhabitants was the fantastic sum of $2200 per head. There is no doubt that this happy result would have been unattainable without the tricks of the advertisers and propagandists. After all, what shall a country covet beyond the liberally interpreted necessities and amenities of life? Each increment to income is less important to well-being than the preceding one and will buy less important additional goods. "Oversaving" is considered such a grave danger precisely because the more goods people already have, the less they need additional goods. Granting that standards of living may change and expand, they do so in the course of successive generations, not every year. But the job here at hand demanded precisely an explosive expansion of the standard of living year by year, by several per cent a year, to keep pace with the explosive rise of productivity, lest unemployment fill the gap between production and demand. The job, in other words, demanded that people be persuaded that an "American standard of living" included cars twice as big as and 50 per cent more expensive than European cars; or that they had better buy a television set lest their children be forced to look at the neighbor's set and thus be estranged from home and equipped with an effective inferiority complex. It is the art and power of such reasoning which has permitted the people of the United States to fully reap the fruits of their dizzy productivity and to continue on their high level of employment as long as more advertising can still sell more goods.

There are only three noneconomic comments to be added. First, the happily solved problem must appear to outsiders as the climax of insanity, as a special blessing prepared by Providence for the too wealthy. The world outside the United States has plenty of worries, but the fear of too much saving because of too much income is not among them. The world is even told in the same breath that America can no longer "afford" to "give away" 5 or 6 out of its 480 billions of dollars per year—less than 2 per cent—unless the recipients use such generosity to build up their military strength and relieve America's military budget to this extent. Nay, realizing that, should the crisis of oversaving break out in America, there would be unemployment, bankruptcy, and famine in the poor countries dependent on sales of their raw materials to America, the world wonders whether the danger would not disappear if America transferred abroad its excess wealth, the source of all the embarrassment. For in the second place, while the problem of annually rising consumption standards has been solved in the recent past by the inclusion of television etc. in the "American standard of living," this fact does not remove the problem from the agenda. Barring a world catastrophe, the problem is bound to recur in ever greater keenness every year of further rise in productivity. After television, what?[4] After the necessary, the comfortable, the agreeable, the superfluous, the silly, what? This, then, is the American dilemma: it lies in the choice between economic stability and mental health, between economic crisis and insanity. In order to keep their economy in its present structure going, Americans must want more and more goods.[5] How stable can such a structure be? And should it be stable, can anyone believe that the rising orgy of commodities will not affect the health of the mental organism, the integrity of the soul? "For where your treasure is, there will your heart be also."

And where in all this is the vaunted liberty of the individual? He is warned in no uncertain terms that, unless he buys the new commodities, his children will acquire an inferiority complex and the American economy will break down. If his economy is free, he himself is not.

4. In 1955 America produced 7.8 million television sets, with a retail value of $1.8 billion. In 1958 the volume of production had shrunk to 5.3 million sets and the value to $1.1 billion—the unit had become cheaper. But was the reduction in volume attributable to cyclical fluctuation, as there was a moderate recession in 1958? The United States Statistical Abstract for 1959 says there were 44 million households with television sets and 5.4 million without them in January of that year; that is, 89 per cent and 11 per cent respectively. The 11 per cent included both persons too poor to afford sets and certain nonconformists—professors and the like— who didn't want them. In the light of these figures, how much can one expect the production of television sets to expand in the future? Sooner or later there must be a point of absolute saturation, beyond which there can be only replacement and improvement, not further expansion. This will be our argument in Chapter VI, where the structural problem will be discussed.

5. The growing difficulty is reflected in the figures for advertising, which have increased by an average of $.5 billion per year since World War II and had reached the fantastic sum of more than $10 billion by 1958.

* II *

Individualism and Society

Society as the Means to Private Ends

INDIVIDUALISTIC SOCIETY is defined as the society in which the individual is the supreme value and end. The very name "individualistic society" is highly paradoxical, in that "society" requires an ultimate cohesion between its members, while "individualism" suggests the sovereignty of these members severally, their emancipation from social or institutional bonds or obligations which might hamper their drive to self-realization. The theorists of individualistic society answer the problem by referring to the individuals' rational understanding of their interest in banding together for the pursuit of common ends and, ultimately, for the more efficacious pursuit by each member of his private welfare. For if life in society makes division of labor possible, every individual acquires greater skill in his chosen line of business or vocation or production, and as he renders the others better service he in turn receives better services from them, thus raising the level for them all. The upshot is that the sovereign individuals establish mutual relations between one another inasmuch as they each promote their private ends thereby.

It was already mentioned that a highly important school of thought, which has continued from antiquity to almost our own day, presents society as the product of a social contract between free, reason-guided, welfare-seeking individuals. These take upon themselves the disadvantages of certain restraints as the price to be paid for the greater advantage of life in society. Other theorists, loath to accept the social contract as a historical fact and preferring an explanation of society in terms of spontaneous growth, still use the idea of the social contract as a norm against which to measure the reality: in order to live in society people must behave as if they were partners in a social contract. In other words, individuals submit to certain disciplines in order better to attain their ends—which thus become the ends of society.

Such theories always take the individual as potentially sovereign and rational; they are perfectly expressive of the logic of individualistic society. For whatever forces may ultimately underlie the existence of society, there is no doubt that the routine reality of individualistic society is created and re-created daily by contract. In the free society of individualism no person is under obligation to others beyond the stipulations of a contract freely entered into and strictly defined in content and duration. In so entering into contractual obligation, the citizen makes use of his reason in the free pursuit of his interest; the contract determines his contribution to the life of the whole and his share in the fruits of the common effort. The reverse side of economic freedom as freedom of enterprise and contract is self-responsibility: no one takes care of a grown-up, able-bodied person if he or she fails to do so. If freedom is defined as choice between alternatives, as is usually and inadequately done in scientific discussion, the alternative to the present contract is another contract with another partner or, in the extreme case, no contract at all when and as long as this appears more advantageous than the terms of the available contract. All this is strictly predicated on the premise that man, being reason-guided, must be left free to decide, as best he can in his own interest, on the direction and volume of his service, depending on the compensation to be received therefor.

The argument may appear to lean too heavily toward the commercial side and to disregard the organic nature of fundamental social groupings, primarily the family. But it is precisely the greatest and most circumspect philosopher of individualism, Immanuel Kant, who defines marriage as a contract between two persons of different sex for permanent mutual sexual satisfaction. We may discount this definition on the ground that its author, being a professor and a lifelong bachelor, did not know better; we may say what happens in this definition is a slight confusion between marriage and prostitution. Nevertheless the logic of the attempt to explain individualistic society as a fabric of contracts, all of which expire either automatically or upon duly given notice—e.g. in a contract of divorce—is instructive indeed. For whether or not this is an adequate rendition of the present reality of individualistic society, there is no doubt that this society develops in the direction thus indicated. The theory may be quite inadequate to explain the fundamental nature of society—it is—but it would not be irrelevant for this reason if it adequately rendered, in logical form, the way people tend to think, to understand their place in society, to interpret the ends they pursue. People may still have other moral resources at their disposal—they do—but if they disregard them and neglect to cultivate them, the oversimplified picture becomes more realistic because the reality itself moves closer to that picture. A fallacious theory is innocuous in itself if it is and remains a purely academic affair; it becomes a historical force if it sums up public opinion and arrays it for action, or if it is accepted by public opinion and permitted to shape and guide it. A fallacious theory may very well spearhead a ruinous practice, precisely because the theory's very birth and growth are already part of that historical process of decline. Likewise a criticism of the theory is meant to be a critique of a practice predicated on the teachings of that theory.

The first and fundamental doubt attaches to the proposition that society can be understood as a means to the private ends of its members. If the private ends of the members coincided on all major counts, this explanation might have a certain degree of plausibility; but the fact of the matter is that the interests, far from always coinciding, cross and oppose one another, that they pit man against man and group against group either as suppliers or as buyers, while certainly also making for the continuation of such an antagonistic association. People are simultaneously both cooperators and competitors or practitioners of countervailing power, and their competitive or market struggle is itself a form of cooperation inasmuch as they have to comply with the rules of the competitive market game. Nobody can improve his welfare by resigning from society altogether except in the rare case of an open frontier. The poorest and most exploited laborer obviously prefers his employment contract to unemployment—else he would not sign the contract—

but this means nothing else than that he prefers his miserable existence to the alternative, death by starvation. In this sense it is true that society serves him as the means to his private "welfare," but lest this suggest undue conclusions to the theorists of individualism, he desperately looks for some other alternative to his contract—and he finds it.

Rationality of Antisocial Policy

The alternative is not resignation from society altogether; it is an antisocial policy in the midst of society. The logic of this conclusion is inescapable. If we assume for the sake of argument that society is to be understood from private considerations, the individual being the supreme ruler, then the society of such individuals is only a derived and conditional value, a means to ends outside itself, a matter of expediency. But then there arises the logical possibility of situations where the supreme individual or group of individuals will not find positive service to the society the best means for the pursuit of private ends, where it is found more expedient to act against the interests of society. It would be incorrect to argue that society in such a case has no value to the member; an action directed against the interest of society in the interest of private welfare is precisely designed to influence society in a sense more profitable to the actor. That is, the individual does have an interest in the life of the society, inasmuch as it is the arena which permits him to prosper at the expense of others rather than alongside of others and through their prosperity. But this is a far cry from the original confidence in cooperation as profitable to all. Exploitation and oppression are possible only in society, and it is they which the rational individual may seek, one can almost say must logically seek. The beneficiaries of exploitation and oppression are sure to be interested in and committed to preserving them—that is, interested in and committed to preserving the life of society in this special form and for this reason. Their victims, likewise, will try to shift the burden or reverse the entire structure without destroying it. This is the true logic of individualistic society.

We have here the more fully reasoned form of the argument

presented in our introduction: a system of liberty supreme tends to degenerate into a regime of liberty for the strong—individuals, classes, and races—at the expense of the weak—individuals, classes, and races; the premise being that there are differences in physical or intellectual or military or financial strength, as there always are. If all are given liberty to seek their private well-being, it is the strong who can best take advantage of this right and who establish themselves in control; and everybody tries to become strong and to supersede the present strong. People are driven by their natural, rationally analyzed instincts. The rational analysis of this or that situation and of the chances for gain that it contains becomes more refined as civilization advances, but the motive remains the same, inasmuch as the principle of economic rationalism remains the same: the use of relations with other people as means to our own private ends; or putting it more bluntly, the exploiting of those other people for our private ends. If man is supposed to build the community as the means to his private ends, then exploitation rather than mutuality is his rational policy. The question that remains is: how safe can be the existence of a society thus constituted, and is not force rather than a contract for mutual service its *raison d'être?*

This tallies perfectly with an important and far too little known socio-political theory of the origin of society, developed in three successive generations by Ludwig Gumplovicz, Franz Oppenheimer, and Alexander Rüstow. To the two former authors it was the sociological theory of the state; to Rüstow, after he had enormously broadened its basis by integrating into it vast prehistoric and anthropological material, it is more simply the theory of superposition (*Ueberlagerung*). It says that society in the developed and differentiated sense of the word—beyond small-scale undifferentiated primitive tribal communities—is produced by conquest, where the conquerors, instead of massacring the conquered or putting out their eyes, establish themselves as the ruling class and the recipients of tribute from the conquered, confiscating for themselves, through the coercive agency known as the state, the excess of production over the bare necessities.

The process may be started, for instance, by some climatic change driving horse-breeding mounted nomads from their steppes into the warmer lands of grain-producing agriculturists, whom their cavalry makes their servants. They become thereby materially interested in the durability and even in the rising productivity of the work done by the conquered. They enter into a kind of partnership with them. Nay, if they decide to increase their own revenues by increasing the efficiency of their serfs, they soon discover that they cannot do this except by leaving to the serfs a share in the larger output or crop. They thus intensify and develop the partnership and gradually transform what began as imperial superposition into a unified although stratified society on a larger scale. One may even doubt that an integrated and highly differentiated society has ever arisen or could ever have arisen otherwise; after all it is the man of violence—Cain, not Abel—who according to the mythical account in Genesis becomes the builder of cities and father of craftsmen and whose descendants (the Kenites) play such a significant part in the formation of monotheism. Hence there is no reason, either in logic or in history, to expect a life of sweet reasonableness in individualism, which is the system where, even though hemmed in by the constitutional game and the market, individuals and groups do pursue their private ends of their own accord under their own responsibility in and through their relations with others.

Our critique has proceeded by developing the unofficial implications and effects of individualism in society. They point in the direction of the law of the jungle. It is these implications and effects which must be added to the official and programmatic picture in order to round it out, lest the official half of the truth presented as a full truth become a total lie. But this in turn means that our discussion of the unofficial truth about individualism will be untruthful if we do not give full credit to the other part of the truth, which is official and by no means irrelevant. We do it in three steps.

There is only a limited coincidence of the logical argument from self-seeking individualism in organized society with the historical and prehistorical argument from superposition. Individualism goes a certain length in the direction of the law of the jungle but includes an element unknown in the jungle and transcending it. This is the law protecting the physical and legal inviolability of the individual—of every individual, no matter how strong or weak socially. The legal freedom of the person may be of little practical use to him in conditions of misery, where he must submit to the stronger man's terms; but even then it remains a potential weapon for the defense of the weak. An intelligent and trustworthy slave often had a life far superior to that of a legally free pauper; but nevertheless the legal freedom of the individual is infinitely superior to slavery, in real or potential practical terms and not only on speculative grounds of philosophical principle. Individualism unfetters the strong individuals but draws, through constitutionalism, a protecting line around the weak such as had not been known before. There is nothing in the formation of organized society by conquest to suggest such a limitation.

This is also the point where the symmetrical correspondence between the two opposite systems of modern rationalist society fails conspicuously. In individualism the strong individual, using social relations with other people as means to his private ends, may take advantage of the weak but must not destroy him; in collectivism the collective, using individuals as means to its own ends interpreted by its leaders, is not kept from destroying those individuals whose freedom or survival does not appear expedient to the collective's ends. Individualism destroys the person spiritually (see the preceding chapter) but protects him legally—no small matter, and decisive in the confrontation of the two systems. For in collectivism there is, in principle, no such thing as a person and his inalienable rights.

Our third major concession concerns the efficiency of individualistic society. The common good is here supposed to be the product of private actions and their interplay. In the classic statement of Adam Smith, it is not from the butcher's and baker's benevolence that we expect our daily meal but from their well-understood self-interest. What in point of fact the private system has achieved in terms of living and health standards is beyond praise; this was emphasized above (and is discussed at length in my above-mentioned book). We are not idealists enough to belittle living and health standards as purely "material"; if man is spirit incarnate, then everything affecting his life in the flesh contributes to the shaping or conditioning of his spiritual life, as can best be seen from the pre-eminence given the healing of the sick in the Gospel stories and in the dual injunction to the Disciples to preach the kingdom to come and to heal the sick.

But once more, to recognize the efficiency of individualism and its results is something totally different from attributing the life of individualistic society exclusively to private considerations crystallized into contractual relations, or from presenting the interplay of private forces as a smooth cooperation in sweet reasonableness. What matters is precisely the unofficial human and social cost of the triumph in efficiency. The classical doctrine of individualism, that of laissez-faire, even if we accept it as the full and exhaustive proof, does not preclude—and in some versions actually demands—that people should be forced to cooperate toward the public good by the pressure of specially designed institutions: competition between businessmen and propertylessness in the case of manual labor so as not to leave them any other way out than cooperation on however unfavorable terms.

Two conclusions follow. In the first place, the cooperation is not conscious, much less intended. Hegel's "ruse of the idea" and Adam Smith's "invisible hand" that "leads us to achieve an end which was no part of our intention" express in respectable language what the cynic Mandeville put more bluntly in the equation "private vice, public virtue." Not only are people pawns in a game which they do not see, as discussed in the preceding chapter, thus making their individualist liberty a make-believe, but their motives are positively misguided. For if they are told that the public good is the unintended outcome of their selfish actions, this does not educate them to any sense of public responsibility but imparts to them a good conscience to sanction their most antisocial actions. The public good is simply lost sight of, whether or not it emerges behind the backs of the agents. If the theory sanctions selfishness as the material

of which the public good is made, its human effect is simply
the justification of and education in selfishness. This has been
pointed out by innumerable writers. Antisocial policy follows
logically.

Rationality of Strikes and Depressions

In the second place, the cooperation of private individuals
and groups in the form of the market struggle can be described
in far more concrete terms by analyzing the situation in which
they find themselves and the problem that confronts them.

The economic life of society depends on an orderly cooperation of capital and labor, however they may be organized.
Capital, i.e. buildings, equipment, and materials, may be held
by private owners or by public agencies or by labor collectively,
etc.; labor may be hired individually or in collective bargain-
ing, or it may be unfree and legally under the command of
capital. But always the economic life of society requires that the
two be brought together for deliberate and disciplined production. In the free rational society of liberal democracy they are
expected to cooperate voluntarily for reasons of well-understood
self-interest. Now it certainly is in their rational interest to
cooperate, but—as was shown above—it is also in the rational
interest of either one to try to improve the terms on which they
cooperate, and this interest is served on both sides by what
Veblen's mordant irony calls "conscientious withdrawal of
efficiency." Two factors determine the income of either group;
first, the absolute size of the national income and output; and
second, the relative share of the group. While the former depends on the steady cooperation of the two, the latter depends
on their struggle, in which each one expects the other to do the
cooperating for the sake of the total income to be divided
between them. Rational society lives in the cooperation of the
strong and the weak, but on the terms set by the strong; and it
is logical for either side to try to be or to become the strong
one and thus to widen the battlefield, which is the life of society.

The strike of labor was not originally, and was not designed
to be, a danger to society. In a competitive economy a strike

against one firm would bring pressure to bear on the employer by driving home to him the truth that his profit and his existence were dependent on the cooperation of labor. Such a strike in a competitive system would not normally affect the larger community, which could continue to buy from other firms. The situation becomes totally different, however, in industry-wide strikes. The public, formerly an onlooker, is now drawn into the conflict because the industry has to shut down. This, in point of fact, is the aim: to increase the pressure on the industry, which may be able to withstand it for a long time, by pressure on and of the public, which may not. The firm loses money, which it may expect to recover after the strike, but the public loses goods or services, which can never be recovered or replaced. Thus the supposition is that the public will force the industry to concessions that will make it possible for the workers to return to their jobs. It follows that the prospects for an effective strike are the better, the more menacing is the grip of labor on the throat of the community, as in coal, railroads, and tugboats.[1]

The strike of labor, spectacular though it is, is not the primary or the most dangerous such attack on the life of society. That distinction clearly goes to the strike of capital. The parallels as well as the differences between the two must be understood. While the strike of labor is a deliberate, concerted

1. There have been several cases in which labor has explicitly spurned the idea of alleviating special hardships caused by strikes—for example, the coal and tugboat strikes; special hardships on hospitals and the like obviously increase the pressure. The telephone strikers, on the other hand, were very considerate. On a previous occasion the present writer has analyzed the problem in two opposite examples, the strike of the chocolate workers in Hershey, Pennsylvania, and that of transportation workers of Shanghai. The chocolate strike was broken and the strikers thrashed and driven back to work by the enraged dairy farmers, whom the workers had not thought of notifying when depriving them of the daily sales of their milk to the factory. The reverse happened in Shanghai in the early 1930's, where the bus and streetcar drivers continued to operate their vehicles but refused to collect their fares, thus enlisting the laughing support of the public, and deserving it by the evidence of their awareness of responsibility to the community. See *Communism, Fascism, or Democracy?* (New York, 1938), p. 208.

action on the part of many, the strike of capital appears as an act of God, like an elementary catastrophe, an earthquake or a flood; consequently it is given an objective name—"depression" or "crisis" or the like. It does not consist in any concerted action by many; it is the joint result of many individual actions given the same direction by the same experience. But essentially depression and strike are parallel, in that in both cases an indispensable element is withdrawn from the service of society because the return to it appears inadequate, with a view to raising this return to a more satisfactory level precisely by the demonstration of its being indispensable.

A moral verdict on either capital or labor would not be in place. Under no obligation to others or to the whole of society, engaging in or refraining from short-run contracts according as this is expedient for survival, what can a businessman do but shut down in order to reduce losses? What shall a worker do but go on strike as his meager livelihood becomes more expensive? What matters here is not individual morality but social morality —that is, the morality of society's institutions, which overwhelms individual morality and forces it to adopt a line of policy unmistakably antisocial. The glaring result is that both capital and labor are withdrawn from production for reasons of inadequate rewards. In other words, the freedom of private interest in both cases means the freedom to disrupt society for the benefit of that interest, with a view to relatively and absolutely improving its share in the national income by reducing that very national income.

The great argument in defense of the strike of labor used to be that if freedom is interpreted as a private right to improve one's lot by an attack on society, society cannot remain free if it curbs the exercise of that right by labor and protects its exercise by capital. But now the general trend of public opinion, even in this country, is toward some control of business fluctuations; and this would imply some control of labor. If national policy underwrites a satisfactory level of employment and production and thus assumes a responsibility which for generations was considered the prerogative of business, then labor's right to reduce employment and production becomes illogical. Nationwide strikes or the threat of them cannot remain a routine instrument of everyday policy if business is deprived of the right to produce booms and depressions. But the reduction of freedom must not be driven to the point of abrogation; it is in order to save essential freedom that the excesses of an unbalanced freedom need to be curbed. Revolt against oppression is an inalienable moral right, and democracy is almost defined by keeping legal channels open for it. The extreme form of revolt remains the strike. Such a dangerous right must not normally be made use of; but it is and must always remain available as a last resort.

In other words, in order to curb the antisocial excess of liberty, one must relieve people of the antisocial situations by which they were trained for such abuse. Liberty was interpreted in a frankly antisocial way because people thrust into frankly antisocial situations were refused any help. Liberty, individualism, privacy as the organizing principle of society—meaning that we are not our brother's keeper—are thus pushing to the point where they disrupt what they are supposed to organize. Individualist society is thus revealed to be the more untenable as it becomes purer, more logical, freer from traditional admixtures. Individualism corrodes society.

Rationality of Self-Restraint?

The question must here arise whether the necessary balance is not found in the properly reinterpreted principle of reason itself. (This obviously will be our own line of approach later, since our critique of rationalism can never mean to discredit reason.) For the time being, what we mean is that the rational pursuit of interest by the individual may be interpreted too narrowly if it is reduced to the assertion of superior strength in the political or market struggle. Are this self-assertion and its strategy really all that reason teaches the free individual? Is he not also taught by reason certain social rules that would balance the antisocial motive of his action, to secure the stability and durability of the social setup in which it is so profitable to him to live? Reason itself might thus introduce a new

48 *Reason and Faith in Modern Society*

factor of long-range perspective into the picture of individuals rationally pursuing their interests in their relations with others. For in more than two thousand years of Western moral and political philosophy, all in terms of man's reason, there has never been any doubt about justice being "the foundation of government," demanded by reason for the sake of peace and stability; or about the irrationality, the unreasonableness, the foolishness of the strong's exploiting the weak and thus inviting disaster. One can then construe rational society as operated by the well-understood self-interest of individuals and groups in driving as hard a bargain as possible, the "possible" being limited by long-range considerations of peace and stability which counsel moderation and justice. Some formulation like this is quite likely to be acceptable to most social scientists today.

The problem repeats itself on a still larger scale in international relations, where the rationally motivated "individuals" are national governments and the theorists of "realism" claim the "national interest" as the only legitimate or rational or realistic guide to action. For they hasten to add that, properly understood, the national interest includes a wise consideration for the needs of others so as to eliminate antagonism, deepen friendly relations all around, and, in one word, make the national interest almost coincident with a moral interest.

But this expedient is full of difficulties. The first thing in this attempt at reinterpretation is its unscientific language.[2] The certainty and sobriety of rationally ascertained facts is what science was designed to bring; on religious dogma there had been dissension, on scientific propositions there is consensus. But a proposition on justice is open to different interpretations, because justice is not a fact and there cannot be a "scientific"

2. It is too often said by humanists and atheists that modern science, on which they stake their hopes and expectations, owes nothing to the Biblical and everything to the classical tradition. Both halves of this proposition are wrong. There could not be modern science had not monotheism proclaimed God as spirit and everything earthly as radically different from him. And the distance between Greek philosophy and modern science can easily be measured if we realize that the Greeks taught wisdom and the moderns teach the certainty of facts.

notion of it if "science" means things tangible and measurable. Physical reality presents us with things and relations but with neither justice nor injustice—things spiritual. We do not form a notion of justice by elongating to the point of purity the blurred and confused elements of justice that we find in a blurred and confused reality, as one may form the notion of a species from generalization of individual specimens; we can discern those blurred and confused elements of justice in a blurred and confused reality only because we have knowledge of the pure idea of justice, which has no physical reality whatever. An altogether different notion of science would be required to make room for the spiritual reality of justice.

In other words, it is not clear just what the reference to the long-range rationality of justice is designed to achieve. The propositions that it is unreasonable for the strong to exploit the weak, that an unjust order of society is *ipso facto* an unreasonable one, that the well-understood national interest includes consideration of the needs of other nations, and that most generally the rational self-interest of individuals and groups includes the social point of view—these propositions may be meant in the spirit of classical political philosophy, where it is difficult to discern whether and in what sense "reason" means the power in the actual operation of the human mind or a norm for its sound operation.

But the meaning of those phrases becomes unmistakable when they are transferred from traditional philosophy to modern social science. The phrases then are supposed to prove that social justice will attract enlightened individuals, groups, and governments because it will make the social, national, or international order that is to serve their ends stable and durable. Fairness in all contacts and contracts will recommend itself because it brings with it the hope of reciprocity; fairness and honesty pay. Karl Mannheim, one of the authorities of an autonomous, scientific morality, comes close to deriving democracy from the most scientific, least ambiguous of all scientific concepts, efficiency, in the following passages: "Planning based on . . . inequality . . . probably cannot last long because these inequalities will create so great a tension in society that it will be impossible to

50   *Reason and Faith in Modern Society*

establish even that minimum of tacit consent which is the condition of the functioning of a system. The necessity of preventing politics from clogging the wheels of planning is one of the factors which, in the long run, make for equality of opportunity in planned society. Planning, therefore, leads ultimately to the spread of democracy in the sense of fundamental equality." Likewise in the international field: "War occurs because men in their activities have not learned to take a long-range view and to think in terms of a real psychology." [3]

All this, and the libraries written in a similar vein, is devoid of logic. Where it holds true, it does so because the partners or adversaries are of approximately or potentially equal strength: they had better compose their differences. It does not hold true where one knows that he is superior in physical strength or in social power or in financial power or in military force, and expects to remain superior for his own lifetime or even for one more generation. Human life is short, and nobody can plan for the life of his descendants in a future much beyond his own death. How long must be the "long-range view" which Karl Mannheim says will avoid war? And far more important, just why should war be avoided at all? In the short range of a lifetime, war may very well pay the victor; why should he then bother to "take a long-range view"? Why should he, conscious of his superior strength, regard reconciliation as more profitable for him than victory, and respect for other people as more advantageous than efficiency in exploiting or extinguishing them?

One may argue that self-restraint on the part of the strong is expedient in the long run because it would save him or his descendants from the revenge of the oppressed; there would be nothing to avenge, and the order as established by him would be stable and durable by consent. But if an unjust order of the community is established by the strong members rationally pursuing their interest and oppressing the weak, then this order is given durability not by righting the wrong but by keeping the weak weak so as to prevent them from rising in vengeance. That such an attempt may fail is clear; there never is absolute cer-

3. Karl Mannheim, *Man and Society in an Age of Reconstruction* (1940), pp. 363–364, 142.

tainty on the effects of our actions. But it is far more important to note that the attempt to keep the weak down for good may well be successful. This very possibility suffices to justify the attempt. The men of power are realists and do not dream the grandiose dreams of organizing the universe for eternity which serve to compensate well-meaning professors for their impotence. A small measure of ruthlessness may bring on revolt. A very big measure of it may deter revolt, nor may it be necessary ever again to use violence. Oppressors have always known how to degrade the souls of their victims by offering them entertainment—circuses in the Roman tradition, which were sorely inadequate technically if measured against modern standards of entertainment, but even so proved quite adequate to their job for several centuries in Rome and for many more centuries in Byzantium. This surely is a sufficiently "long-range view" to satisfy the quest of durability.

More generally, while history produces many examples of revolt, doubtless encouraging the belief in the expediency of moderate and just rule, history produces on the other hand many more examples of revolt not attempted, despite or because of shocking conditions. Those revolts that did come off have a more sensational appeal to our attention than those that did not; but the latter should figure as facts in history no less than the former. If we count that way, it will become clear how good a chance, for how long a period of time, suppression can count on; and hence how rational a policy of suppression is if it musters enough strength and guards itself against weakening in ruthlessness. In other words, moderation and justice are not parts of well-understood, carefully thought through self-interest; and the paradoxical society of rational individualism, if it lives as it does without an excessive use of physical force, must live on residual sources other than rational individualism.

Traditional Inhibitions

We have argued in these two chapters on individualism that the rational pursuit of self-interest by enlightened individuals is self-defeating, in that it destroys both individuality and civilized society. At this point we want to guard ourselves against two groups of possible misunderstandings.

In the first place, we are far from saying that the picture as here presented is fully realistic. It is, rather, an experiment in applied logic, deduced from the one pure principle of rational individualism. But if not a complete picture of reality, it is not quite unrealistic either. For in pursuing the effects of that one principle, we have singled out for observation the force that modern society has proclaimed as its guide and norm and of which it boasts every day in uncounted speeches and editorials. This situation suggests two conclusions. On the one hand, residual sources of a nature much different from rational individualism modify and mitigate the picture. That is, people are, in point of fact, considerably better than their cherished self-interpretation would have it, or than they would be if their rational individualism had completely overcome their traditional motives and "inhibitions." Nay, not aware—in an age of engineering—of the quiet work of the past in the present, they are prone to mistake for rational individualism everything they find in themselves and their actions. That is, they mistake for rational individualism a complex of motives some of which check and mitigate it. Not only are they better than their program but for the same reason their program appears to them better than it is.

On the other hand, however, this strange confusion reinforces the danger. The fact that we can live with a program of rational individualism is now fully attributed to the program itself rather than to the furtive and unconceited mitigations and inhibitions coming from elsewhere. Hence the program appears justified by its effects and can be pursued with ever greater vigor. Being consciously cultivated and praised, it naturally gains more and more room in the mind, at the expense of those traditional forces which linger on in the mind but are disowned and denounced as irrational, and are certainly not renewed. Rationalism is—anyway in the modern Western world—an aggressive revolutionary principle, which tends to purify, sharpen, and narrow its own understanding of human reason by critically corroding residual traditional admixtures. This picture, however, is somber. If rational individualism corrodes individuality and civilized society, the end of the road will sooner or later be reached. How far are we advanced toward it?

This brings us to the second main point. It is our thesis that modern man is misguided precisely by his belief in the supreme principle of reason, in the light of which the waning traditional forces appear as "irrational." This thesis may be misunderstood as an advocacy of irrationalism and an attack on the principle of reason. But a critique, however radical, of the historical career of reason in society is not an attack on the principle of reason. On the contrary, the argument proceeds by reasoning at every step; that is, it uses reason in the attempt to improve the past achievements of reason and to correct the too narrow conception of reason itself which lies behind the shortcomings. No nobler job is known to science than the re-examination of its methods and premises. Scientific progress need not confirm or conform to past scientific achievements; it may and does occasionally modify and rebuild the methods and preconceptions of fundamental propositions and is not subject to any other tests than those of logic and as much verification as the always complex and often ambiguous nature of history allows.

It is an eminently rational scientific question whether man is a rational being in the narrower sense—that is, self-sufficient through the use of his reason on the plane of his natural life— or whether his faculty for receiving revelation and rising in prayer and meditation is essential to his personal and social life. If his reason is not self-sufficient in that narrower sense, then his reliance on it misguides him into actions and policies which are dangerous to the life of society. In this case, if modern society manages to live on despite the disruptive influence of its official rational individualism, its survival must be traced to the still continuing influence of religion, even though this is officially denied in theory and neglected in practice. It would follow that a systematic theory would have to derive the objectives of social life from the frowned-upon religious inheritance, to explore these objectives in logical argument and conceptual language, and to translate them into adequate institutions and policies. For the objectives of life, peace and justice, are spiritually given beyond question, and they demand to be accepted and explored by rational theory. But institutions are never revealed; they are altogether a matter of rational building. This is the program toward which the last third of our book is designed to make a modest contribution.

At the present point, however, where the rationality of our procedure is being explained, it is essential to stress the fact that the decision between the two alternative explanations, the rejection of social rationalism, is not a dogmatic but a rational decision. That is, social rationalism is rejected because, when put to the test of logic and verification, it proves inadequate to explain the life of society. The adoption of the alternative "hypothesis" is nothing but the logical effect of this critical inquiry. The life of society cannot be understood if we try to derive it from social rationalism, for, when thought through, this principle leads to such absurd antisocial conclusions as we have here studied, and its official adoption by secular society leads to effects in history which are disastrous enough in themselves and would be far more disastrous if it were not for the mitigating influence of still-surviving but supposedly irrelevant religious forces.

* III *

Individualism
and Scientific Regularity

THERE are at least two different factors which closely connect
individual liberty as understood by modern social rationalism
with the scientific enterprise.

On the one hand, the mind must be free to ask any question
and to attempt any answer which may be suggested by the
growth of science and the further forward urge working in it.
The growth of science has its own logic, which would not be
able to assert itself if the mind had to obey a different law. The
coincidence in history of the growth of individualism and the
rise of science bears out this relationship and has always been
understood.

On the other hand, the scientific enterprise promotes individualism. The autonomy of the individual, which is the program of individualism, materializes, as it were, through science.
For if religion is discarded as heteronomous—as an arbitrary
law foreign to man—the individual must be given orientation
and guidance by science, which is the alternative. Liberty as a
mere empty space to be arbitrarily filled by the individual's decisions and choices cannot be conceived; to act according to his
dunklem Drang, his instinctive urge may be sufficient in special
situations but not for life as a whole, either individual or social.
But then man needs standards and directions, suprapersonal and
interpersonal, to give him certainty and communicability. To
the autonomous individual they can be given only by science,
because scientific truth is ascertained by the reason which is
every man's natural endowment; it is the elaborated and systematized form of common sense and is in principle accessible
to every individual who trains his mind for such studies. If religion means divine truth, science is human truth. To the extent

that man organizes his life according to scientific principles, he is then free. Or is he?

The scientific enterprise began with the natural sciences and in them had its greatest triumphs and the main source of its glory. The natural sciences, of course, are not concerned with external nature alone but also with man, inasmuch as he is a creature of nature; i.e. they are principally concerned with his biological health. The physical and chemical processes discovered by the sciences concern man's life inasmuch as they are employed in the production of goods for his use. It is these two usages of science which have changed the aspect of the earth, opened new horizons to man's life, and borne out their authentic human origin and purpose. (This was already discussed in the preceding chapter.) But of course the scientific fields apparently more remote than medicine and technology are no less vitally needed if the system of knowledge is a system; the directly useful branches of knowledge could not stand or develop in isolation from the others. The glory is that of all science, not of some sciences.

The admiration, awe, and worship in which the natural sciences are held is most curiously illumined by the fact that the likeness in stone of Albert Einstein can be seen among the saints and martyrs of the faith over the entrance to the Riverside Church in New York. Indeed, it is the sciences by which modern mankind expects to be saved from its ills and forebodings, as former ages expected their salvation to come from the power worshiped in religion. In such an intellectual climate, is it permissible to say that in this world, which hopes for salvation through rationalization of individual and social life, science itself has gone irrational?

The Irrationality of the Natural Sciences

Reason incorporated in science is supposed to shed its light into the dark corners of our existence, ferret out what cannot stand up to the light, and clear up what is damp and dusty. Reason in science is supposed to be the truly human force in man, that through which he rises above the unreasoning animals and emancipates himself from inscrutable forces of doom and grace superior to him; that through which he becomes autonomous, his own master. Instead, it is science itself which has become autonomous—that is, has emancipated itself from man and has embarked on a course of development increasingly heedless of human reason. One may say, increasingly unintelligible to man. In its dynamic logic every step drives to the next and drags, as it were, the human mind to discovering it. The great scientists figure out formulas and apply them but understand them as little as the layman, if understanding implies appropriation by living man rather than mechanical production and reproduction of magic figures. The scientists find themselves in the tragic position of being enslaved to the products of their mind, which they hate and denounce but cannot stop, like Goethe's Sorcerer's Apprentice. *"Herr, die Not ist gross."*

It is not true that this development could not have been foreseen. A wise man foresaw it four centuries ago. Leonardo da Vinci, whom the world reveres along with one or two others as its greatest genius in art, knew how to fly and navigate under water but destroyed the traces of his knowledge lest mankind be tempted by its reckless lusts to use them for its self-destruction. Leonardo was far from being an orthodox Christian; he was one of the earliest believers in reason. But he still breathed an air which was saturated with insight into the ambivalence and moral frailty of man's mind; he knew that knowledge must not be proclaimed supreme and left unguided because it might be abused by lusts. The Nazis made systematic scientific experiments in the behavior of people under torture; such studies may quite possibly yield instructive results in psychology and physiology, and no objection is possible if knowledge is good in itself.[1]

Atomic science now has taught man how to blow up the world. In search of the key to the mystery of creation, we have hit upon destruction. The scientific difference between the two

1. Otto Hahn, the inventor of atomic fission, knew at least what he was talking about when he said it again (according to a report in the newspaper *Die Welt* of July 3, 1954): "Science cannot act differently. Its task is to explore the world, its reality and truth, regardless of whether mankind therefrom experiences good or evil."

is small, but they are essentially one. It is all contained in the famous proposition of the theory of relativity which equates energy with matter. God laid the foundation of the world by transforming His creative energy into substance; we transform substance back into blind energy. But we know as little as ever of the mystery of creation, which is to make something formed and alive of nothing, of empty energy; we make nothing of something, although the scientific law of preservation of energy certainly holds in this case too, since the evaporated, dispersed energy is energy still. To science, unmaking is as worth studying as making; unfortunately it is easier.

Of course the moral frustration implied in this development has not been lost on the really great minds, the great discoverers themselves, who had seen new problems and broken new paths. While the public was in raptures over the triumphs of the human mind—meaning everybody's mind—and more and more impatient over the failure of the social sciences to emulate the new physics and teach us at last how to establish harmony among men, the great minds were in the grip of their sense of wonder and awe at mysteries which, they found, became more elusive as one seemed to come closer to them. Planck's last years were filled with such considerations; Einstein has repeatedly suggested that the moral problem is not a scientific but a religious problem; and to Niels Bohr the new physics is the straight avenue to religion. Among leading modern physicists such sentiment is widespread, if more or less inarticulate; and at least two of them (Pasqual Jordan and Karl Friedrich von Weitzsacker) try to demonstrate to the layman what they regard as the religious implications of the new physics. But among those who only identify themselves with the mental achievements of others, blinding pride and presumption are mounting.

There was a time when people realized that a great student of nature or medicine or history or the law not only knew facts but possessed insights and wisdom which lifted him over ordinary men to a dignity all his own, despite the personal vanity which often accompanied it. Insights and wisdom are not born into man; they grow and mature in him and with him through his work. And the work does not mature without the marks of suffering and defeat on it; a Christian knows that there is no other way to understanding. But no wisdom, no maturity, no personal growth is required for scientific greatness today; one either is a great physicist at twenty-three, endowed by nature with the extraordinary brain power which this requires, or one will never become a great physicist. The scientist as such is a man of power without responsibility. As a scientist he disclaims responsibility for his knowledge, which he regards as morally indifferent. Nay, human presumption has taught him to believe that his knowledge, the power of his mind, will liberate man from his ills. The Biblical legend (Isaiah 14:2) has it that God's most beautiful angel, Lucifer, the "Bringer of Light," when he set himself up as God, was thrown into the underworld to reign over the forces of destruction.

The Spurious Autonomy of the Social Sciences

In this situation the social sciences are harangued with the exhortation to speed up their development along the lines so triumphantly trodden by the natural sciences. Scientific morality will make us good, not by a moral effort of the whole person and his will power, still less by a religious effort—a rededication and regeneration—but by a mere intellectual effort, the training of the mind, which does not hurt. It is as easy as that.

The social sciences, like the natural, claim autonomy, and not only in the general sense, discussed before, that the reason inborn in man and elaborated in scientific enterprise is a specifically human force, thus equating autonomy and humanity. Beyond this, the autonomy of the social sciences is meant in a methodological sense, fencing off an area of studies where everything is explained and intelligible within the field and no recourse to outside factors is needed. In other words, the social sciences are not interdependent and interlocked but stand side by side, independent of one another; so much so that many academic curricula do not demand a course in social or political science of an economist, and vice versa. That is, to understand—and manipulate—economic life one does not need to understand anything outside economic life.

This is most paradoxical, and a very recent development. Until about 1650 or 1700 there was no autonomous science of economics, and economic problems were discussed as what they were: social and political problems, problems in political science. Economic activities were directed to socially desired ends, either by tradition or by the authorities, and were made intelligible by an inquiry into these ends and into the technical ways to attain them. They were not autonomous, determined by merely economic considerations; they were the technical side of social and political arrangements. No greater revolution has mankind gone through than the emancipation of economic activities from social and political guidance and their orientation toward inherent technical criteria and institutions such as "the" market, demand and supply, efficiency. That is, the responsible managers were exempted from noneconomic criteria and norms if they increased efficiency and thereby the quantity of goods.

The big change was reflected, first in the splitting off of "political economy" from the earlier comprehensive political science, and then in the tightening and narrowing of "political economy"—a demonstration of things economic in a sociopolitical framework, as in Adam Smith's work—into "economics." By the same token, naturally, the rump political science, equally impoverished, became more narrowly technical and autonomous too; like economics, government was now measured in terms of efficiency—that is, in terms of power. Meanwhile the youngest of the social sciences, sociology, appeared on the scene with comprehensive integrative ambitions in the work of Auguste Comte, who proclaimed that the human mind and institutions, having matured through the religious and the metaphysical stages, had now entered the "positive" stage; but in the execution of the plan sociology was bound to become positivistic in the narrow sense of the word, as in the neighboring sciences, which it claimed to comprehend but found already emancipated and autonomous. The result of the development, then, was a group of departmentalized social sciences, each autonomous in its own field and organizing this field with refined acumen and inexhaustible accumulation of material.

If the new intellectual situation is thus shown to be the exact mirror of the new reorganized departmentalized reality, the question must be raised: How much and what can the thus organized social sciences teach us? The answer is that they can teach us nothing fundamental but are confined to dealing in secondary matters—that is, such matters as can be settled in the individual field of activity without recourse to outside forces or events. This, however, is the case of the less grave problems exclusively. For the really grave problems are never confined to the individual field; they cross from one field to another and thereby reveal the unity underlying the several specialties. The great depression of the late 1920's and early 1930's broke the stamina of German democracy; brought fascism, a new form of government, to power; and thus produced the Second World War. The great depression, however, did not necessarily spring from purely economic causes, since the dislocations of the First World War in all probability contributed powerfully toward it. More generally speaking, there is no reason whatsoever to believe that political phenomena must always have political causes and economic phenomena economic causes. While in the laboratories of the natural sciences things are carefully controlled so as to change only one factor in a set of conditions and watch the one effect of the one cause, it is logically impossible in the history of society to attribute one of innumerable simultaneous effects to one of innumerable simultaneous changes at an earlier moment of time. All one can do is make the vague and empty statement that the whole of the later situation is the effect of the whole of the earlier one.

It is true that causes of a limited weight are likely to produce effects within the limited fields; but events of greater weight do not come under this rule. This then is our point: the autonomous sciences can adequately deal only with events of a significance sufficiently limited to keep within the autonomous field. Or, in other words, science presupposes that the events studied by it do not affect the routine operation of the neighboring field. For example, government and society must continue undisturbed in the event of an economic disturbance which must be exhaustively discussed by economics. For if they are disturbed too, then anything may happen, and there is no reason to believe that economic measures will remedy the economic disturbance in the manner tried out in the case of the minor disturbance. "Major" and "minor" designate differences in degree; but here they become differences in principle, minor problems fitting into the limitations of the autonomous science and major problems reaching beyond this limitation.

But where do they then reach? The answer cannot be into the field of political science or sociology, because these operate under the same restrictions as economics. The various disciplines stand side by side, it is true, but there is no logical or methodical link between them. The problem is that of transition from one field of study to the other, or of the translation of social forces from the special form of their appearance in one field to a different form in the other field. There is no specialist for such translation or for the study of the links that connect the several fields in reality, on the strength of the trivial observation that neither man nor society are as strictly departmentalized in reality as they are in the theory reflecting that reality.[2]

Nay, as the very notion of translation suggests a common ground of experiences and emotions to be expressed in different languages, so there must be a deeper ground underlying the economic or political or social crisis. The analogy of a social organism readily lends itself to the explanation of the difference between a localized condition—a cut finger, e.g.—and one that spreads from the place of origin to the total organism and may kill it. Treatment goes with diagnosis, of course, and may or may not work on symptoms while attacking a deeper layer of the sickness that grips a deeper layer of organic life. But all such considerations have no room in the modern social sciences, which are constitutionally unable to inquire into the nature of society or its sicknesses, but can only discuss limited localized problems of any one special discipline, on condition that the other manifestations of social life explored by the other special

2. In an ingenious venture—presented with greatest modesty and therefor apparently without making an impression—Hans Neisser has united economic, sociological, and political analyses into one systemic picture: "Stability in Late Capitalism," *Social Research,* Spring 1954, pp. 85–107.

disciplines offer no simultaneous problem. The health, balance, and durability of society, the all-important and only practical study in a time of general crisis, does not interest the conventional social sciences; despite all the historical evidence to the contrary, they proceed on the assumption that the life of society is always assured and so needs no care. They are rich in material and sophisticated in analytical technique; the one thing for which they do not care is wisdom, insight, understanding.

The complete absence of an underlying doctrine of man, which would spiritually unify the several disciplines, and the splitting of social life into several practical aspects each of which constitutes one such discipline, imitate the procedure of the natural sciences in breaking up the unity of the physical event into its several "aspects" or "sides," as studied by the several sciences. This program is clinched by the famous phrase "other things remaining equal," which is just as far-reaching in its significance as it is innocuous in appearance. This phrase is precisely designed to assure the tractability of the social problem in the methodical manner of the natural sciences by at least ideally isolating the social event, as the physical event is isolated in the practice of the laboratory. We imagine that the social event occurs in a context where nothing else happens, e.g. that there is an economic disturbance but no strain on social cohesion or government authority.

It is a most unfortunate but unalterable fact that, while tests in the laboratory seem to be capable of any degree of intensity—what about the huge atomic laboratory which is the Nevada desert?—the analogous isolation in thought of a social disturbance to make it accessible to scientific "observation" can be applied only to mild cases. The obvious reason is the organic unity of man's mind beneath all the different manifestations of his life, in contrast to the mechanical nature of the processes which allow the triumphs of physical science. A set of social sciences which disregards the organic unity of man's mind for the sake of reducing him to an agglomeration of unrelated activities should at least be credited with a self-effacing loyalty to the lead of physics and chemistry, instead of being constantly exhorted to follow that lead.

Another way to describe this methodological situation is to say that the autonomy of the social sciences is suggested by the experience of prosperity, when each of the several fields of social life functions smoothly within its own boundaries and is protected and supported by the smooth functioning of its neighbors; there is no change in context. The two formulations can be combined by enlarging the notion of prosperity to include such minor disturbances as the healthy resilience of the structure can absorb without shock. It is, of course, highly significant that the social sciences are more right in prosperous than in adverse conditions—that is, more right when they are less needed.

The ruthless optimism of the age in which they originated is conspicuous particularly when contrasted with our own considerably more skeptical climate of opinion.[3] And this optimism goes far toward demolishing or at least ignoring the limitations on the scope and validity of the propositions hedged in by the phrase "other things remaining equal." Indeed, the more we are inclined to take prosperity as our normal condition, the more shall we be inclined to drop that limiting clause or to give it an altogether trivial meaning. This tendency furthermore will find powerful psychological support in the vested interest which the social scientists have in the unlimited validity of their sciences. An enormous and rapidly growing investment in acumen and descriptive research keeps a constantly growing number of students busy and drowns out in their minds any of the fundamental problems—the nature of society, the constitutive power in it, the health and durability of society—which their sciences are constitutionally unable to handle.

Scientific Manipulation of Democracy

The hoped-for reward for the loyal adherence of the social sciences to the lead of the natural sciences is the discovery of laws of human and social behavior analogous to the laws of nature. In more strictly positivistic parlance, the metaphysical

3. Chapter IX of *Freedom and Order* traces the origin of the social sciences to the doctrine of preordained harmony which is the philosophical version of that optimism.

implications of the term "law"—who gave that law?—are replaced by the descriptive term "regularities"; this hardly means a difference in the approach. The analogy to the regularities in physical nature, of course, does not stop there; man's interest in the social regularities is not academic but practical. The old socialist adage "Knowledge is power" characterizes non-socialist theory as well, the more so since socialist theory—or rather Marxist theory—is really only the climax of general social theory, in this as in other respects. The power which knowledge conveys is in the technical application of scientific propositions so as to control and manipulate the forces that figure in the proposition. If we know how man and society must be expected regularly to react to one or the other stimulus contained in one or the other situation, then we can work out such techniques as will make them react in the way we desire. If we are quite sure that we know what pattern of social life is to be desired, we can produce that pattern by producing those conditions to which the desired pattern is the reaction. To quote Karl Mannheim once more, we can then produce a "smoothly working social process" which gives the individuals their "peace of mind." The more optimistic we are—i.e., the more the optimism incorporated in our sciences conveys itself to us—the more ambitious will our promises to others become.[4]

This is the grandiose vision of scientific democracy, which inspires the most advanced and ambitious of our social scientists. It is all in line with the theory of the Marxist "vanguard," which understands itself as the vessel of final scientific reason and makes it its appointed job to lift the people to the level of this exalted understanding by the use of whatever means appear expedient. And it is, naturally, in line with the attitude of the natural scientists, who use their knowledge of the elements to harness them into the service of man. The great and decisive difference between the natural and the social sciences, of course, is that the elements tamed by the former are unmistakably the

4. Jacob Burckhardt, *Force and Freedom,* Chapter III, Section I (written in 1869): "Indeed, there are wiseacres enough who imagine that *they* would dictate the programme of culture to the State, once it was completely united."

means to the scientific end, while in the case of society man is not only the means properly manipulated for the attainment of the scientific end but also the ulterior end beyond the scientific end. If this were not so, and where it is not so, it would certainly be impossible to speak of democracy, no matter what other merits might be claimed for the arrangement. Even so, the democratic character of the arrangement may be doubted, in view of the fact that the people as object of scientific manipulation can at best only trust but can hardly examine the measures applied to them. The responsible masters of the treatment are —in this utopia of scientific democracy—the social scientists, and this role would make of them enlightened despots rather than democratic representatives. Karl Mannheim's way out is the suggestion that the planners would and should "plan for freedom"—e.g., leave certain areas of unplanned activity between those others held under strict control so the total process still operates smoothly and "according to plan"—freedom being defined by him as absence of planning. But such "planned freedom," of limited scope and in a strictly supervised context, is a safety valve rather than a democracy. Nor does it help to refer to democratic elections putting the planners in control and possibly recalling them in due course; the means of information and propaganda are quite sure to be the last to be left unplanned by the planners, and where they are planned, the results of elections are a foregone conclusion.

More promising as a way out is a closer inspection of the source of the plan. If this is to be the most mature fruit of scientific studies systematizing and refining but certainly not violating the common man's common sense, then one may say that the persons in charge are the representatives of the common man —elections or no elections. The fully developed fruits of reason may be beyond, but cannot be contrary to, common understanding. The scientific law is, by definition, autonomous human law. In this sense one may call it democratic, although this certainly would be a democracy different from congressional or parliamentary democracies, not only in institutions but in philosophy.

But now this happens to be the Hegel-Marx theory of liberty: "recognition of necessity." Disregarding with Marx and

Engels the facts that in Hegel's idealism "necessity" is not understood as the causal or functional law of science, the uniqueness of man is here found in his insight into the lawful structure of the world, including the law which controls himself. All creatures are blindly driven by the blind necessity of nature; man alone, by virtue of his reason, rises to intellectual participation in the rational processes of nature and, by understanding and accepting the necessity of their governing him, receives this necessity into his will and makes it a self-given law. This analysis will be further pursued in later sections of this book.

What we wish to emphasize here is the wide distance we have traveled from individualism to an autonomous law which leaves no room for individualism. Or if this be individualism—if the law of autonomous reason is interpreted to be the mark of liberty —then there is no more difference between individualism and collectivism. After all, individualism in the popular understanding and historical origin of the word stands for the liberty of the individual person. But the law of natural necessity, whatever it may be, is certainly not a respecter of persons: it must and does wipe out individual differences as irrelevant and establishes as essential the things the individuals have in common rather than those that mark them off from one another. Nay, in claiming that "man" by his reason makes the oppressive rule of natural necessity a self-given law of his rational nature, we certainly have not spoken of the individual person and his particularities but of the species, or in sociological aspect, the collective. Only of collective man can it be said—in this immanent criticism— that he makes the natural necessities of his life his self-given law and freely submits to them; it does not make sense to say the same of individual persons, as if their submission to the rationally understood necessities meant the fulfillment of their individuation.

A scientific argument cannot, in principle, produce more than is potentially contained in its premises; the premise determines or at the very least limits the result. That is why the decisive thing in the development of science is the new question; there are no new answers where there is no new question. The question in the scientific approach to man and society is, and must be, put in such a way as to isolate, through the clause "other things remaining equal," the several sides or aspects or functions or activities of man in society; man is dissolved into his component parts. The whole, naturally, would then be a composite of these parts, and social scientists will generally agree that such composition would crown their efforts and merge the several social sciences into a comprehensive science of man in society. But synthetic man is at best collective man; he certainly is not the free person in free society. Nor can one arrive at the individual person by introducing differences between the exemplars of the species in regard to size or weight or sex appeal or intelligence or the thousand other features which these individuals may show in different measures. For what makes man an "individual" is not the different measures in him of the qualities which he shares with all other men, but that in which he is "indivisible" and distinctive; and this has been eliminated at the outset of the surgical operation by which he was divided into his component parts for scientific processing of the raw product and final composition of the finished parts. Eliminated by the division of the parts, it cannot be restored by their composition. Science leaves no room for individualism.

Rationality Versus Liberty [5]

Science leaves no room for individualism because scientific necessity leaves no room for liberty. The planners may decide

5. The following books about the crisis of education have impressed the author: Fred Clarke, *Education and Social Change,* 1940; also his memorandum on "Church, Community and State in Their Relation to Education," *Oxford Conference of the World Council of Churches,* 1938; Wilhelm Flitner, *Die Abendlaendischen Vorbilder und das Ziel der Erziehung,* 1947; William Ernest Hocking, *Experiment in Education: What We Can Learn from Teaching Germany,* 1954; Theodor Litt, *Individuum und Gemeinschaft,* 1925; Jacques Maritain, *Education at the Crossroads,* 1948; Walter Hamilton Moberley, *The Crisis in the University,* 1949; Arnold Nash, *The University and the Modern World,* 1944, with an excellent bibliography; André Schlemmer, *The Crisis in the World of Thought,* 1940. The first two chapters of Eugen Rosenstock-Huessy, *The Christian Future, or the Modern Mind Outrun* (1947), including among other sections "The Soul on the Highway," give the most graphic and most profound presentation of the crisis known to me.

to leave a few activities unplanned and may call this "liberty," but nature has not decided to leave anything to chance. The Heisenberg effect has now for decades served as a topic for sermons on the foundation of liberty in physical nature or similar themes, but social scientists have not yet discovered any analogous indeterminacy in man; and if they did, it would not prove anything for individual liberty. Indeterminacy is not liberty. Liberty is the liberty of a self to realize, manifest, fulfill its distinctive creative power in a distinctive act, however modest, beyond the natural necessities. How this should be possible must be discussed presently; for the moment, it may suffice to summarize the entire lengthy criticism in the trivial proposition that natural necessity and liberty are mutually exclusive in logic by definition; and that, hence, the reduction of man to an agglomeration of natural necessities denies the possibility of his creative liberty as a person, no matter how much acumen is invested in the heroic enterprise to prove that acceptance of necessity is the true and only liberty—the liberty of the collective, which is defined precisely by the absence of personal liberty. Necessity rationally understood and submitted to is freedom? It is, if man's nature is rationality; it is the limit of man's freedom if man's nature is in his individuality. The quality of rationality, characterizing as it does the race, cannot constitute the uniqueness of individuality. Speaking sociologically, this rationality, being actual only in an intellectual elite even though potential in every member of the race, cannot constitute individuality, which does not coincide in any sense with intellectual gifts and training and is the property of every member of the race. Speaking religiously, man's rationality, however limited or widespread in reality, is limited in power and intellectual reach by its integration into the human self; man's reason is not God's reason.

If we equate rationality with necessity and individuality with creativity, we have thereby delimited the problem of this book. Creation is the act of putting there something that could not have been predicted. If it can be predicted it is there potentially. But *Hamlet,* the B-minor Mass, the dome of St. Peter's, etc. could not have been predicted. This fact is perfectly compatible with a high appreciation of the sociology of the styles and forms of art. And even on the most modest level and without any lasting incorporation in an objective work, individuality cannot be predicted, nor repeated for that matter. The essence of scientific control is predictability and repetition; the essence of the scientific method is to make things over so as to control them; the claim of science is that its rule is all-inclusive and permits of no exception. This claim, on closer inspection, turns out to be pure dogma, unverifiable in experience and contrary to logic. The truth is that science, in order to apply its method, concentrates on things tangible and measurable—such as the economic interest of a specific person or group in a specific situation—and ignores things spiritual because they are outside its chosen method, and then proceeds to declare nonexistent that which it chooses to ignore because it cannot deal with it.

That which science chooses to ignore is the spiritual life of man, the core of his person, the center of his creativity, the seat of his responsibility. If science is right, man is not responsible because he is not free; his actions are the necessary effects of causes that work on him and through him but do not originate in him and hence are in no way his responsibility. The objectives toward which he is scientifically to be conditioned are ascertained scientifically too—that is, practically without anybody's responsibility; or in a different version, at best under the scientist's responsibility for the correctness of procedure. Responsibility is replaced by the certainty which is promised by the scientific method. It is thus being replaced because responsibility is now revealed to be an atavistic, prescientific illusion. Man is that strange and grotesque animal which can have illusions—even the illusion of being responsible for the lawful processes of nature in him, the reverse side of his illusion of being free from the laws of nature in him. Social science thus emancipates man from the yoke of responsibility for his actions: everything will be fine if he stops bothering about it.

The one thing that may still be added is a brief discussion of the end to which man is thus led with his own approval. If man denies that he is free and responsible, this has the effect of killing his freedom and responsibility. He may have been less free and responsible than he thought he was—this at least is not contrary to logic; but he can never be more free and responsible

than he thinks he is—this would be contrary to logic. For freedom and responsibility imply an action, a moral effort, a dedi-
cation, and cannot be had at a cheaper price. Where I will not
serve, I am sure not to serve. If I claim to decide I may, and am
perhaps likely to, be frustrated; but by not wanting to decide, I
am sure not to do it. I am then carried down the river of necessity to which I have surrendered—"liberty is acceptance of
necessity"—toward its goal, which I implicitly make my own.

The goal is either decay and death, or totalitarianism, or
both. According to the great Spengler, who anticipated our
critique of science a generation ago, it is both, a rationally
organized and irrationally justified totalitarianism being the
last, possibly long-lived, phase in the natural cycle of human
societies from birth to death under the law of nature. According
to the still greater Karl Marx, the goal is a rationally justified
totalitarianism beyond and above any possible conflict of the
past—a picture of life fulfilled, which others may easily equate
with death. Modern academic social science can lend itself to
either one of these two interpretations, but it has not elongated
its short-run analyses into an independent picture of the future,
true to its far more modest, positivistic attitude. An exception
is, e.g., the sociologism of Mannheim, a form of Marxism where
the biting drink of revolutionary proletarian power is watered
down to a mild professorial rule. A generation or two ago Social
Darwinism suggested a similar goal through writers like H. G.
Wells and Julian Huxley, where sexual selection by a scientific
board would produce bigger and better men, thus enormously
improving upon the clumsy and wasteful selective processes of
nature, which always need millions of years and myriads of
deaths and lost germs to attain their goal. In comparison, one is
almost tempted to count poor little Dr. Kinsey among the in-
dividualists when he presents the zoology of human sex as the
implicit norm of sexual ethic, with such regulative forces as love
or consideration of family life strictly ignored as scientifically
irrelevant. All these are results of the "scientific method."

It is impossible to deny the logical possibility of man's destroying his freedom by denouncing it as unscientific; the possibility is borne out by too many examples in literature and too

strong tendencies in reality. But does this consideration not condemn us precisely to that cynical naturalism, or at least that helmless relativism, which we have just found in the worshipers of the scientific method? Will it not come down to saying that man collectively does change in essential character so as to be a different being at different times, free in the past but unfree now? Or perhaps, in a different turn of thought, that man collectively can change himself by changing his ideas about himself? Nothing of the kind. Man can give up his freedom only because he is free; his freedom includes the freedom to give it up. The result would then be that he becomes unfree sociologically and historically; but he remains free ontologically and can historically resume the freedom he gave up at any time, in principle at least. If man chooses to behave like an animal, this does not make him an animal; it makes him something far below the animal. For man remains free and responsible, and it is precisely his freedom which lifts him ontologically to the uniqueness of his position on this earth and may make him morally as wicked as we know only he can be. In a way the animals are good, for they live their lives as appointed and cannot sin. But their goodness is trivial because they cannot sin. Contrariwise, man is not good but free because he can sin; if he gives up his freedom he sins—which is precisely the test of his freedom.

Are we then saying that the social sciences are wrong because they deny man's freedom? We are far from saying that; we do say that their truth is sorely incomplete and becomes a grievous lie if presented as the whole truth, but is an important part of the truth if properly qualified. The reason is that man's freedom is certainly not absolute, as is God's; it is more or less narrowly qualified by the material conditions of his life, which are under the rule of nature and are being explored by the social sciences. In other words, man is conditioned by material conditions, which limits his freedom; but he is not determined by them, for his freedom transcends the natural conditions of his life. The sculptor's hammer must comply with the structural requirements of the marble in order to give the marble the new spiritual form, but this spiritual form does not follow from the structural requirements of the marble but testifies to the artist's creative freedom.

Knowledge of conditioning forces is indispensable; it becomes arrogance and usurpation if it claims to determine and control man and his work. If the social sciences made allowance for man's freedom, their positive studies of the limits of freedom would be in their proper place. But the trouble with them is not only that they forget whatever mental reservations, if any, they may have had in favor of liberty, but go so far as actually and positively to discourage and disparage liberty, seduced as they are by their luciferic ambition to control and manipulate man and the world. For those who dream themselves in the magnificent role of using unlimited power over man's soul to free him from ancient ills and give him happiness are themselves ignorant of the glory and agony of liberty, and they destroy its glory because they think its agony is an ill. The tragedy is that the same intellectual individualism whose dynamic openness created their sciences also cut them off from the profundity of personal liberty and left them with nothing but that ignorant and inflated positivism of which they boast as the "scientific method." These antagonistic developments can be shown in a survey of the various social sciences.

Methodological Survey: Psychology, Sociology and Anthropology, Political Science, Economics

Psychology, which was strangely left out of Comte's plan of the positive sciences, has certainly made good as far as positivistic method and program are concerned. Its general thesis seems to be that our decisions are not really ours, that they issue from natural drives or forces or instincts, which we share with all the other animals under the laws of biological nature and which can be studied and explored and thus applied to useful purpose. For they may be given specific shape and direction by the "milieu" or by the particular configuration of interests or by sexual frustration or by biological inheritance, which in turn may or may not be open to modifying influences further back. Our decisions, hence, are predetermined and pass through us to their appointed results in our actions. This, of course, does not preclude that in passing through us the individual motivation may be combined with other motivations coming from other sources into a more complex picture of motives and actions, which in this particular combination is not found in other cases and may be described as individual.

No doubt, psychology in individualistic democracy will hope to proceed from the study of simple cases to more complex ones, thus taking account of human multivariety and possibly building up a system of psychological typology, which may then intertwine with parallel endeavors in sociology. Complex causation, however, is no nearer to being freedom than is simple causation; both are deterministic, both give irrefutable evidence of the absence of freedom by permitting psychology to predict and control human action. If psychology knows the forces that go into the making of our decisions, it can predict, control, and modify them at will. It can, by adding advertising techniques to a given set of conditions, make us buy things that we neither need nor want; it can, by propaganda techniques, make us accept slogans which we know are not true; it can, by appropriate pressures, make man over into the image desired or deemed expedient by anyone in control of the psychological apparatus of "communication," not to say education.

The one thing that psychology cannot do is use its techniques of control to make us ourselves; for it does not know that there is such a thing, and it does not care to know because such knowledge would explode its structure of control. If the name suggests that psychology tries to understand man's "soul," it is precisely the soul that must be discouraged by being told that it is an unscientific residue. But the truly grotesque thing is that the scientific technicians themselves, while they would never deny in theory that they are conditioned like everybody else, do have the ambition of deciding what people should be like and must be made into. It is their mastery of their science from which this ambition accrues to them; knowing the techniques, they feel they are—or will someday be—competent to set spiritual goals for man. Their approach protects them from suspecting that, in thus setting themselves up as the judges and saviors of others, they may be motivated by vanity and lust for power. The latest fashion of their science is invariably proclaimed as the truth that speaks through them. That the next fashion, not to speak of the real truth, may teach something entirely different and recommend a different approach to people does not trouble their conscience.[6]

What makes things still worse is the conflict with depth psychology. Through Nietzsche, Freud, and Jung there has been the rediscovery of the human soul, its repressions, compensations, and sublimations, its life in anguish, despair, and hope, its language and imagery, its storehouse of individual and collective experiences. This is far too great a wealth for anyone to really know and master completely, and plenty of dissension and strife is unavoidable. Nor should we be overmuch troubled by obvious borderline violations, when the imperialism of the great discoverers claims to unlock with their key the mysteries of society, history, and religion. The mirror of God in the human soul does not explain God, but the rejection of the claim does not affect, e.g., the doctrine of the archetypes. All this, however, is far below the dignity of our academic psychologists, who, with very few exceptions, regard as unscientific speculation what is too rich, too profound, and too complicated for their laboratory tests. For it all amounts to the insight that the border line between human liberty and human serfdom has become quite fluid because, in principle, one can now excuse any vice as sickness, just as one can present almost any sickness as guilt.[7] One cannot speak about the human soul without speaking about its freedom and the limits of its freedom.

Sociology is the specific instrument which Comte has forged as the tool of social unification and integration—of that

6. At least three times in my life span so far the physicians have completely reversed their judgment on the drinking of milk. I can only draw the conclusion that either the first and third phases or the second phase recommended something harmful to health. Truths seem to be the more apodictic, the more short-lived they are.

7. Cf. Wilhelm Kuetemeyer, *Die Krankheit Europas. Beitraege zu einer Morphologie,* 1951; and above all Eugen Rosenstock-Huessy, *Heilkraft und Wahrheit,* 1951.

"progress" in unification and integration which modern "progressive" large-scale technical society has made possible and which neither Comte himself nor Saint-Simon before him nor Durkheim after him have ever mistaken for progress in the direction of individualism and liberty. Nor has the very differently motivated Max Weber ever succumbed to that modern confusion. Spencer in England and Sumner in America one generation later used the hypothesis of natural evolution as a highly speculative framework for the presentation of the stages through which society, like an organism, has to pass on its way from primitive homogeneity to higher forms of differentiation and integration, which develop and require new social organs and should lead to an equilibrium between the two opposite tendencies—that is, between freedom and order. In Spencer this crystallizes into an explicit program of laissez-faire in economics and pacifism in politics; in Sumner there is, after the description of religion as an early erroneous pseudoscience, a positive appreciation of religion as a powerful means of social discipline and morality, which may or may not be replaceable by equally strong and more scientific means in modern society.[8]

What is startling in both cases is the absence of any discussion of modern technical society in its specific features and tendencies—those tendencies which stood at the beginning of sociology and constitute its central problem. For what Spencer opposes to the military type of society is not the technical-industrial type— which may easily converge with the former—but the business type, which may or may not be technical; it is the bourgeois type but not the scientific type. Hence also American sociology, while strong and invaluable on the descriptive side, can hardly be credited with a contribution to the discussion of liberty in modern large-scale society. Continental sociology, contrariwise, is rather pessimistic as to the liberty which is dear to the hearts of

8. A thorough and circumspect history of "The Theory of Religion in American Sociology" is given by Dr. Oliver Read Whitley in his doctoral dissertation, which the author and the Graduate School of Yale University had the great kindness to let me see. I owe much enlightenment to Albert Salomon, whose forthcoming history of sociology promises to be a landmark of scholarship.

men like Durkheim and Weber and sheds a tragic light on their work. Finally, Mannheim in his supposedly democratic program of "the planned guidance of people's lives on the basis of sociology with the aid of social psychology" has not even a reference to liberty or individualism, though the benevolence and moderation of the planners is supposed to "plan for freedom" by voluntarily leaving certain less vital areas outside their grip.

Sociology had described the primitive stages of social evolution almost deductively and certainly speculatively or hypothetically. Now anthropology began to verify or rather refute such speculation, with the result that organic evolution had to give way to cultural history, in the center of which there is religion as the doctrine of meaning and purpose. Men like Malinowski in anthropology and Merton, Kingsley Davis, and Howard Becker in systematic sociology had thus a new approach to religion in society, from their understanding that such values and virtues as the life of society must know and commend can be established only by religion. Strictly speaking, there are then two sociological functions united in religion: the answer to the question of meaning and value; and the unifying, socially integrating effect of any common belief, no matter in what. The Durkheim answer (implicit already in Comte) to the question of meaning and value—to the effect that what people worship in religion and what really transcends, disciplines, and ennobles their lives is their society itself, in whatever disguise—is thus left behind and the door is flung wide open. In this framework, on the basis of the ideas of creativity and brotherliness, the approach to personal liberty for the first time becomes at least possible, after having been barred by the merely socially integrating function of religion in the teachings of Comte, Durkheim, and Sumner.[9]

9. But this, however gratefully to be acknowledged, is really all: society needs a religion and creates it. There is much noble anguish and sadness in Malinowski's confession that, convinced though he was of the need for religion, he could not bring himself to that surrender which it required. Maybe he could not because his scholarly endeavors were directed toward "religion," a function of society, rather than toward the true God, Who is meant not in "religion" but in the Christian religion. For as one examines these studies of religion, what they seem to say is that man

78   *Reason and Faith in Modern Society*

Political science was originally the mother of the social sciences, comprising as it did everything that was required to establish a healthy and vigorous community, including such study of the principles of justice as should give both the freedom of the citizens and the order of the community the direction toward the good which of themselves they did not have. One can say that political science was applied ethic, where the method of application, of course, was determined by the technical structure of the material of which that community was built. Being applied ethic, political science was not autonomous. It is supposed to have become autonomous through Machiavelli; he is praised as the beginner of realism in political science.

This credit, however, is of more than doubtful validity. On the one hand, even Machiavelli cannot be more realistic than St. Augustine eleven hundred years earlier, who in striking analyses described Machiavelli's reality as "the City of the World" governed by the "Love of Self," but intermingled with the "City of God" governed by the "Love of God," and defined man as suspended between the two. On the other hand, Machiavelli engages in lengthy discussions of the virtues required for the public good, and his work, far from being neutral on values,

---

decides for religion in general as necessary to his life and then, more specifically, for a particular religion. It is as if we believed that man, in a first step, becomes man and only then American or Chinese or French, whereas it obviously is the other way around: man becomes man only through being American or Chinese or French. Hence also the confused notion that the more dogmatic forms of the high religions should give way, in our own day, to more directly ethical and humanitarian forms, which command the religious devotion of modern man. Is this really a development of religion, is it not rather its evaporation? Sociology has gained greatly in realism by discerning the "function" of religion, but what sociology can thus explore is not "religion," far less Christianity, but at the very best the social function of religion. And even that, if it is to advance beyond mere generalities, presupposes an understanding which is not a cognitive but a religious act and requires a commitment of the person rather than an "objective" process in the mind alone. It is tragic to see the noble souls of great scholars groping in vain for the comfort of faith to be restored to them by an extension of the same scholarly studies which have destroyed their faith by subsuming it under societal phenomena.

is an eloquent plea for the happiness and honor of his city. If this be realism, then it is certainly very far from the positivism widespread in modern political science, which explores facts and institutions and, where judgment enters, uses as its only yardstick the national interest regarded as a fact. This, of course, is so because the matrix of political science has been emptied by the emancipation from it of the other now "autonomous" social sciences. The rump political science that is left is thereby in constant danger of being reduced from the moral to the technical level, where the political aspect of human freedom cannot be given an adequate discussion. The bewilderment into which political science was thrown by the rise of fascism clinches the point.

It is only fair, on the other hand, to report that the moral tradition of political science, its close relationship throughout the ages with political philosophy and history, still asserts itself or perhaps asserts itself again in our own day. While all the other social sciences arose with the claim to autonomy by emancipating themselves from the matrix of political science and were thus given by their very origin the direction toward positive and technical studies, the great themes which political science has discussed throughout the ages continue to fascinate the minds of educated students. Political science, not being purely "modern" in origin, is not purely modern in method and nature.

Most marked and most successful is the modern scientific tendency in what is nowadays significantly called economics, while it had been until relatively recently "political economy." After eliminating the vestiges of deism and idealism which still used strongly to tinge the teachings presided over by Alfred Marshall, we have now arrived at a system of teachings coordinated under the assumption that what rational man does is maximize his income (and the utility of consumption). The terminology is to suggest that a different type of behavior is possible and can happen; it is not illogical but only irrational from an economic point of view. This is considered a substantial improvement over the naïve assumption by eighteenth- and nineteenth-century economists of "economic man" as a kind of species in nature, if not the climax of natural evolution.

But the words "rational" and "irrational" in the modern
world are strongly laden with bias; "irrational" is a scientific
term for "absurd," undignified in rational man. And the terminology is not of a merely declaratory nature, as an aesthetic judgment would be purely declaratory; there is every reason to
assume that this terminology, commending one and disapprov-
ing another policy as it does, becomes an active force in the
education of students, even though this may not be anybody's
conscious purpose in using such terms. If the terminology implicitly dissuades the behavior it calls irrational, this outcome is
in line with the material interests of the profession. For such a
behavior is by definition beyond the explanatory reach of economics; it is an irregularity where regularity is needed; it is
prohibitive of prediction where the age of manipulation requires
predictability. The more successful the call to rational economic
behavior and away from irrational behavior, the more successful
will be the verification and practical application of the economic
propositions derived from the premise of precisely that behavior.
As a human being, the student will be prone to conform to the
type of behavior which, if generalized, makes his professional
training more valuable; as a student, he must wish everybody
else to conform to that behavior. The age of manipulation has
created the vested interest of students in scientific methods of
prediction and control, which require standardization, collectivization, and mechanization.

The means to the end of maximum income is maximum efficiency in the use of labor by the laborer or of capital by the
investor or of the available resources by the manager, etc.
Maximum income through maximum efficiency, or rising income through ever rising efficiency, is the one accepted rational
behavior, which permits predictability and control. That is,
man's life is appraised as a means to the end of production.
Were life an end in itself—and inasmuch as it is—it should
measure its value in terms of, say, satisfaction. For to repeat,
man lives on the goods he makes, but he lives in making them;
and while satisfaction in personal work may coincide with
technical efficiency, it is far more likely to conflict with the

changing demands of fluctuating markets and revolutionary technology. But it is precisely in this conflict that the modern materialistic and collectivizing interpretation of rationality makes efficiency the mark of rationality and deprecates satisfaction in work as a private selfish goal. This conflict was discussed above in a different context; it occurs here again as the quite fundamental problem in the subjection of man to scientific law which requires his reduction to quantitative and collective standards.[10]

Disregarding the relationship of man to his work and thus justifying—"by amputation"—the assumption that maximum efficiency and maximum income are the rational objectives of rational man, the use to be made of that income is the rational problem that economics finds on the demand side of the market. The first alternative is between spending and saving; the second alternative, if the choice is spending, lies among the many goods that are for sale. Economists, insofar as they care at all, like to stress the study of these alternatives as their contribution to the study of, or even the education to, democratic freedom: in democratic society people are free to buy what they please or to save as they please. The trouble with this freedom is only that it exists in Soviet Russia as in the libertarian camp.[11] So democratic freedom cannot be defined as "consumers' freedom." Far more important, however, and typical of the prevalent indifference to the problems of freedom, is that, immediately upon describing their consumers' freedom and savers' freedom, econ-

10. The distinctions and classifications here suggested have been worked out in my book *Wirtschaftssysteme und Gesellschaftssysteme*, 1954, and earlier suggested in an article "Comparative Economic Systems," in A. Dudley Ward (ed.), *Goals of Economic Life*, 1953.

11. We must add the minor qualification that the West, in addition to this "consumers' freedom," also displays "consumers' sovereignty," i.e., the determination—within limits—of the sizes of supplies and of the sizes of the industries producing them by consumer demand; while in a Communist system the official plan is sovereign in this sense and may override the wishes of consumers. The importance of this distinction is somewhat controversial, however; cf. Barbara Wootton, *Freedom Under Planning*, Chapter IV.

omists proceed to develop the economic laws which these two freedoms obey, in strictly mathematical form and with an elaborate apparatus of three-dimensional figures.

Still worse, the fundamental drive to maximum income through maximum efficiency as the standard of rational behavior is ambivalent in itself. Is this maximization rationally sought in the framework of the individual units of business firm or household, or in the framework of the unified total of all production plants or households? The Communist contention is that collectivism is a higher form of efficiency; and while there is no way to prove this from experience, neither is there one to refute it. The two systems do not yet stand on the same footing, Soviet communism being a hundred years younger than American capitalism.[12] Is productivity greater in the system of individualism? If so, is stability more doubtful in this system? [13] What about incentive under communism, and what about stabilizing measures under individualism? No unequivocal answer to such questions can be given. But if we decide that individualism is preferable on moral or spiritual grounds, we imply the superiority of Communist efficiency and become guilty of that irrationality which is ready to sacrifice efficiency and income to dogmatic whims and which we ourselves have just denounced as undignified and unscientific in rational man. In the world of modern thought, such a dogma would hang in the air, rooted nowhere, suspended nowhere, connected with nothing, derived from nothing, illogical, absurd—but nevertheless a human possibility if suggested by the frantic desire to escape the drift toward collectivism which lurks in the argument from efficiency.

Nay, if there is no logical way of deciding the issue between individualism and collectivism, or—the same thing—if either one of the two claims to be the last and final word of scientific

12. Cf. my book *Wirtschaftssysteme und Gesellschaftssysteme.*

13. This same question can be given a quite different form: What is the time span during which income should be made a maximum? As between the individual plant and the unified total of all plants, so as to the shorter or longer period of efficiency and income, the decision is arbitrary, not tied to any logically necessary criterion. In this form the question is fully discussed in a special section of Chapter 5.

reason, then modernity is back, after a few centuries, at the point from which it started: the ambivalence of dogmatic belief, the insolubility of the conflict in logic, and the ensuing dissension in practice. Scientific reason was supposed to be unequivocally certain, and rational life consequently harmonious. Now the modern world is torn between two dogmas which are presupposed in two rival social systems and which demonstrate that human reason is not any nearer divine reason than the reception of revelation in man's limited mind is near the source of Revelation—or, more generally, than religion is to that which is meant in it. This is where modern social science is led by its own dialectical development, which its own positivism ignores.[14]

To sum up: All the social sciences have this in common: that they dismember the physical, social, and moral organism and study its various organs separately under the impact of varying "stimuli" or the like, thus learning to control the behavior of persons and groups. This procedure presupposes that man and society are the sums of these organs and reactions—in other words, that there is in man no irreducible personal center, no seat of spirit and decision, no spontaneous action and genuine responsibility; and that whatever may appear as such is merely a reflex of ancient superstitions of which an educated modern mind rids itself. In still other words, man appears as standardized, rationalized, collectivized; an interchangeable specimen of a species created in principle by the industrial revolution which

14. In order not to have to concede to itself the disaster of its positive method, academic social science in the Western world seems more and more inclined to treat Marxism as nonexistent, instead of investing every intellectual and moral effort in the study of it with a view to overcoming it. It is difficult to see how one may hope for victory by ignoring the enemy. The many hundreds of prodigally financed research projects on Soviet Russia or other Communist countries only confirm this. "Research" in this context means a purely positivistic study of statistics, first-hand reports, and documents, on the assumption that to Communists their Marxist theory and philosophy mean as little as any philosophy means to the researchers. An occasional attempt at interpretation of policies in the light of their Marxist background then founders on lack of knowledge and understanding of Marxism. Cf. my articles "Soviet Politics and Power," *Social Research,* March 1951, and "On Academic Liberty," *Christianity and Crisis,* July 7, 1952.

made efficiency the supreme goal of life and to this end suppresses in man whatever may thwart efficiency: spontaneity,
imagination, personality, individuality, moral norms, and moral
inhibitions. The industrial revolution suppresses these qualities;
the servile social sciences ignore them and accept the man of
the industrial revolution as the norm of man, the subject of
their studies. It need hardly be added that he is also the man of
totalitarianism, as the social sciences produce the techniques for
the operation of totalitarianism. This picture is indeed a far
cry from the liberty that made it possible. There cannot be a
spectacle more ironic than man using his liberty to enslave himself and in addition interpreting his slavery as real freedom, on
the strength of the proposition that science is his nature and
that life according to one's nature is freedom. It is all a matter
of definition in an age that has lost its standards of value.

Positive Significance of the Social Sciences

After this criticism the question comes up again: Are the
social sciences wrong? When this question first arose, the answer
was that they were right, as could be seen from the fact that
people do yield to the manipulating pressures worked out and
applied by the social scientists. What they study is the limits of
man's freedom, and these are of extreme importance for us to
note if we care for freedom. But if this is all they study, if they
leave out the freedom that is thus limited, then the study of
the limits of freedom easily degenerates into the study of how to
tighten the limits and destroy freedom. This answer, naturally,
is not final nor comprehensive enough; it needs to be supplemented. If the social sciences can be abused, thus putting their
validity to the test anyway, to what legitimate use can they be
put? (We need not repeat that Mannheim's answer, claiming
that the social scientists themselves will put their techniques to
beneficial use, is no answer because it merely changes the purpose of the application but not the system of the sciences themselves. In other words, Mannheim believes with the totalitarians
in all-inclusive manipulation; the future of mankind, he says,
depends only on who will seize and use the apparatus of manipu-

lation—"selfish, power-hungry men" or unselfish scholars? To us the point is that, while the social sciences give some truth, they deny and suppress the essential part of the truth—man's freedom—and become guilty of pernicious error.)

The analogy of the physical sciences can help us make our point, precisely because the social sciences continue to imitate them and construe society in the image of physical nature. There was a time, a generation or two ago, when biologists and physical scientists confidently expected to explain the mystery of life, possibly to create some life, through the appropriate combination of the physical and chemical processes which they discovered in the living organism. No self-respecting scientist shares that belief today. But this obviously does not mean that physical and chemical processes are irrelevant to life in theory and practice. If those processes do not create life, their failure still brings disease and death. Organic life has been kindled in physical nature and depends for its preservation on the correct interlocking of innumerable processes in physical nature, as evidenced by the fact that the sicknesses of which life may die are legion. The physical and chemical processes are not life, to be sure, but they are an integral and indispensable part of life; they do not originate life, but they condition it and their failure kills it. The doctor to protect and preserve life has to keep them going; their study is essential to the defense of life.

The relationship between the social sciences and the life of society is analogous to that between the physical sciences and biological life. Political, psychological, sociological, economic processes keep the life of society going, although it cannot be deciphered by those disciplines or reduced to them or derived from them. A failure in any of those processes produces uneasiness, disease, and crisis, which may be localized in the field of origin or may spread to engulf the whole of that society or civilization. Examples were studied in an earlier chapter. It is the first business of statesmen and administrators to watch the technical processes and turn or replace the switches in the immense complexity of modern society so as to keep the processes going and properly interlocking. The life of society, like the life of the organism, is embedded in nature and in that quasi nature as which the economic and other processes are presented by social scientists. The mystery of social life, of person and community, is not deciphered or exhausted by any of the social sciences but is conditioned by the natural and quasi-natural processes whose laws they so accurately describe. What they teach us, then, is not how to understand the mystery of social life but how to defend it, to protect and preserve it by defending, protecting, preserving, or readapting the institutional structures and processes in which that society lives. They teach the necessities that have to be met in order that there be personal and social life, and the necessities that immediately attach themselves to any new fact, action, and decision so as to drive from it to its logical consequence. For there never is a moment when the operation of natural causal forces is suspended; they are always at work and always have to be watched by those responsible for life, society, spirit.

Nay, often enough the causal laws, the forces of nature and quasi nature, seem to be in exclusive control of human and social action as described by the social scientist. Determinism then seems to be fully warranted, and the liberty of decision to be ruled out. But they are not. They seem to be if and when we choose to bow to necessity—that is, if and when we decide not to make use of our essential freedom. Most of the time our freedom to change our life is indeed dormant, and we drift along under scientific law toward the goals of natural or social life, which are decay and death, or possibly totalitarianism, as discussed earlier. In the absence of freedom, the law as taught by science is supreme, and its supremacy then looks like the definition of man and society. But we are ruled by necessity only because we have freely chosen to submit to it, so what is false ontologically appears correct historically. The entire picture is then to be explained in terms of necessity, and it will bear out a scientific prediction in such terms. In case we do not make use of our freedom, the deterministic social sciences are right, and their spokesmen eagerly expand the territory over which they rule by telling us that we are not free and should not succumb to the illusion that we are.

Theory of Liberty

The doctrine of man that underlies the sciences denies man's creative freedom. But there is no logical difficulty involved in assuming that there is in man an irreducible personal core, a center of responsibility, a potential power of decision which is often so dormant as to suggest that it does not exist but which comes to life intermittently in very specific conditions and then adds its own authentic contribution to the set of effects studied by the sciences. This unexpected contribution then deflects the course of events from that which was expected. Langmead Casserley in a fine book [15] has made the point that the free will of man is one among the many conditions that govern man's action or rather its outcome, and as great and unsuspect an authority as John Stuart Mill is invoked by Casserley to bolster up the case. This reasoning is quite realistic in limiting free will to a rather narrow scope in society and history, reserving most of the field to the strict rule of determining laws. Without having any quarrel with this view, we think it even more realistic to assume the complete eclipse of free will for long stretches of time and its occasional strong reassertion under particularly trying conditions, and only in such emergencies. The doctrine of free will in these two related versions is worlds apart from that utopian idealism to which free will is will as free as God's, and against which the emphasis on man's subjection to all sorts of forces and powers is a matter of common experience. The second of the two versions gives a large measure of plausibility to scientific determinism in all routine matters under somewhat normal conditions and clearly singles out the exceptions as found only in exceptional situations. Once more, no logical difficulty is involved.

The problem, after finding a formal opening in the wall of scientific determinism, is rather in filling it with a plausible human content in a second step, and then in linking this human content to an adequate principle of systematic thinking as a final

15. Langmead Casserley, *Morals and Man in the Social Sciences,* 1951. See esp. pp. 196 ff.

step, which must be left to a later chapter. If we follow the above argument, freedom is something actual and alive only in exceptional situations under heaviest pressure, as a great moral and intellectual effort, where only such an effort can avert the course of events from the road to disaster down which they are heading. To the Marxian and general scientific theory that liberty is the acceptance of necessity, on the ground that what is is scientifically necessary, we oppose the definition of liberty as transcending necessity, rising above necessity in a great moral effort instead of succumbing to it. For if liberty is not simply another name for necessity, it must mean exemption from and transcendence over necessity. In other words, liberty is creative. We do not say that liberty is the creative power; we cannot say that because liberty can also be used for destruction. But liberty is the form of creative action which breaches the fortress of determinism; the content of that action must be discussed later. Creative action is unpredictable by definition; the mobilization of the normally dormant power confounds calculations predicated on the assumption that liberty is too dead ever to upset them.

Liberty transcends necessity but does not remove it. Transcendence is something different from elimination. Necessity is everywhere and always present; the question is only whether and when it is in exclusive control—which is most of the time—and whether and when it must share control with the reawakening creative power. The forces of natural causation, never dormant and never suspended, move in on the unexpected result of unexpected action and begin their work anew on the new level. All the personal and group interests that are forever lying in wait for their opportunities accommodate themselves and explore the new situation and begin to exploit it and gradually to grind it down, until finally the new has run its course and exhausted its vitality and is in turn faced with the ever recurring dilemma of decay or renewal. That is, the creative action itself, transcending as it does the necessity, cannot afford to ignore it; it is conceived in the social, political, economic, psychological material whose inherent tendencies are taught as scientific laws or regularities.

For all this, liberty, or the creativity as which we have now tentatively interpreted it, is not "acceptance of necessity"; it still is transcendence of necessity, because it realizes something unknown in the known material. To create means to put there something that had not existed before. Man does not create, of course, as God does; he does not add to the stuff of the world, he only transforms it. But he does create new meaning where there had not been any. He does that by giving the material a new spiritual form which conveys meaning where the former existence of that material had not been meaningful. We have above referred to the trivial example—trivial in the reasoning, not in the making—of the artist. Michelangelo finds a block of marble, a dead, meaningless piece of nature; he gives it a new form, the form of a David, which has been there ever since and has told its tale to uncounted visitors: a work of distinct and unmistakable meaning. In so doing Michelangelo could neither ignore nor violate the physical structure of the marble, or of his hammer for that matter; he would never have created anything if he had not obeyed their demands. But in thus accepting necessity, he transcended it by incorporating his spiritual creation into that material. The acceptance of necessity thus is the indispensable condition of the creative act, but it is not the creative act. For no study of that necessity could ever have predicted the David, who springs from the head of its maker as Athena springs from the head of Zeus; the world has been richer by this David ever since. The artist's creative freedom is not in the laws of nature but above them; liberty transcends necessity.

There is no difference in form between artistic creation and the political creation that is the main object of our study. The material that the creative statesman has to respect and obey is the given social and political structure, together with all the aspirations, undertakings, and commitments which sustain it and are sustained by it. The creative act uses this material to give it a new form that expresses a new meaning: a new vision of community quickened and justice achieved that opens new horizons and inspires people with a new mission, a new hope, where there had been the apathy of hopelessness, the expectation of the end, either in a great catastrophe that is seen waiting further down the road or without any catastrophe for sheer reasons of moral exhaustion and cynicism.

The parallelism with the work of art continues in the greatness of the spiritual effort that genuine creation exacts; it demands concentrated energy, devotion, and sacrifice. But this is true in a specific sense in acts of political or international creation because the effort required to make them become possible is an eminently moral effort. The rise above the familiar necessities is a rise above our past, including our past achievements and failures; in the light of the emergency the achievements are not good enough, and the failures may be fatal. The rise to the new level, hence, is the beginning of a new life, a regeneration, where new forces may accrue to personal life and give it a new meaning by giving it a new purpose, while the regeneration of society may add a new span of time to the life of the spiritual organism. This has been described by the great historians of our generation, Rosenstock-Huessy and Toynbee; in the latter's brilliant formulation it is the "creative response to the challenge of the emergency."

In retrospect, it may be easy to pretend that the effort and achievement were necessary and logical if without them the unsolved problem would have wrecked the life of the society—in other words, that there was nothing creative because everything was necessary and logical. The test, then, is in the question: Could the new have been predicted? Was it predicted? Can regeneration be predicted? Is regeneration more natural and logical than the alternative, the march down the road to the vast graveyard of history?

The achievement of the freedom that is creative freedom may further be belittled by pointing to the element of selfishness in the motivation of the action. Idealists, who think of man as God, may believe that complete unselfishness of political action is a human possibility and the yardstick of value. The point of view of this book, however, which is the Biblical tradition, is as far from that illusion as can be. It is to save the community from doom that the creative statesman acts; if this be called selfish, the word becomes irrelevant. What matters is the distinction between a policy that enhances the self—the individual or the organized community—over other selves at their expense, and a policy that reconciles the claims of this self with those of other selves by lifting the problem to a higher plane, where threatening conflict can be absorbed into the common pursuit of farsighted goals. The principle of justice is not identical with unselfishness, but on the contrary with the affirmation, recognition, delimitation, and reconciliation of rights on all sides of the problem. The fact that selfishness is not simply rejected but accepted, lifted to a higher plane, and thus ennobled makes the freedom of creative regeneration a human possibility. But the rarity of this possibility becoming actual explains its omission from the scientific picture of "regularity" and gives it special distinction as the manifestation of man's transcendence over the world of nature of which he is a part.

PART TWO

Is Communism the End of the Dialectic?

* IV *

Dialectic of Reason

From Individualism
Through Communism to Democracy

Marxism's Historical Theory of Itself

ENOUGH has been said in the first three chapters to establish three propositions. First, the program of rationalist individualism is self-defeating on all levels if taken at face value and if logically pursued to its inherent end. Second, these ultimate effects have been delayed and hidden from consciousness by the continuing work of the Christian moral tradition, acting as an "inhibition" in the pursuit of individual interests and for a while even "blurring" the conscious argument of individualist rationality by slipping in traditional contents.[1] Third, the official program—that is, conscious valuations and aspirations of people—has the upper hand, in the long run, over the unofficial residual admixtures, which it denounces as irrational and reactionary, so the program appears in increasing and increasingly disastrous purity.

If rational individualism—the private pursuit of private interests as supreme in personal and social life and its acceptance as supreme by social science—is thus self-defeating, its very defeat clearly shows where victory would go: to collectivism, which is its dialectical opposite. The loss of individuality and the threat to social and moral cohesion in a system

1. According to John Dewey, this "compromise" resulted in "dumping our actual human problems into the lap of the least developed, the most immature, of all our modes of knowing: politics and ethics," so the science of human affairs "is not a 'science' but an ideological reflection and 'rationalization' of contentious and contending practical policies." (*Commentary*, October 1947, p. 382). It can be seen that, as far as the facts are concerned, this description is in perfect harmony with the above. Compare also the third point made above.

of individualism as well as the standardization of human thought, first in theory and then gradually in practice too, point to collectivism as the adequate organization of an essentially already collectivized world.

Now this is anything but a new discovery. It is a restatement and reillustration of the Marxist dialectic, which teaches that individualism is not full rationality but only the first phase in the development of rationality, a transition to and preparation for the final phase, which is rationalist collectivism. For collectivism is not only the opposite of and alternative to individualism but its dialectical opposite, growing from the same general presupposition in the same general climate of society. Rational society is to be defined by the rational pursuit of interests, either individual or group, and its dialectic as seen by Marxism is in the fact that adventurous individualism, after its initial pioneering triumphs in an unexplored world, proves more and more inadequate in an already tightly organized world. Marxism draws an enormous intellectual and moral strength from the fact that it recognizes the preliminary contribution of its adversary—that is, the adversary's assignment in a special phase of the historical development—while individualism has no intellectual access to the collectivism which is its undoing, and reacts to it with incredulity and fury rather than with reasoned argument. So much the more must the Marxist doctrine of that transition be the first subject for our critical study, before we proceed to the examination of the Marxist solution in its different layers.

In what follows we shall present, in streamlined form, the logical transition from capitalism to communism—or perhaps better, the urge in the rational institutions of capitalism toward communism, in which the forces of unbalance and unrest should come to rest. We shall present this movement in the spirit of Marxism, improving upon the actual presentation of the Marxian case by the Marxists themselves and illustrating the positive meaning of some Marxist ideas by contrasting them with the opposite ideas. Only after this full presentation shall we proceed to our own argument.

Marxist reasoning is best presented on two levels, one of

philosophy—the dialectic of reason; the other of sociology—
the dialectic of bourgeois and proletarian interests and institutions. Not that we mean to suggest in Marx any idealistic
supremacy of dialectical reason over material class interests;
the greatness of Marx is precisely in the way in which logically
successive ideas emerge as the specific contributions of successive sociological figures—that is, classes—which hit upon
those ideas as the fulfillment of their specific class interests.
But the fact that these historically successive class interests produced a dialectical logic of ideas is the very core of Marxist
materialism, and it can be fully and critically appreciated only
if the two are distinguished in analysis, without in the least
implying independence of the first from the second.

Individualism and collectivism are interlocked because they
are united on fundamentals and derive from this essential unity.
Their difference is in the interpretation and application of the
principle of autonomous reason which underlies both of them,
as it underlies all modern civilization. In an autonomous society
the natural reason inborn in man is considered sufficient to
organize the perfect and durable life. We have called this the
principle of social rationalism.

The rule of reason did not succeed at once, however, in
eliminating traditional evils. So the further development of
reason, its gradual victory over ingrained inhibitions and
vested interests, its scientific refinement and courageous application, must be trusted to complete the job in the future.
It is not reason which failed its trust, it is now argued, but
the incomplete, unsatisfactory development of reason. Salvation from evil is still ahead of man because full reason is
still ahead. An almost mystical belief in the redeeming force
of history follows from the basic belief in reason as the redeeming force in human life and merges historically with the belief
in evolution as producing progress automatically in all sections
of nature, including society.[2]

The Enlightenment proper in its—philosophically, not

2. The spread and power of Social Darwinism in the second half of
the nineteenth century is difficult for us to recapitulate after only fifty years
have lapsed. Marx had planned to dedicate his *Kapital* to Darwin.

politically—radical wing—i.e. the Encyclopedists rather than the skeptical Montesquieu and Voltaire—had expected redemption not from history, of which they did not have a strong sense, but from reason in the sense of a natural, essentially immutable endowment of man. The idea of progress was more or less implied in this belief, as progress through developing knowledge. This idea was soon worked out as a theory or philosophy of history. As early as 1750 Turgot published his brilliant sketch under the characteristic title *Discourse on the Successive Progresses of the Human Mind.* Progress—a unilinear progress within rational society—was invoked to encourage the doubters and appease the impatient. Hegel transformed the idea of rational progress from a straight to a dialectical movement, and Marx used the dialectical movement of reason as a revolutionary weapon. But the more logical all this is, the more should it elucidate the argument of which the first step is the rule of and trust in reason. Belief in history is derived from it to reconcile preliminary disappointment with the belief in the redeeming power of reason by making reason itself a progressive force, whose development is first—in the West to this day—interpreted as a unilinear, then as a dialectical, and finally as a revolutionary movement.

This, then, is the place of Marxism in the picture of modern civilization. Marxism does not simply teach a progressive straight development of reason to greater efficiency, but a development from a lower to a higher stage of reason. That is, Marxism does not blame the injustice and disorder of bourgeois society, which claims to be the rule of reason, on reason as such, but on an undeveloped preliminary form of reason, on bourgeois or individual reason. Autonomous reason, drawing the lesson from its preliminary failure as individual reason, is thus driven to its own fuller understanding and unfolding as collective reason, and in practice overcomes its initial shortcomings by substituting proletarian socialism for bourgeois individualism. This shows on the one hand the unity, and on the other hand the conflict in the unity, of the two systems.

Both systems thus believe in the world's preordained harmony, which has been obscured by the rule of unreason and will become manifest as reason comes into its own. In the eyes of bourgeois democracy, the present framework is essentially rational and harmonious, and it will attain perfection by further straight progress. Marxism denounces the bourgeois belief in the essential harmony of the crisis-stricken bourgeois world as a vicious "ideology," a profitable distortion of the truth, a "rationalization" of the unrational. But if there is no harmony in the present, Marxism is the more convinced that there must and will be, of scientific necessity, harmony in the future because man is rational. Marxism promises the final harmony in the future as a result of rational action which rational proletarians, victims of the unrational bourgeois order, will take to revolutionize it and erect a truly rational structure. To the bourgeois belief in natural harmony here and now, Marxism opposes the belief in the causally necessary proletarian harmonization on the next stage of history. The institutions of this expected harmonization by communism are opposed to those of the alleged harmony of liberal democracy because communism follows from and opposes democracy.

Bourgeois Democracy

Bourgeois democracy is the rule of individual reason. Reason is the general principle of harmony. It lives in the universe and in every human mind and thus permits man to discover the laws by which the universe operates and to partake intellectually of its harmony. It appears as that through which we share in the universal good. In following our reason, we integrate ourselves into the life of the whole; there is no conflict between our individual interests, controlled as they are by reason, and the interests of the whole. Reason works both in us and in the universe. And this reason, whose proud possession man now opposes to the abject self-humiliation of the Middle Ages, is naturally understood to be individual reason, the reason incorporated in all individuals severally. They have it, or in the less optimistic earlier version, they can and must be educated by an "enlightened" elite to develop it.

In order to follow their rational interests, individuals must

LEWIS AND CLARK COLLEGE LIBRARY
PORTLAND, OREGON 97219

be free. The liberation of the people is the liberation of the reason in all persons, and it will thus produce a harmonious order. Order, far from being the (dialectical) opposite of freedom, results from freedom. This is the un-Christian position implied in liberalism. It denies the existence or relevancy of the "irrational" forces in man which may sweep his rationality; or rather of the forces of evil, of greed and presumption, which may corrupt even the mind because the mind is not above the always ambivalent aspirations of the human self, but in them and at their service. That is, man's reason is not supreme, as is God's reason. But, claiming to be supreme, man's reason denies that man's liberty is the liberty of both the good and evil forces in man. The politically decisive step from medieval society to modern society is precisely this reliance on freedom as the freedom of the good.[3]

The second decisive step is that of toleration. If all individuals are to be free in order to make their spontaneous contribution to the life of the whole, they must be tolerant of one another's motives and the society must be tolerant of them all. While the underlying doctrine is un-Christian and Christianity is far from being a public function in autonomous society, the practice is not anti-Christian because of the principle of toleration, which follows from that of freedom. As a personal motive among other motives, Christianity is respected and private instruction in it is permitted, even though

3. The integration of the mind in the self and all its personal and social aspirations is the great lesson of the sociology of knowledge. Unfortunately, the sociologists were unable to bow to their own insight, and they claimed to discover ways to unbiased knowledge through sociology. Morally, the very attempt again proves the supremacy of interest over reason, the use of reasoning for the service of interests: or is it not true that the power of sociology is precisely in the interest of sociologists; that they have invested in it their studies, education, and incessant intellectual efforts; and that on it depend their reputation, influence, and income? The problem is not one of (human) reason but of religion, as worked out by Paul Tillich in his essay "Logos und Kairos" (in the volume *Kairos. Zur Geisteslage und Geisteswendung,* 1926)—the Christian religion producing that unique position in which the believer with all his historically most legitimate aspirations stands under the ultimate judgment of the Cross, that is, of self-negation for the sake of pure love.

the Jeffersonian expectation is that the rational mind of free men will progressively expel the dogmatic element—that is, the religion—of Christianity and will retain only the morality, inasmuch as it appears justifiable on rational grounds.[4]

More generally, toleration permits and liberty materializes in the growth of personality, which is the greatest among the achievements of the age of rational humanism. A wealth of human possibilities thus becomes real, and a wealth of spiritual and cultural movements ensues. It appears that the rule of individual reason, because of the ingredients of liberty and toleration in it, is not at all a rigid form, as is that of collective reason. The rule of individual reason is, in point of fact, so flexible as to appear completely subjectivistic and to approach spiritual confusion and moral chaos in the end, where anything must be tolerated, however absurd, on the premise that in the long run the logical power of the truth will assert itself in reason-endowed minds. In the long run, this preliminary relativism may lead to chaos rather than to self-assertion of the truth, and it will then yield to the forceable imposition of some intellectual and social pattern, for obvious practical reasons. This is precisely the doctrine of Marxism.

In its political and economic applications, the principle of individual reason is much more rigid because a system of institutions can be operated only according to adequate rules, which have often been compared with traffic rules in a city. The principle of individual reason here incorporates itself in the private interests of free individuals as the motor force in society. Nothing else is needed for social life, because the private interests of rational man are rational. This leads to laissez-faire capitalism and to democratic government, however limited originally.

Laissez-faire is the realization of the freedom of private interests in the fields of production, commerce, and finance. These private interests being supposedly rational, their unchecked freedom is supposed to improve the economic situation of man and society. Order here follows from freedom through the operation of the anonymous price mechanism. Private in-

4. On this, see Chapter X.

dividuals, each caring for himself, naturally find themselves in competition with one another, and competition is the vehicle of order in the original version of laissez-faire capitalism. Price expresses the intensity of demand and determines the income of the suppliers. Free individuals hence seek to invest their labor or capital in such goods as will meet the most intensive demand of the others, because they themselves will then receive higher income. In this way the production of the various goods and services attracts or discourages producers, with the relative and changing intensity of the demand expressed in changing prices. This is the coincidence of all interests in the short run. In the long run, producers will technically improve their services to consumers, thus advancing under the pressure of competition to more efficient methods of production. For technical reasons, such progress normally requires larger and larger units of production; it is these which cheapen the unit of output by making the total output disproportionately larger.

The way from the many small units of production to the few large ones is the way from competition to monopoly—and, far more important, from individual work in small-scale production to collective work in large-scale production. The dual result of capitalism is rising productivity, testifying to the reason in man, and mounting economic disorder and social conflict, testifying to his unreason. Economic disorder arises from private piecemeal considerations in the conduct of essentially collective large-scale production in interlocking but separately owned and managed units of production. Over-all and long-range considerations of government and public opinion invade the purely private domain only gradually. Social conflict mounts because the formerly independent individual workers are now collective workers, employed on short contracts in big plants; unchecked freedom permits the financially strong to overwhelm and control the financially weak. Collective organization of the weak only gradually permits them to partake of some of the benefits of individualism. In terms of social morality, economic disorder and social conflict mean that the public good, supposedly a natural by-product of private interests, is sacrificed wherever private interests feel that their profits or wages will be increased by withdrawing from production rather than by contributing to it.[5]

Discussion between reason-endowed free individuals is supposed to ascertain the common good, which is their common interest. Such discussion again requires personal freedom and the political freedoms therefrom derived, and is organized into some form of representative government wherever societies have grown too large for direct participation by the citizens. In case of dissension, the majority of rational persons can be presumed to be nearer the truth than the minority. The more rational the citizens are, however, the more can government—defined as ultimately coercive power—be reduced to a minimum (according to Jefferson), because the citizens can be trusted to do spontaneously what is rational. This applies primarily to economic activities.

The liberal trend toward minimum government has been reversed in recent decades by the effects of social and economic disorders, which have forced government to increased activities in wider areas. At the same time, the foundations of democratic government in individual reason are being shaken by the standardization of the people in mass society. The giant machines of the press, the radio, the movies, the political parties, do the thinking for us, weaken the force of rational personality, and mold people into an amorphous mass, which can easily be manipulated.

Marxism

The (dialectical) drive of reason from its individual beginnings to its collective consummation has already been suggested. It is unreasonable to have many different centers of reason thinking and acting independently and often at variance with one another; economic disorder, social conflict, and the frequent impossibility of arriving at any majority decision in deeply cleft parliamentary bodies all refute the claim to final rationality put forth by individualism. This is not to

5. Cf. Chapter II.

dispute that mankind acted rationally in trying individualism out. Individualism abounded in pioneering adventures, groping discoveries, and experimental inventions, and it created the atmosphere of scientific rationality. But it is precisely individualism's overwhelming success through which it becomes antiquated. For as all those brilliant discoveries coagulate, it becomes clear that they must all be geared to one another because they are all pieces of one truth and one reason, unified, perfect, collective.

The Hegelian character of the concept of collective reason is obvious. But it does not remain speculative, idealistic; in the materialistic system the truth is objectified in the organization of society. Hence the concept of liberty loses all meaning in this system. Once there is the objective truth, liberty remains only the freedom to err, toleration the toleration of error; they make no sense. (The often-referred-to parallelism to Catholic doctrine must not be exaggerated; the truth of Christian doctrine is a purely spiritual one, "not of this world," and therefore without obligatory institutional consequences, except by way of abuse. The Marxist truth is "material," practical, tangible, and is found primarily in connected, disciplined, unified, collective action in every phase of life, but then also requires conformity of thinking lest dissension disturb the unified action.) But Marxism can tolerate least of all the Christian religion, teaching as it does the moral frailty of man and the corruptibility of his autonomous reason—that is, of his reason unguided by suprarational truth. In the light of this clash between ultimate opposites, rational individualism along with the ensuing scientism really appears only as a halfway station on the road to autonomous rational collectivism, the unified system of reason, which, being scientific, is infallible in principle though amenable to further perfection within itself.

Historically, according to the doctrine, collective reason incorporates itself in those who suffer most from the disorder and injustice of the system of individual reason, the working class. It is they who, deprived of their small private property by that injustice, are thereby emancipated from the corrupting force of private property and are enabled to rise above the plane of inadequate individualistic thinking to the plane of collectivist thinking. They are taught collectivist thinking and unified action by their experience in collective work and common misery; they, and only they, free from the illusions of private owners, recognize the dependence of their individual welfare on the welfare of all in the world-wide division of labor. Hence, universal collective reason assumes the special historical form of the workers' revolutionary "class interest," which becomes the motor force of history and imparts to the individual worker a sense of universalism, of participation in the unified life under the guidance of the unified truth.

The "correctly understood" class interest of the propertyless collective workers, in contradistinction to the illusions of trade unionism, aims to reorganize all means of production as their common property and to unify the management of the entire system. Socialism thus eliminates the class conflict between owners and nonowners by unification and equalization of the people. The final consummation of this true industrial community, according to the doctrine, will be achieved by communism: everyone contributing according to his ability and receiving according to his needs, as in the family. Meanwhile, the preliminary form, "socialism" proper, still needs the appeal to private incentives through a drastic differentiation of wages and salaries within the unified system. The planned economy aims to eliminate economic disorder by an all-inclusive plan of production executed by unified management in the interest of all and under their control—all are co-owners.

In its application to government, the collective reason incorporated in the workers' class interest establishes the "workers' democracy" and thus achieves "the jump from the realm of necessity to the realm of freedom." In the workers' democracy the interest of everyone is supposed to merge into the scientifically ascertained interest of all; and individual liberty, in the sense of personal spontaneity, hence can be said to "wither away" before the liberty of the whole for lack of a separate function; while the state—required in a class society to keep down the oppressed majorities and protect the system—must likewise "wither away" for lack of any further function. The

final form of political life, then, is anarchy—the free, un-
coerced cooperation of reason-guided men educated by the collective requirements of their industrial work.

The no-state phase of Marxism repeats item by item the
vision of heretical Christian sects which taught that the redeemed need not be coerced by government, police, or penal
code; and this ultimate vision of Marxism corresponds to the
minimum-government vision of Jeffersonianism, which equally
refers to the rationality of citizens as the alternative to government. The difference between the two systems is simply in the
fact that to Jefferson, in an industrially undeveloped world,
individualism was the rational principle; to Marx, in an industrially developed world, that principle is collectivism.

In order that history achieve the homogenous proletarization required for communism, capitalism is supposed not only
to expropriate the many in favor of the few, but also to simplify
and equalize all functions. Marx and Lenin expected mechanization to achieve precisely this, both in the system of production and in that of administration. Sociologically, the "withering away of the state" implies the absence of a special, trained
governmental bureaucracy, which will no longer be needed
once its functions become simple enough for workers to take
turns at them. Equality of functions thus forms the basis of the
workers' democracy.

The workers' democracy, however, according to the doctrine,
still needs the coercive agency of the state for its self-defense
so long as class enemies, though stripped of power and property,
are not yet eliminated or merged into the working class; nay,
so long as a hostile environment persists. In its relation
with the world outside the working class, the workers' democracy thus constitutes itself as the "dictatorship of the proletariat." It is defined as the coercive agency of the state
employed for the first and last time in history by the huge majority in the interest of the huge majority. According to the
original doctrine, however, the dictatorship will not be needed
for very long, because capitalism merges all nations into its
world market and they all are thus being given huge proletarian majorities aiming at the workers' democracy. The end

of the dictatorship, which is the rule of fighting reason, is anarchy, the undisputed rule of victorious reason.

Sovietism

The Marxian prophecy has fully materialized on its negative side: social and economic disorder threatens us all. As a consequence, everyone in the Western world has become more or less interested in some form and degree of centralized control to rescue him from such disorder. But this has not happened in the positive form expected by Marx.

Modern capitalist society is anything but homogeneously proletarian. It is too highly diversified to permit of the proletarian way out of the crisis. Agriculture remains outside the class conflict and the ensuing proletarianization: the small farm is modernized in itself by small machines and supplemented by cooperatives for a number of large-scale activities. In industry and administration, an increasingly complicated mechanization produces a greater rather than a lesser stratification of functions in all countries, including Soviet Russia, and raises the managers, organizers, technicians, accountants, and middlemen to positions above those of workers. The result is that there is no proletarian majority in any country, and the simple coincidence of the working class with society and of the workers' democracy with proletarian interest fails. In other words, history produces a cleavage between the principles of democracy—meaning majority rule—and those of uniform proletarian socialism, which originally seemed to converge. In this dilemma, communism chooses the pole of proletarian socialism (and social democracy chooses the pole of democracy).

The Soviet Union, in order to establish a proletarian, atheist, socialist system in a society where there is no proletarian majority, has to give a new meaning to the originally defensive and transitory "dictatorship of the proletariat." In addition to stamping out the minority, the dictatorship now has to reshape in its own image the life of the majority itself. It has to build the house, as it were, from the roof downward. It is fitting that the dictatorship, definitely of secondary importance in the original version of Marxism, should now be given the assignment of constructive, creative initiative in the recent version of dialectical materialism. Accordingly, the dictatorship is tightened, intensified, and much prolonged in duration.

Still, the deviation from the original version should not be exaggerated, since even in the original version the underlying idea of collective reason is lifted above mere social experience to the speculative plane. Even there infallibility does not attach to democracy as the experienced will of the majority of individuals, but to the "correct understanding" of rational collectivity, whether the majority is already mature enough to rise to such understanding or not. The sense of mission is derived from the doctrine of the dialectical course of history and does not depend on approval by those who do not yet understand it. If the workers' democracy is not yet the state of the huge majority, it is the state in the "correctly understood" interest of the future huge majority, and they will make it their own once it succeeds in making them rational.[6]

This state, hence, is not conceived as a state like other states but as their dialectical mirror, their heir and undoing. Being designed by history itself to undo the other states and only then to undo itself, it must not give up its sovereignty in the midst of others. At the San Francisco conference the United States insisted on the veto power because a still largely isolationist Senate would otherwise not have acceded to the United Nations Charter; but one could conceive the United States renouncing the veto power in a somewhat normal world. The Soviet could never give up the veto; it must not permit itself to be outvoted by capitalist states on any question it may consider vital to its revolutionary mission.

While the Western nations, however hesitatingly, regard the United Nations as a step toward final unification, the Soviet cannot possibly attach to the United Nations any programmatic significance. For Marxism, the embryonic form of the future world organization is not the United Nations but the Union of Soviet Socialist Republics (USSR)—a name commonly understood to mean "Soviet Russia" but in fact meaning the

6. For an elaboration, see the following chapter.

"Soviet Union," chosen with consummate skill for its omission of any reference to any particular country or nation, and basing the "union" on social ("socialist") and political ("Soviet") homogeneity. That is, peace and harmony are to be had only on the other side of the Communist revolution; there can be no peace and harmony in the world of private property, and no compromise is possible. The USSR itself, far from merging into the United Nations, is the superior alternative to the United Nations.

This principal and ultimate expectation does not preclude a highly flexible policy in the meantime; that is, it does not preclude temporary membership of that same USSR, or rather of some of its member states, in the United Nations. But this is so only because the world represented in the United Nations is considered sure to collapse under the weight of its economic disorder in the near future. In this sense, while the West struggles for some reorganization to escape collapse, Marxism can wait and can meanwhile quite honestly engage in peaceful collaboration with its future victims. But even the most pleasant experiences in the United Nations, where capitalism and communism stand side by side, could never refute or set aside the long-range expectation; this expectation would be affected only if the West could convincingly demonstrate a new and impregnable internal stability. The ideologists of the United Nations, of world federation, and of pacifism, in their hopes for reconciliation and integration in the present world, never see Soviet policy in proper perspective because they ignore the fact that the Soviet Union, according to its own basic philosophy, is not a part of the present world at all but the whole of the future world.[7]

7. If one sees the foundation of the United Nations without illusions, it is neither narrow nor hopeless. The Soviet is in the United Nations pending the collapse of the Western world. If there is no such collapse, the Russians can and will cooperate. It would be the end of their philosophy anyway. Even here it cannot be sufficiently emphasized that Marx only takes up and translates into collectivism motives of thought that had arisen in the individualist branch of rationalism. The international totalitarianism of Marxism had been preceded by the universal republicanism of Immanuel Kant, who had made "Eternal Peace"—in a book under

The massive sense in which this is true can best be seen from the definition of genuine internationalism as proclaimed by the Polish Communists in the struggle against Tito's nationalist heresy. To a Western mind, internationalism means loyalty to a spiritual authority, however vaguely conceived, which is higher than any national interests and is to be appealed to from them. In the struggle to give that authority institutional form, it will always have to be remembered that no political power is acceptable as supreme to the Western mind; the power of the United Nations of the future will always have to bow to the spiritual authority behind and above it, which is only reflected in it. This may be so because the supreme principle of Western society always remains the reason in the individual, or because of far-reaching effects of Christian tradition and church history.[8] Contrariwise, the materialistic conception literally defines internationalism as loyalty to Moscow, the seat of a moral authority greater than that of Warsaw or Belgrade. It is Moscow which "correctly understands" the interests of the Polish and Yugoslav proletarians, which neither they themselves nor their Communist representatives can possibly understand so well. Collective reason is totalitarian, even internationally.

---

this title—dependent on all states adopting a republican form of government. The difference was only that Kant was somewhat more optimistic on the possibility of this happening peacefully, because of his more optimistic appraisal of the natural reason in man, and of course, Kant's conception of the republic was not totalitarian. But the parallelism of the two cases is overwhelming. In both cases peace depends on first staging one more revolution on a world scale so as to have international homogeneity established under the law of reason, which is harmonious by definition, while variety in forms of government is then irrational by definition and bound to produce conflict between them. There is no geographical or other limit to the totalitarian ambitions of rationalism. The League of Nations, of course, was established under this philosophy, destroying as it did the two Central European, more or less autocratic empires for the sake of peace, and keeping Soviet Russia outside for the same reason; it was not a league of republics, but at least one of liberal governments. The United Nations has given up the dogmatism but is extremely weak ideologically, as shown above.

8. Cf. Chapter VI.

The Fallacy

The totalitarianism of the Communist program is derived from rationalism, which is the totalitarianism of reason. A check on Soviet power, to this way of thinking, would be tantamount to a check on reason. The dictatorship of the first phase, hence, must not be checked, and the statelessness of the final phase need not and cannot be checked; complete rationality is infallible. In the hands of erring, vindictive, power-hungry men this doctrine is a fearful thing; to themselves and to their followers they appear godlike, the climax and center of world history, the saviors of mankind, under obligation both to destroy their enemies by any means that appear expedient, and to make over all other people in their own image by any means that appear expedient.

The atrocities in which the regime engaged, therefore, were not accidental but were required by the underlying logic of its system. The millions of dead in the civil war and in the attack on individual farming in 1932–1933; the millions deported, silently disposed of, or in forced labor; and the terror which such dealing with opponents struck and was designed to strike into many more millions—all this does not count in the balance against the eternal bliss of all future generations, which is supposed to be secured precisely by such methods. There is no personal ethic left; ethic is logically reduced to political expediency in the hands of the powerful, who claim to liberate mankind from its ills by enhancing their own positions. No Marxist dialectician understands the deep ambiguity of power, its real dialectic.[9]

9. Fairness demands our adding (1961) that since Stalin's death these methods have been completely abandoned, as far as we can see. Pasternak and many others who would not have survived under Stalin did survive now. A general relaxation of internal policy has taken place, parallel to the conversion of production to consumers' goods, under the pressure of the terrorized and starved masses. This introduces a new structural element into Soviet sociology and policy. One may hope for, and even consider likely, further progress along this line. As long, however, as there is no reform of the Constitution, a return to the policy of terror remains legally possible. It has happened before; cf. the following note. At the same time,

Sociologically, the fundamental fallacy is the assumption that the only possible division in society is that between owners and nonowners; the denial that there can be a vested interest in government or any other exalted function in a society without private ownership; the blindness to the fact that it is functions that convey power—in capitalism through property which reserves the highest functions to the owners and their deputies, and in communism directly. The irrationality of the abuse of power for its own defense and enhancement cannot be checked where it is considered impossible by definition.

Philosophically, the fallacy lies in the assumption that man is essentially rational and becomes fully rational after conquering the mysteriously seductive power of private property. According to this strange doctrine, the workers, saved from the temptation of private property by capitalism, come to understand the oneness of reason and the ensuing all-inclusive unity of rational society; but before all workers are raised to such a full understanding, their "vanguard," their dictatorial government, is so raised. At one with the will of history, they can neither err nor abuse their power; the scientific man is born who does not need and has no use for liberty and raises the others to his own plane. The more the moral danger to man and his mind is argued away, the less it can be guarded against.

This is what has happened to a great and noble dream at the hands of scientism. The dream is that of justice established and community recovered from a world where injustice is rampant and community torn. The dream inspired the early martyrs, and it continues to inspire uncounted millions of persons in all countries. Justice and community, however, are not to be found in the vocabulary of science; not they, but rather rationality and causal necessity, are invoked by scientific socialism. If this doctrine, in the scientific age, conveys to the movement the confidence in its final victory, it ruins the meaning of that victory before it is won.[10]

---

moreover, China has reinforced the Marxist terror under the regime of Mao, the strongest Marxist theoretician since Stalin.

10. In *Freedom and Order* (1947), p. 180, this author, after weighing the then available evidence, arrived at the discussion of a possibly more

The current analyses of conflict of ideologies are for the most part inconclusive because the authors usually give us only their personal preferences without an objective criterion of choice. It does not help us to be told that the liberty for which our side stands is preferable to anything else if this liberty is presented as the liberty of rational man and thus invites criticism in terms of a technically superior rationality, which is supposed to avoid the remaining technical irrationalities of individualism. The trouble is that the two opposite systems do not confront each other by mere chance, as might be the case on the plane of nationalist power politics alone, but are connected logically and in historical causation. This is the point announced in the introduction of this book. The specific manifestations of Western rationalist liberty in economic disorder and social arbitrariness would have been bound to produce a collectivist reaction somewhere in the world, even if there were no Soviet Russia or if we had smashed her. And it is Russia's despotic equality, a protest against the West's inordinate liberty, which drives people to embrace Western spiritual liberty and the liberal constitutional democracy to which it leads. This is the circle in which we are caught: the two conflicting ideol-

---

hopeful future because, in the 1930's, the Soviet system had shown definite signs of deviation from Marxist orthodoxy, and the exigencies of war and postwar policy led to the proclamation of the milder versions as binding upon Soviet policy in the neighboring Slavic states now under Soviet hegemony. Representative of this trend was the official announcement, after the first conquest of Finland, that Finland, not being an industrial-proletarian country, could not be Sovietized, as also the solemn assurances given small farmers in Poland and Czechoslovakia. This line of policy seemed to be yielding rich dividends and thus to bid fair to be continued. However, it was discontinued, obviously because it implied a relaxation of the controls which might become dangerous to the "monolithic" logic of Communist organization. Tito's Yugoslav nationalism was denounced, among other things, as defection from Marxist economic teachings in agricultural policy; strict collectivization of agriculture now again appeared as the only permissible line of action. This was one among many signs of Marxist orthodoxy being restored. The critique of the Marxist orthodox doctrine in the earlier book (pp. 277–285) coincides with that presented here. A similar relaxation after Stalin's death is referred to in the preceding footnote.

ogies produce and reproduce each other because they are connected causally. It follows immediately that it is logically impossible to decide for either one of the conflicting systems, since
such a decision would be a decision for the source of the opposite system as well.[11]

The trouble, in other words, is not with the conclusion
but with the premise. Man can become fully rational only if
he is potentially rational; and that he is potentially rational
is a proposition which by no means originated with Marx. Nor
is there any logical possibility of arguing that the system of
individual reason, because it includes the great virtues of
liberty and toleration, is more true or more logical than the
system of collective unified reason. It must be clearly seen
that there is no logical solution of the conflict because the
criterion of logic itself is drawn into the conflict of dogmas
and loses its absolute validity. Marxist thinking denies the right
of traditional "static" logic and can never be persuaded to accept refutation by means of such logic. Like the two systems of
logic, the two social systems are in logically insoluble conflict.
For one cannot say that emphasis on the individual is better than
emphasis on the community, or liberty better than equality,
or that the reverse is true; either position is dogmatic, and there
is no superior principle to which either one could appeal against
the other. The truth is that the two systems advertise each
other's shortcomings in terms of rational standards accepted by
both and interpreted in dogmatically opposite ways. Either
one of the two opposite systems would tend to produce the
other as the mirror of its own sins if that other did not yet
exist. But the sin, in both cases, is fundamentally the same:
claiming God's autonomous rationality for the frail creature,
man, whose reason is conditioned. The difference in belief between the two systems is considerable and should certainly not
be belittled, but is not decisive in the logic of the case. It
makes little sense for those who sow the wind to complain that

11. This paragraph was first printed in an article published in 1949. In
1950 the four French Cardinals issued a pastoral letter to comment on
the Pope's encyclical on communism, where they argued that the Holy
Father, in criticizing communism, could not have sided with capitalism
because that would have meant siding with the source of communism.

the whirlwind which they reap is worse than the wind, though this is true enough.

The Antidotes of Constitutional Democracy

But the story of the transition from rational individualism to rational collectivism is not complete in the version presented by Marx. Everybody knows that the picture of the present world is different from the one drawn by Marx, much as Marxists are naturally anxious to argue the difference away. The fact is that the threatened organism of Western society has produced antidotes. By no stretch of the imagination can the resulting system still be subsumed under the heading of individualism. In an institutional sense of the word, it might be more correct to say that institutions of individualism have become regulated and balanced by collectivist admixtures—e.g., in the organization of labor and the labor market—and by centralizing admixtures—such as controls over an even flow of purchasing power and investments. All of these have by no means been invented by democracy, but they testify to the increasing social and political power of democracy to push individualism back to its main bastion in free enterprise. The reforms, it should be noted, are correctives; they are not meant to be and can never become substitutes for the institutions of individualism; what they do is smooth and even out the operation of the institutions of individualism and give their material benefits a wider dispersion. Clearly, both the elimination of cyclical disturbances in the formation of income and the redistribution of income presuppose that the total output which is the physical content of such income continue to be produced in the traditional ways. Else it might shrink in the process of reform. We have described the new reformed structure in considerable detail elsewhere,[12] so these few words must suffice here.

The total structure is known as liberal democracy, where

12. Cf. my book *Wirtschaftssysteme und Gesellschaftssysteme,* 1954, and a number of later articles, the most recent and most elaborate being "Après le Succès du Capitalisme—Où Allons-Nous?," *Economie Appliquée,* 1959, No. 1–2.

the word "liberal" stands for individualism both constitutional and economic, and the word "democracy" for a sense of community and concerted action. Individualism is the core of free enterprise in the midst of all those collectivist and constitutional admixtures, in charge of efficiency and progressive productivity; and individualism is also, on the other hand, the constitutionalism which keeps the democracy from going collectivist or totalitarian—an aspect so important as to make it quite plausible that Carl J. Friedrich prefers the name of "constitutional democracy" to the conventional "liberal democracy." Both aspects of liberal democracy are clarified by the exact contrast with the self-styled "people's democracies" of the Soviet orbit.

It was the democratic ingredient in liberal democracy which made it possible for the underprivileged of liberal individualism to exert political power and use it for the betterment of their economic and social condition, thus removing or mitigating the ills which were supposed to drive them to Marxism. And it was the constitutional ingredient in liberal democracy, long belittled by collectivists as "formal democracy," whose spiritual and moral significance was driven home to them by the contrast with the extraconstitutional rule of the police in the "people's democracies." This is, in briefest summary, the story of how the spell of Marxist collectivism was broken and the working masses of Western individualism were won over for liberal democracy, thus driving Marxism to the underdeveloped countries. This statement may be found too strong in view of the continuing Communist allegiance of a majority of the industrial workers in France and Italy—countries, however, where the democratic mitigation of capitalist individualism is strangely retarded. The West in general can be said to have averted the Marxist prophecy by reforming itself; or in Marxist ideology, where the spiritual aspect of constitutionalism does not count and major developments must be reduced to merely economic forces, by bribing the workers into giving up their revolutionary birthright for a meal of lentils.

Would it then be correct to say that, as far as the West is concerned, Marxism rebounded impotent from reformed individualism? The question has two layers, and on both counts the answer is that this does not follow at all. In the first place, Marxism has been a most powerful positive factor in Western life. It has not simply been an adversary, in the manner of one nation being the adversary of another nation, thus exerting a negative influence by its external threat. Marxism has been a formidable critic from within, whose bitter denunciations got under the skin of Western life and stung it into adopting precisely those reforms. The pressure of an undirected dissatisfaction and unrest that, without Marxist guidance and codification, would have sufficed to bring victory to reform is altogether unlikely; and it is a purely academic question because the historical evidence leaves no doubt that it was the threat of subversion which made reform indispensable if the threat was to be averted. Disraeli spoke of the two nations in the nation which had no common ground and not even a common language, and he did not forget as a prime minister the insights of his radical past, thus symbolizing the first wave of social reform—the one in the labor market. The second wave, the introduction and gradual enlargement of social security— outside the labor market—was inaugurated by Bismarck in the explicit combination of his social insurance acts with the "act against the subversive aspirations of the Social Democratic Party." The latter act formed a repressive weapon against the revolutionary party sponsored by Marx and Engels, while the former act was designed to give the underprivileged of capitalism a positive stake in the existent state of things, so they would not need to turn to revolution. Likewise in this country, after the great crash, the controls over purchasing power and investment were explicitly meant to demonstrate that democracy is quite capable of steadying the flow of economic activities without giving up the principles and institutions of constitutional democracy which the Marxist critics denounced as incompatible with economic stability.

In other words, the threat coming from Marxism could be repulsed only by accepting the Marxist criticism; the quarrel was not over the right or wrong of the criticism but over the possibility or impossibility of taking action on it within the constitutional framework. The West's affirmative answer was right; but it was the right answer to a question laid before the West not by its own insights but by Marxism, and indeed answered by Marxism wrongly. It still remains true that the question was Marxism's. Whether or not there are Marxists in Western countries, Marxism has become an integral part of the West's life. Nobody has expressed this more succinctly than Lord Acton, when he said: "The promises of socialism have supplied the best energy of democracy." In a way, one can also present the development as the real fulfillment of the Hegelian dialectic with its emphasis on the enlightened Prussian monarchy and its highly educated liberal officialdom which would dialectically arch over and reconcile the clash between bourgeois society and its proletarian victims. But anyway, the relationship between Marxism and constitutional democracy flows from the dialectic between the systems of individualism and collectivism—that is, from their antagonistic unity.

We can here see the way in which world history works. As long as things look all right, a few independent minds and consciences may be aroused by injustice and suffering but they will not be heard or heeded. As injustice and suffering produce their own reaction in growing tension and internal or external danger, it becomes clear that it is the moral structure itself of the world into which we have run head on and which will mercilessly smash us if we insist. But to do so needs tools, and the appointed avengers of violated justice always are the victims, no matter what their own ideology and principles would be in case their assignment carried them to victory. After all, according to the Old Testament, God used even the Assyrians to drive His chosen people back into loyalty to His covenant with them.

The relationship of Marxism to the West, we said, is far more direct and organic than that between Israel and Assyria; but what matters is the attack on an unhealthy structure, not the positive principles of the attacker. That is, Marxism's own program need not be at all right in order for its criticism of us to be right and to strike home. Nor does our Western world appear as exceptionally bad in the light of this story; the hardening of a once smoothly working system, the pride that goes with achievement and success, are the ever repeated stuff of human history, and the final judgment on the West will not depend on that phase of failure but on our capacity for transcending it and thereby mending our ways. To use the well-known Toynbee categories: creativity there is in history (and was partly explored in Chapter III) but exclusively in response to the threat of the emergency, never spontaneously at a time where such creativity is not strictly indispensable for survival. That the Western world responds to the challenge shows its spiritual vitality. But the challenge to which it responds is Marxism's, and its threat did not originally come from without but from within, from the victims of our injustice whose vengeance was to be made the driving power in Marxism. Thus our first question regarding the significance of Marxism to the Western world is to be answered to the effect that the reform of the Western system is the creative response to the Marxist emergency.

This, however, only makes our second question more urgent: How did Marxism originate from the Western system? The answer is a matter of dates in history. Marxism is a century old. It was far from creating the socialist movement at that time, but on the contrary explained its mission as giving orientation, direction, and coherence to the revolutionary impetus of the existing labor movement; it grew with that movement, captured its undisputed leadership twenty years later, and has ever since been the chief antagonist of the Western social system in its very midst. The bifurcation in Western history, the parting of the roads, thus was in mid-century, and the preparation for it even earlier, filling the first half of the century: since then there has been an organized, growing, fabulously dynamic force proclaiming itself as the alternative and rival of the Western system within the same historical framework, thereby awakening the West's conscience and prodding it to reforms. The all-important point is that revolutionary socialism was born, and was given its Marxist education, when there was no liberal democracy as yet. It was born of capitalism, not of liberal democracy; as Marxism was the dialectical fruit of capitalism, so liberal democracy became the dialectical fruit of Marxism.

It is only natural that Marxism ignores everything that distinguishes democracy from capitalism. It is capitalism that gave it birth, and it is capitalism whose continued existence is expected to give it growing strength and final victory. Its own theory of capitalism and of itself—in other words, its theory of the property question as the center of history—makes it blind to the changes effected by constitutionalism and democracy even in purely economic matters, and this blindness is essential to its prophecy and its fanaticism. It is equally natural that the apologists and diehards of capitalism should interpret liberal democracy as incipient "serfdom," unable as they are to realize that vaccination uses the deadly poison to immunize the body; or that the surgeon's knife, when cutting out some dangerous growth in the "calculated risk" of the operation, does not necessarily continue to cutting the patient's throat; [13] nay, that the operation gives a chance of renewed life while its omission would be sure death. For it is precisely the transformation of capitalism into constitutional democracy under the impact of Marxism which immunized the West and deflected the menace to the Eastern countries, white and non-white, where it found an incipient capitalism parallel to that of one hundred years earlier in the West, reinforced by racial bias and without the constitutional and spiritual preparation for its transformation into democracy.

What we just called immunization can be described without metaphor and much better as a true dialectic. Historical dialectic is the emergence of the new from the conflict of the old—in this case, the emergence of constitutional democracy from the clash of capitalism and Marxism. Contrary to the Marxian claim, the mere clash between the two is not dialectic at all; it is nothing but a vicious circle and has here been presented as such. But Hegel conquers Marx, inasmuch as the logically insoluble conflict between those two systems gives rise to a new form of life superior to both. This proposition, however, is of purely factual validity; we do not say at all that this one event proves any historical law of dialectic, in Hegel's or anybody else's sense. In other words, progress to ever higher forms of

13. Cf. *Freedom and Order,* p. 5.

life is not at all secured by a law of history—which incidentally would amount to saying that there is nothing worth admiring in this special achievement because progress is enforced anyhow and always by a law of history. Nor do we say with another possibility of Marxism or Hegelian thinking that no further such achievement is either possible or required because this one brings the final and supreme consummation of liberty and precludes further conflict once and for all. Finally we do not regard the battle as won, in view of the unfinished condition of the work, particularly in international and intercontinental relations. To later chapters must be reserved the discussion of what this purely factual and still unfinished dialectic of Western society signifies in principle and how it is to be understood and construed in the framework of history.

In the present context, however, it cannot be overemphasized how great is the harm done the cause of liberty by the refusal of the Western democracies to recognize a truth as simple as this dialectic—with or without this dreaded name —and thus to wrest this mental weapon from usurpation by the adversary. The philosophy with which both capitalism and democracy introduced themselves and with which they have justified and explained themselves to this day is that of the Enlightenment. As man awakens to the reason which is his nature and emancipates himself from superstition and bondage, he engages in rational production for the service of others and for his own income, and he gets together with his fellows for reasoned exchange of experiences and opinions on such things as concern them all and demand concerted action. If this is what his rational nature suggests to man to do, then any alternative suggestion is by definition against reason and nature, and capitalism and democracy are the final word in the rise of the human race.

Then, however, there is no way of accounting for the plunge into something as unnatural and unreasonable as communism save as sheer accident. In the Marxian picture of history, capitalism has a signal place; it makes the decisive contribution toward the prerequisites of communism by collectivizing in industry the workers' work and soul, and it has finally to give way to communism because its own root in private property prevents the final completion of the collectivized world. But in the picture of history as seen by capitalism and democracy there is no room for communism—that is, the very existence of such a powerful reality explodes the belief in nature and reason to which it runs counter. Ignominiously, the study of Marxism is shrunk away from in many academic institutions on both sides of the Atlantic under the pressure of a highly emotional public opinion. The awareness of one's own indubitable intellectual inferiority reinforces the emotional fury of the reaction, which goes far toward making outsiders—and the intellectually curious—suspicious of the West. Hence the importance of making the connection between capitalism, communism, and liberal democracy intelligible in the wider horizon of the different manifestations of modernity, as attempted here.[14]

14. Some readers may have been disappointed not to find in this streamlined survey of Marxist thought any reference to the theory of value and exploitation, which the Marxists, following the lead of Friedrich Engels, regard as one of the two most important chapters in the system— the other being the economic interpretation of dialectical history, which underlies our presentation of that system. The reasons for the omission have been given in detail in a technical discussion in my *History of Economic Doctrines*, Chapter VI, particularly pp. 173 ff., and before that in my collection of essays under the title *Kapitalismus und Sozialismus*, 1931, p. 144. Those reasons were summarized, in the German version of this book, in a three-page note on Marxian economics, which is omitted here.

V

Dialectic of Society

*Economic Planning
Without Proletarization*

Marxism and Humanism

SOCIALISM in general and Marxism in particular arose as the left wing of bourgeois democracy. Under our eyes Marxism has been transformed into a doctrine of totalitarianism, without in the least giving up its claim to represent the consummation of democracy. Nay, Marxists are emphatic in denying any totalitarian leanings in their system. They refer to their objective as a stateless society—that is, a society without coercive agency, in which the rational nature of man would take over and nobody would be coerced because everybody would act in accordance with his own clear insight into his interest, which is work under the rational plan. What distinguishes Marxist doctrine from conventional anarchism, they say, is the insight into the needed historical preparation for that goal. It is history itself, centering in economic history, they say, which uses its own not always soft methods to educate man for the rational stateless life, irons out the conflicts of interests between individuals and groups, and makes solidarity possible by evolving such institutions as to make the interests of everyone coincide with the interests of all others. What the Marxists themselves add, they say, is only this insight into the inherent tendencies of history, and the ability to translate the insight into teachings and actions aimed to protect, promote, and speed up the necessary movement of history to the happy denouement.

Not only the end, but also the way to the end, in this explicitly antivoluntaristic, materialistic doctrine is set by the grand design of history, more specifically of economic history, which is plainly said to be part of natural history and thus to "partake of the strictness of the laws of nature." The system as a whole, hence, can be described as traveling on two tracks or extending through two floors: the empirical-sociological, which is basic, and the philosophical, the one of meaning. Not that there is a separate doctrine of meaning, still less a separate origin of meaning; the point is precisely that meaning is involved in the goal and then in retrospect in every step preparatory to the meaningful goal. In the famous Engels phrase, mankind's "jump from the realm of necessity to the realm of freedom" is still "necessary." It is the inherent causal logic of the economic-social facts which produces the fully meaningful facts in the end. But the analysis then must distinguish these two layers. The analysis of meaning achieved, of liberty attained, will be reserved for the next chapters; and the present chapter will concentrate on the socioeconomic development in which the meaningful goal is inherent. This analysis continues the one of the preceding chapter.

While the objective of Marxism is philosophic and the earlier writings clarify it in philosophical analyses of great profundity, the bulk of the classical writings are economic. The Communist Manifesto was published in the year 1848, and it marks the transition from the earlier to the later phase. But it would be wrong to assume, as is too often done, that the results of the earlier phase do not survive in the later phase; the philosophical objective gained in the earlier writings is put to the test by concrete application to the facts of society in the later writings.

The philosophical idea underlying the entire system is that of the gradual dialectical unfolding of the nature of man as the vehicle of economic reason. Originally man realizes his nature in a primitive but harmonious way. His rationality not yet being developed, he is controlled by his instincts and lives a life of tribal solidarity without efficiency and without individuation and tensions. This doctrine of primitive communism as the golden age was suggested to Marx and Engels by the writings of an early American anthropologist, Lewis Morgan. The dialectic of history, the drive on and on to the final communal rationality, is introduced by private property breaking into the primitive natural harmony, fencing off pieces of the land, and concentrating all effort and hope on the more and more efficient utilization of the individual pieces. Thus what had been united is rent apart and what had been lying dormant is drawn into fierce movement. Alienation of man from man and thereby of man from himself is the mark of private property, restlessly driving on to its climax in capitalism, inventing technological industry as its ultimate triumph, and then tipping over into the communism required for the operation of fully developed industry. It is in communism that mankind, after its long migration through the desert of alienation, comes to itself, in a life of rational community or communal rationality; alienation leads up to and ends in full rational realization.

The central notion of the Marxist system, hence, is that of alienation. Alienation is the content of what we call history; prior to it there is primitive realization, beyond is full rational realization. The dialectic of alienation, its relentless drive ahead, the development of all man's rational faculties in its service, the widening and deepening of the insight into the technical, social, political, ideological conditions of private success, and the final overcoming of alienation and inauguration of realization through the growth of the industry which is alienation's greatest invention—this is the Marxian formula for the history of man. Coined by Hegel, "alienation" is discussed by Marx in no less striking terms of man's "real life," with his productive work in the center. If no stone of the Marxist theoretical structure remains on the other, the very concept of alienation still serves as the key to a sufficiently comprehensive and profound analysis of the crisis of modern society in terms of man's spiritual life.[1]

1. The first three chapters of this book could come under such a heading. Cf. Paul Tillich, "The Person in Technical Society," in *Christian Faith and Social Action,* edited by John A. Hutchison, 1953. It is worth noting that the current texts on Marxism, whether sympathetic or sharply critical—even quite scholarly texts such as those by Paul Sweezy on the one side and M. M. Bober on the other—seem to be perfectly innocent of any knowledge of the doctrine of alienation, as of the dialectic in general. Like the entire Marxist literature and most of the anti-Marxist literature, they make of the dialectic, because its content is an economic interpretation of

The final overcoming of alienation, which material conditions had at last made possible, was the declared objective of Marx's life work. Conditions, he says, had made it not only possible but also "necessary." But it is interesting to see that, at least in Marx's earlier writings, this word "necessary" is highly ambiguous, because of the coincidence in the dialectic of the causally necessary with the morally necessary—that is, the final identity of the "is" and the "ought." The word, covering both, thus means sometimes the one and sometimes the other. So much so that the two, at least in the early writings, do not really coincide; "conditions" permit the overcoming of alienation but do not guarantee or enforce it.

Marx is quite emphatic on the distinction. He deplores the "dehumanization," the "complete loss of man" under capitalism; and he bitterly denounces the "vulgar communism" which, he says, instead of restoring to the worker the means of self-realization and abolishing the proletarian mode of existence, "is nothing but the generalization and completion of such an existence, . . . denies the personality and thereby proclaims kinship with that private property which is the denial of personality" in the propertyless masses of the people. The self-realization, humanization, and personalization of the worker require that "private property be abrogated in a positive way: that man appropriate his own nature and his own work in a broader sense than that of material possession alone." [2] Common property, hence, is the

---

history, an economic doctrine and deem themselves excused from studies in philosophy or intellectual history. One cannot warn too emphatically that, whatever usefulness for special studies there may be in such books, there is in them nothing of the fierce greatness of Marx, and the picture as a whole is distorted. As to the economic interpretation of history, it was not invented by Marx, of course; many seventeenth-century authorities from James Harrington on, and most eighteenth-century writers including Adam Smith and the authors of *The Federalist,* make use of it. What Marx did was to integrate it into the dialectic.

2. The quotations are chosen at random from hundreds of similar passages in Marx's early writings. A good edition, originally in two volumes, in which several of these writings were published for the first time, with a scholarly introduction by S. Landshut, is *Karl Marx, Der Historische Materialismus,* edited by S. Landshut and J. P. Meyer, Leipzig,

indispensable prerequisite of man's self-realization but does not guarantee it. But on the institutional basis of common property a humanizing effort becomes possible again and necessary as well, lest we perpetuate under common property the depersonalized existence imposed by private property. Marx's greatest adversary, Proudhon, had expressed exactly the same idea, much as the two differed on institutional consequences to be drawn from the principle.

Now our point is that in *Das Kapital* this very idea is preserved and emerges in the strategic passage of the entire Marxian work, the incessantly quoted chapter "Historical Tendency of the Accumulation of Capital." There we find the definition of what the final socialization is to achieve: it is to "restore . . . individual property on the basis of . . . the common possession of the earth and the means of production." [3] In this phrase individual property is not meant in the legal but in the human sense, as the ultimate objective which the legal and institutional arrangements under socialism, here defined as "the common possession of the earth and the means of production," are designed to serve. Institutional socialism is the means to spiritual humanist individualism.

With this program Marx stands in the great tradition of modern liberal and humanist thought and shares all its shortcomings. It is true that he denounces the bourgeois belief in the natural harmony of all private interests under a regime of laissez-faire and bourgeois democracy; but he replaces it by the scientific theory of a causally necessary—that is, preordained—

1932; now in a second edition under the title *Karl Marx, Die Fruhschriften,* herausgegeben von S. Landshut, 1953. The same year 1932 also saw the publication of these writings in the *Gesamtausgabe* of the Marx-Engels-Lenin Institute of Moscow. The long delay in this official publication in the original German and the longer delay in any translation into English show that these writings were anything but popular among Marxists. The English translation bears the title *Economic and Philosophic Manuscripts of 1844,* Moscow, 1959. These writings are popularly known as the Paris Manuscripts.

3. *Das Kapital I,* Chapter 32, p. 837 of the Modern Library Giant edition; Chapter 24, section 7 of the fourth German edition. The passage again is ignored in the Marxist literature.

final harmonization toward which the history of society is driven by modern technological industry and in which it will attain its end and rest.[4] This is Marx's version of the general belief of modern man in the redemptive force of the historical process.[5]

Common property emerges as a necessary result of the causal process of history; it grows out of the force with which modern technological industry asserts itself as the dominant power in modern history. The divisive element in modern history, private property, first puts industry on its track but then becomes more and more incompatible with the intrinsic tendency of the industrial process toward collective unified management, as is evident from the economic crises which periodically disrupt the growth of industry. At the same time the social aspect of a society based on private property becomes more and more accentuated as one of class division, of social injustice, since large units of production cannot be privately owned without excluding the majority of the people from ownership. For both reasons, social and economic, the institution of private—that is, divisive—property is in conflict with the structural requirements of industry and is finally overridden by them. In this way common property, the precondition for man's final liberation, is presented as the scientifically necessary result of history. One may very well call the ultimate idea which the theory tries to develop social democracy, as opposed to individual or bourgeois democracy.

The great socialist claim, of course, is that the elimination of private profit, the emancipation of the workers from the supremacy of private capital, gives them that individual independence which private property withholds from them. But this, in the first place, is true only if economic oppression is the sole conceivable form of oppression; otherwise it is quite possible for a man to receive what is called the "full product of his labor" without, however, feeling personally free to worship God, or marry a foreign woman, or oppose the official candidates at elections, or criticize the economic interpretation of history. In other words, only with the narrowest understanding of the economic

4. Cf. *Freedom and Order,* p. 248; *Communism, Fascism, or Democracy?* p. 96, and below, Chapter VII.
5. Cf. Reinhold Niebuhr, *Faith and History,* 1949.

interpretation of history, which is not Marx's, can the problem of personal liberty be made to disappear. But secondly, as Marx's own argument makes clear, socialization of property itself is at best only the condition for making individual independence possible; it does not make it inevitable, it is not a guarantee. Otherwise original tribal community of property prior to in-dividuation would have been an organization of individual independence, which it clearly was not. The historical contribu-tion of capitalism was to emancipate man for the first time, even though the fruits of liberty were distributed most unevenly.

Our problem, then, is the relationship between the institu-tional means, common property, and the human objective. It seems that the human objective is gradually submerged by the means, which are of a heterogenous character. And this again is so because Marx interprets human rational nature, which after all produces those institutional means, in such a manner as ultimately to bar his own spiritual objective. Marxists, then, may be right in disliking and ignoring Marx's early thought, if his spiritual individualism proves to be consistent indeed with He-gel's spiritualism from which it is derived, but inconsistent with what he claims to be the unfolding of the rational nature of man in the process of collectivization through history. If so, the change that has taken place is not un-Marxian in itself; it would only bring out the full implications of the idea, much as it would thereby destroy the original intention of that idea. This is not the only example in history of an idea developing its own in-herent logic to full historical force beyond the intentions of the author, once it has been released by him.

The Empirical Argument

If, according to Marx, socialism is the institutional arrange-ment which is to serve the human objective, the overcoming of alienation, the history as conceived by Marx in realistic terms needs a social force to drive toward that institutional arrange-ment as the fulfillment of that force's own aspirations. This historical force is the class interest of the proletarian workers.

Institutions, according to Marx's conception of history, are

not aspired to because of their general desirability but because
they appear as the rational fulfillment of special rational interests. The trick which history uses is to make the special class
interest of the proletarians the general interest of society by
making the proletarian class more and more identical with the
whole of society. The reader may be reminded that these two,
socialism and the proletariat, were joined only by Marx, assert-
ing that socialism is the necessary end toward which the class
struggle of the proletariat must strive. This is precisely what,
under the name "scientific socialism"—socialism as the necessary
result of the enlightened labor movement—has ever since been
opposed to "utopian socialism"—a recommendation of sweet
reasonableness to well-meaning bourgeois capitalists and governments, which, according to "scientific socialism," could not be
well-meaning enough to sign their own death warrant by advo-
cating socialism. "Scientific socialism," then, has to prove two
propositions: (1) that late capitalist society tends to become
proletarian; (2) that proletarian workers tend to become com-
munistic. Some auxiliary propositions will be added as we
proceed.

Marx expects the unification of the whole society in a proletarian existence in which all preproletarian, preindustrial groups
are leveled. He thereby uses property as the sole criterion of social
stratification and concludes that, as almost all members of society
lose their original small properties and become employed in the
huge industrial establishments owned by the few, the proletariat
more and more becomes identical with the whole of society, and
the "dictatorship of the proletariat," designed to stamp out
counterrevolutionary interests and attempts, becomes the dictatorship of the huge majority and in this sense a democratic dictatorship. What appears as the dictatorship of the proletariat in its
relationship with outsiders is "workers' democracy" in its internal relationship.[6]

6. Addition, 1961: It would be wrong and unfair to reduce all Marx's
sociology of classes to the two-class scheme of owners and nonowners. There
is a wealth of keen observations and analyses, scattered throughout the
writings of Marx, about the survival, transformation, and even revival of
numerous middle-class functions. A systematic presentation gives a most

The argument is not complete before we add the contribution which Marx and Lenin expect of the development of
technology. New machines would simplify all functions in production and administration to the point where a special training
for special functions could be dispensed with. Not only would
the monotony of labor be eliminated by a regular change of jobs,
but neither in production nor in government would there survive a bureaucracy—that is, a group of specially trained people
whose job it is to direct the activities of others. The bureaucracy
would "wither away." But "bureaucracy" is only the sociological
name of what, since the rise of the rationalistic monarchies in
the earlier centuries of the modern age, has received the name
of "state." The "withering away of the state" then means the
free accessibility of functions in government and administration,
the elimination of the time-honored distinction between rulers
and ruled, and the direct participation of the people in the
actual use of power.

Nothing in observable reality points in this direction. As the
machines get stronger, they get more complicated, and while
labor under the machine gets simpler, work on the machine
demands higher technical skill, higher engineering knowledge,
higher organizational art, and more accurate accounting; a new
stratification of function arises. Likewise the whole society in

---

surprising and impressive total; cf. T. B. Bottomore and M. Rubel, eds.,
Karl Marx: Selected Writings in Sociology and Social Philosophy, London,
1956. But the more we must give credit to Marx the social analyst on this
ground, the more weird is the result for Marx the political prophet. The
two sides are really not reconciled, for in the dialectical future, which is
supposed to emerge from the present, the rich picture of the middle
classes is blotted out and no trace of it is to be found in the structure of
communism as established after a brief intermediate period. In other
words, the more numerous and technically important these middle-class
functions are now, the more severe must be the unifying proletarian
pressure. This is the reason why, in our outline of the dialectical development as given above, no reference to this chapter in Marxian sociology
is found. Moreover, and primarily, this chapter is implicitly disavowed by
both Marx and Lenin in their prediction of the simplification of all functions in both production and political administration so as to make higher
training for higher functions unnecessary, as discussed in the following
paragraph in the text.

this age of mechanization becomes more rather than less complicated and demands higher professional ability of the administrators in all countries of the world. But nowhere to the same
extent as in the Communist countries, which, according to an
often quoted sentence by Lenin, must be operated like big
machines. In non-Communist countries many sections of society
follow their own spontaneous law of growth, and especially in
the economic sphere the impersonal, anonymous mechanism of
the market still organizes activities to a large extent, although
this does require careful supervision and, in special conditions,
deliberate intervention. Finally, in the Western countries the
development of agriculture, the fundamental branch of production, shows an autonomous tendency to modernization
through small machines and cooperatives, i.e., outside bureaucratic and proletarian collectivism. The proletarian unification
of the people that Marxism expects and requires does not ma-
terialize.

But in Communist countries the market has no regulatory
function, and the control of economic activities entirely devolves
upon the bureaucracy, just as every other phase of life is strictly
supervised and directed toward the objectives proclaimed as
binding. Bureaucratic functions and ambitions are thus all-
pervasive and are still spreading, the whole presenting itself as a
fully bureaucratized society, as Max Weber had predicted in a
pamphlet in 1918. One would be justified in defining Communist society as bureaucratic collectivism if this were the whole
story—that is, if it were not for the tremendous drive and dynamic located in the utopian and pseudoreligious elements of
the system. (Cf. Chapter VI)

The deviation from optimistic Marxian predictions, furthermore, is most conspicuous in the international scene. Marx had
expected that the principle of free trade, which is the international arm of laissez-faire, would unify the world market on the
antithetical basis of private property and thus drive the whole
of mankind along the road to an all-inclusive socialism. National
differentiation, which became more accentuated as capitalism
advanced, destroyed this vision and put a further severe limitation upon socialist rule, wherever established. Finally, the fact

that it was first established in an undeveloped, preindustrial country completes the enumeration of the causes which make communism the achievement of a small minority.[7]

The dictatorship of the huge majority—that is, the "workers' democracy" as Marx envisaged it—was to have been of relatively brief duration only. In the already quoted paragraph of the strategic chapter in *Das Kapital*, Marx brings that out quite clearly by saying that the revolutionary expropriation of the few expropriators is an "incomparably" easier and shorter job than the preceding transformation of the entire people from one of small owners to one of propertyless workers by capitalist expropriation and concentration. But if a minority dictatorship is substituted for the dictatorship of the majority, the duration of this regime must grow proportionately because a new task accrues to it, namely that of re-educating the members of the majority itself to a "correct" understanding of their class interest. The "coexistence" of the Communist state with capitalist states in the same world, naturally, serves as a further vindication of prolonged dictatorial rule.

The upshot is that history missed the predicted course of proletarian unification. So Marxism, convinced of its own superior knowledge of the course that history ought to have taken and must some day still take in the near future if it is to attain its dialectical goal, substituted the dictatorial rule of a minority for the democratic transition to a majority socialism envisaged by Marx.[8]

Totalitarian Democracy

Even in the original Marxian conception of workers' democracy, the significance of "democracy" is highly equivocal. It is

7. These two paragraphs summarize the discussion in Chapters IV, V, and VI of *Economic Systems and Social Systems*.

8. I offered this explanation of the change in the meaning of Marxism many years ago in my book *Communism, Fascism or Democracy?*, New York, 1938. I still think it is correct but do not think that it is complete. Already in that book I called attention to the inadequate interpretation of democracy by Marx, which I have developed in more recent writings and discuss in the next sections of this chapter.

not genuine democracy as we understand it, for two interrelated reasons. The first of these—the sacred liberty of the person and the rights that flow from it—can be discussed only in a later chapter, although they must be kept in mind here as well. Secondly, true democracy is supposed by Marxism to rest on the most complete social conformity, or rather uniformity, as the only guarantee for that social equality which precludes group conflict. An almost mathematical example of social equality in quite different "pluralistic" social patterns—an un-Marxian social equality—would be that between industrial workers communally owning their plants by way of cooperatives in large-scale production, and small-scale farmers individually owning their fields or cattle. Or the factory jobs may be "controlled" by labor unions for distribution among the members—Perlman's theory—parallel to that individual ownership in small farms. In Marxism, only uniformity is supposed to make political unity possible: the proletarian pattern of life in endless repetition in all spheres of life, because in it alone solidarity of all interests to the point of their complete merger flows from the institutions into the souls of the men operating them. The spirit of the machine is not individuality but collectivity.

Qualitatively different people may be perfectly capable of living side by side on a footing of social equality, under the common belief in a common principle of human equality, as in the above examples. But such differences are suspected by Marxist materialism of giving rise to clashing group interests and thus of disrupting the unity of society. This mistrust has occasionally borne strange fruit. In the first wave of intellectual curiosity and enthusiasm for the Russian experiment, many of the themes of Marxist argument were widely discussed all over Europe after the First World War, and one of them was the alleged danger to social unity inherent in the differences, or as the Marxists invariably and characteristically put it, the "contradiction" between the sexes, and the ensuing necessity for using all means of social pressure to minimize that danger. The authentic result at that time, certainly not of Marxist institutions which did not exist in Western countries, but of an atmosphere full of Marxian problems, was a women's fashion that

—with due respect to the ladies—put the belt not around the thinnest part of the body but considerably lower, so that the circumference of a slender woman resembled that of a stout gentleman—a triumph of democratic equality. In more recent Soviet movies the admiring spectator could still see how the pretty star fell in love with the glamorous machine—that is, with collectivism.

So the class interest of the workers is conceived as a completely homogeneous magnitude. This is the proper understanding of the word "collective." The collective interest is not the sum total of individual interests, however parallel they may be; it is supposed to be a higher form on a higher plane. (Hence also it becomes possible to oppose the "correctly understood class interest"—to be discussed presently—to any chance interpretations of a nonauthoritative character which the class interest may be given by individuals or groups of less enlightened minds.) What the collective interest means is a completely unified rationality and homogeneity, over and above any qualitative difference which may prevail in reality.

Speculative in its form of thinking, this doctrine is correspondingly arbitrary when translated into materialistic practice, which it is not in the original Hegelian form, where idealism and spiritualism keep the "objective spirit" an ideal reality, a matter of "interpretation" (Marx) rather than of deliberate political incorporation. This is not to deny but to trace the Hegelian origin of this crucial Marxian theory. On the other hand, Hegel was not Marx's only inspiration, and the Hegelian tradition is not the only way to Marxism today. Rousseau's distinction between the will of all and the general will, which is a higher and purer reality, was translated by the French Jacobins into the doctrine that one had the right and duty to "force people to be free"—the phrase is Rousseau's. Marxists rightly list the Jacobins among their precursors. It is interesting to note that, while the German way to communism is via the Hegelian worship of the state as incorporating reason (*objektiven Geist*), the typical French way to communism is via Jacobin rationalism, a despotic individualism which dialectically changes into its opposite, collectivism. This turn had been achieved even before Marx on French soil by Auguste Comte, the founder of sociology, since he understood society as rational collectivity although without proletarian features; hence Marx rejected Comte as undialectical but was influenced by his "positivist" antimetaphysical program. Such despotic individualism, forcing people into a pattern of institutions supposedly incorporating liberty, is the special temptation of the United States in the struggle against communism today.

It is thus logical for Lenin to describe society as a big machine which must be run in a unified manner and cannot tolerate any freedom of individual cogs, which could, in human terms, only be freedom for error. Once reason is fully realized and truth discovered, freedom loses its meaning. Rationalism thus culminates in dictatorship, which is the logical social incorporation of what, philosophically, is collective reason correctly interpreted. The class interest of the proletarian workers is identified with collective reason, in which the nature of man comes to its full realization. Somewhere along this dialectical route the objective which the entire process was supposed to serve has been lost to sight. The collectivism of the means has overwhelmed the humanism of the end. There is in the concept of the collective no room for personal liberty; not man but society is now the ultimate end.[9]

Marxian humanism and its belief in the dignity and liberty of man relied on the conservative element in the dialectic. In order for there to be progress, the achievements of the preceding stage must be carried over into the subsequent stage; if they are not, we only have change, possibly an exchange of values but not that growth and fulfillment which we call progress. Marx did believe that human dignity and liberty, which bourgeois individualism had first developed in its struggle against feudalist superstitions, would be preserved and generalized by socialism. He was convinced that his proletarian man would not give up this great achievement but would appropriate and develop it. A strange case of idealism indeed; there is no automatic process,

9. In Hegelian phraseology, liberty is *aufgehoben*—that is, preserved in changed form; literally "raised"—that is, raised to a higher plane and thereby also removed (as in "raising the siege").

and liberty must be willed and defended if it is to be preserved. But the class interest into which the worker is supposed to merge all his individual aspirations is homogeneous, and no spontaneity is possible in a system of complete unified rationality.

The "Correctly Understood Class Interest"

The next question is that of the interpretation of the proletarian class interest itself. The original intention of an unrefined economic interpretation of history—whatever doubts may be raised about it—can be said to be democratic in the sense that it regards social and political programs as rising out of the experiences and natural aspirations of the common people in their daily lives, as opposed to idealism, which regards the products of mental processes inaccessible to the common people as determining their history. The expectation of the working class being raised to the position of an overwhelming majority clinches the point. But Marx himself found it necessary to annex a considerable measure of aristocratic idealism to this democratic materialism, as he did in his doctrine that "the communists . . . fight for the attainment of the present purposes and interests of the working class but represent in the present movement at the same time the future of the movement"—obviously because the working class itself does not correctly represent its own future; that "the communists . . . are the theoreticians of the proletarian class"; that in the beginning they—the Communists, not the proletarians—"recognize nothing but the misery in the misery" but soon "discern in it the revolutionary subversive side which will overthrow the old society." If Marx calls the Communists "the theoreticians" of the proletariat, whose task it is "to represent in the present movement at the same time the future of the movement," there is no reason to doubt that he meant this exactly as he said it.[10]

Accordingly, communism teaches that the laborers by themselves would never achieve anything but a primitive "trade unionism," which finds its objectives within the pale of capital-

10. Cf. the "Note on the Doctrine of the 'Correctly Understood Class Interest'" after this section.

ism—"crumbs from the table of the rich"—and that hence the workers must be educated to an understanding of their socialist mission in history by the socialist party, their "vanguard." The materialist, economic basis of the entire system of thought is not thereby given up, since the socialist party can so educate the workers only by taking their experiences, the hopelessness of all their aspirations within capitalism, as the starting point of the education. A mere theoretical instruction would achieve as little today, he says, as it did in the past when exploitation and misery always tended to make men revolutionists, but the absence of a collectivized existence and a collectivized pattern of work made it impossible for the people to establish themselves as a socialist community. The point is, however, that even today socialism could never be achieved without a difficult and far-sighted interpretation of those experiences as well. The workers have to be explicitly taught that they can realize their natural aspirations only by pursuing their unified class interest beyond capitalism because their naïve "trade unionism," a junior partnership in dying capitalism, could never prevent its death and could never survive it. But a conception of a completely changed world requires a high degree of abstract constructive thinking and is beyond the reach of untrained minds. Thus the indispensable and really strategic task of "correctly" explaining to the workers their "real class interest" devolves on the Marxist party, the proletarian "vanguard."

The vanguard, as interpreted by itself, consists of men completely identified with the average proletarian not so much in their social background—which from the time of the founding fathers in many cases has not been proletarian—but through their highly trained minds, which have outgrown the bourgeois matrix of their education and enabled them to see the great denouement of dialectical history being prepared in contemporary events. Their identification is with the essence rather than with the empirical imperfections of proletarian life; they look through the trade-unionist illusion to the Communist reality of the future and understand that their special assignment is to maintain, in all the bewildering distress of proletarian life, the clear vision of the true and only way out. In other words, they represent the "correctly understood" proletarian "class interest," in contradistinction to the empirical reformist misunderstanding of it—the true reality as distinguished from its superficial appearance. The universalist man, rather than the particularist of the trade-union local, is the one whom history wants to produce and with whom the vanguard is identified. One may very well see in the doctrine of the vanguard the key to all subsequent developments in the Marxist movement.

The Marxist intellectuals are qualified for their strategic assignments by a study of the norm for man that emerges from the nature of large-scale industry. They are in charge of protecting that norm against confusion with the empirical worker who approaches it only potentially, not yet in fact. The distinction between the dialectical proletarian existence and that pure essence of collective universalism which is to emerge from the dialectic and bring it to its end creates the gap which is filled by the Marxist student, whose dialectical understanding anticipates the future in the present, the essence in the existence. The worker now appears in two different forms: the empirical worker is not revolutionary but must be revolutionized, while the authentic class-conscious worker is the model to be emulated and imitated. The active part, hence, is that of the vanguard; theirs is the main responsibility before world history, and theirs consequently must be the power in due course.

Reserving the analysis of the vanguard argument to the following chapter, the discussion of the proletarian class and class interest may be summarized here by saying that not indeed the empirical working class, but a distilled, purified, stylized, idealized image of it is the goal of history and the norm in which man is to be made over. For only the proletarian worker, deprived of property as he is, has no stake in any particular piece of the world and is thus enabled to enjoy precisely that balanced, fair, comprehensive vision which private owners and anyone who dreams of becoming a private owner cannot have. Only the propertyless see the world in correct proportion and understand their own place in this world not as individuals but as members of the collective. That is, they see the possibility and necessity of perfect rational solidarity in a world-wide division of labor where everyone's private welfare directly depends on everyone else's. Once more, this picture does not represent the empirical worker. Nevertheless, in order for such qualities to crystallize in the "class-conscious" worker—that is, the worker as he should be—these qualities in however blurred a form must be found already in the empirical worker, and the emphasis on him, then, has not simply statistical but moral reasons in the doctrine of Marxism.

It is useful to contrast the Marxian doctrine with that of Britain's Fabian Socialists. They, and the Labour Party which they inspired, have never appealed to the workers' class interest but always to the conscience of people of good will—the Labour Party more often than not to the Christian conscience. The negative attitude of the Fabians toward the proletarian class interest is summarized in the words of one of their three leaders, Bernard Shaw: "I hate the poor and burn with impatience to exterminate them." This is a quip, as expected from the great playwright and scoffer, of course, but it is more than a joke, as also expected; it contains a polemic against Marx. What it means is that misery degrades man rather than giving him a potentially wider and more balanced view of the world, and that therefore there is no sense in finding anything potentially admirable in the proletarian worker and making him a model and norm for man. It can obviously be argued that Marx does not do that either, as far as the empirical worker is concerned, since he concedes that the empirical worker does not correctly understand his class interest—because of his misery and lack of education. But then the fundamental difference in nationally typical ways of thinking stands out in great clarity: the difference between the speculative approach of the German Marx through an admittedly hypothetical concept of the worker as he should be, and the sober empiricism of the British interest in the worker as he is and should not be.[11] Be it noted that the former concept —the worker as he should be—became the ruling ideological figure in countries which have only a very limited experience

11. Ferdinand Lassalle, the founder of the socialist party in Germany, had likewise spoken of the "vices of the oppressed," for which the oppressors were responsible.

with workers as they really are, while the latter concept—the worker as he is—was employed to arouse consciences in the countries with the most stable and advanced democracy.

Note on the Doctrine of
the "Correctly Understood Class Interest"

In the summary of the *Communist Manifesto* given in its concluding section, the following is said about "the relationship of the communists to the already constituted labor parties": "They [the Communists] fight for the attainment of the directly given interests and purposes of the working class, but they represent in the present movement at the same time the future of the movement." In the same vein but more explicitly, Marx says in *Misery of Philosophy* (Chapter II, Section 1): "As the economists are the scientific representatives of the bourgeois class, so the socialists and communists are the theoreticians of the proletarian class. So long as the proletariat is not yet sufficiently developed to constitute itself as a class of its own . . . so long as the productive forces are not yet sufficiently developed in the womb of the bourgeoisie to let shine through the conditions which are needed for the liberation of the proletariat and the formation of a new society, so long these theoreticians are nothing but utopians. . . . But in the measure as history advances and hereby the struggle of the proletariat becomes more marked, they need no longer seek science in their heads; they have only to account for that which happens every day under their eyes and to make themselves the organs of these events. . . . So long as they are in the beginning of the fight they see in the misery nothing but the misery, without discerning in it the revolutionary subversive elements which will overthrow the old society. But from this moment on [i.e., when they discern the revolutionary element in the misery], science becomes the conscious product of the historical devleopment." The Communists, hence, are "the theoreticians of the proletarian class," they are "science."

In *Neue Zeit*, the scientific weekly of the German social democratic mass party, edited by the scholarly Karl Kautsky, this doctrine—as far as I can see—has not been mentioned one single time in the thirty-odd years of its publication. It has been mentioned, however, in the younger parallel periodical of the Austrian party, *Der Kampf*. After the Russian Revolution, the non-Communist (and nondialectical) philosopher Max Adler tried to wrest the doctrine from the Communists (*Der Kampf*, 1918, pp. 44–45): "If consciousness is determined by social existence, then not only the wrong consciousness is so determined but the deliberate correction of it, the correct consciousness as well. It is true that social existence produces in its every step a quasi-natural, merely reflected or instinctive feeling of the masses [in German, *Massenmeinen*], which still represents a lower, rather passive stage of social consciousness. It is not yet that consciousness which has arrived at the idea, at theoretical clarity, and . . . at the distinct direction of a will conscious of its goal. . . . The necessary transformation of the first into the second form contradicts the materialistic interpretation of history so little that it is precisely the latter which gives us the insight into the necessity of such a development. For it is not at all the automatic effect of the mere social existence which provides the progress from the instinctive to the correctly oriented [*zielbewusst*] consciousness; this is achieved only by the fact that with that passive mental reaction of the masses from the subfoundation of social life [*gesellschaftliche Untergrund*] rises, at the same time, a critical consciousness, which radically transmutes the former. . . . Contrary to that original wrong consciousness of the proletariat it was the historical achievement of the *Communist Manifesto* to bring the proletariat the knowledge of . . . its true interests. . . . Likewise now once more it is only . . . theoretical insight . . . which can give the proletariat its proper consciousness." According to this presentation, then, the theoretical consciousness of the proletariat "arises from the subfoundation of society." This attempt of an educated and thinking man makes clear the hopelessness of a democratic Marxism. According to Marx it is "the theoreticians," according to Lenin's always practice-oriented mind it is the theoreticians organized "bureaucratically" as a cadre of officers, who educate the proletariat to "correct consciousness."

After Lenin, George Lucacs in *Geschichte und Klassenbe-wusstsein* (Berlin, 1923) unfolded all the depth and width dimensions of the doctrine of the correct consciousness; this is the most erudite book of the Marxist literature. This is not contradicted by the fact that Lucacs got into trouble with the ruling vulgar propaganda of the party, and—good collectivist that he was—ruefully confessed his ignorance of Lenin's and Stalin's teaching in a long article in *Under the Banner of Marxism;* he also promised not to reprint his book. The vulgarization of Marxism had already set in with Engels, was energetically continued by Lenin, and reached with Stalin its lowest point so far, which permits it to inculcate a version of *Dialectical Materialism* into children in elementary school. This again does not preclude a broad and much ramified discussion in Russia and does not diminish the credit due the two Jesuit scholars who present the entire development in all its details: A. Gustav Wetter, *Der Dialektische Materialismus: seine Geschichte und System in der Soviet Union,* Vienna, 1952; and a briefer work, I. M. Bochenski, *Der Sovietrussische Dialektische Materialismus,* Munich and Berne, 1950.

After completing the German version of the present book the author became acquainted with several learned contributions to the discussion. He wishes to record his appreciation of Isaiah Berlin, *Karl Marx* (Home University Library, 1953); Ralf Dahrendorf, *Marx in Perspective,* 1953; Heinrich Popitz, *Der Entfremdete Mensch, Zeitkritik und Geschichtsphilosophie des Jungen Marx,* 1953; and two survey articles in the altogether scholarly *Studien uber Marxismus* of the German Evangelical Academies, edited by E. Matzke, 1953—one on "Epochen der Marxinterpretation," mainly concerned with the German development, by Erich Thier; the other by Iring Fetscher, with the corresponding French discussion. The well-known book by Jules Monnerot, *Sociologie du Marxisme,* 1948, mainly quoted for the parallel it draws between Marxism and Islam, is not profound enough in its discussion of religious problems.

The Sociology of Economic Planning

This chapter so far has discussed the two Marxian propositions about the proletarian worker: (1) capitalism tends to produce an overwhelmingly proletarian society; (2) the proletarian worker tends to be or to become a Communist. This is the sociological pole of the Marxian argument. It is supplemented by an economic argument, the argument from the economic crisis. The crisis, according to Marx, is caused by the inadequacy of private property and the market to the operation of a large-scale industrial system, and it can be remedied only by unified management under common property. This argument, naturally, assumed increasing propagandistic importance in recent decades, when the stunning collapse in 1929–1933 discredited unregulated capitalism, as predicted by Marx, while the prediction of growing proletarian homogeneity ran into trouble, as shown above—unless the misery of that very crisis itself would still force social development back into the proletarian channel. Anyway, the shift from social democracy to Bolshevism was clearly accompanied by a shift of emphasis from Marx's social criticism—exploitation can be averted only by common property —to his economic criticism—economic crises in modern industrial systems can be stopped only by common property. Those who did not feel they were victims of exploitation and particularly did not accept the designation of proletarians were victims of the economic crisis, like everybody else; they were supposed to be attracted by proof that the crisis could be stopped only by unified operation of the total industrial structure, as promised by communism.[12]

12. The Marxian argument rests on a diagnosis of the crisis which it is here not necessary to reproduce. In point of fact, several partly conflicting diagnoses are offered, among which the theory of the falling profit rate is most popular with Marxists. It says that the very mechanization of production, replacing manual labor by machines as it does, diminishes the relative opportunities for exploitation of labor and thus reduces profit to the point where profit-hungry capitalism ceases to operate the system and must be replaced by communism. Now this theory is logically untenable: it overlooks the growth of total output as the very effect of mechanization, which makes it possible for prices and money wages to fall and for profits

The key to the problem, then, is on the one hand the economic necessity of proportionally coordinating the dynamic industries and on the other hand the sociological question of finding in industrial society the group capable of establishing such
over-all controls because they would fit into the general pattern
of institutions to which that group looks for the satisfaction of
its own interests and ambitions. According to Veblen, that key
group would be the engineers, who understand machinery and
whose ambition and pride is in seeing it work smoothly, while
neither business nor labor understands anything of machines and
their sole concern is so to influence their operation as to get
more money out of it. According to Mannheim, the key group
is the social scientists, who realize the necessity for some co-
ordination of action in all fields of modern large-scale technical
society including the economic field, and who also are distinguished from the other groups by the wider and more balanced
outlook which they gain through their studies and by the constant exchange of opinions and points of view.

to grow in absolute amounts so that the profit rate need not fall. (Cf. for
this and the other points in this footnote the summary given in my *History
of Economic Doctrines,* pp. 148, 157 ff.)

A second Marxian theory on the economic crisis, known as the theory
of the industrial reserve army, must be credited as the first to see that an
unregulated system of free enterprise, far from securing a high level of
employment through the operation of the competitive mechanism, normally rests on a sufficiently large reserve of unemployed to keep down the
wage of the employed in favor of profit. But again, as in the preceding case,
the argument disregards the constant rise in productivity and total output
which makes a simultaneous rise of both wage and profit possible.

That Marxian theory of the crisis which is the really important and
still unexhausted contribution is the disproportionality theory, whose
foundation is laid in the famous production schedules of the second volume
of *Kapital*. The price mechanism, which is the regulatory device in an
unregulated economy, is not infallible; as it fails in certain other cases,
so it also fails to regulate the production of durable equipment in its relationship to the production of current goods. Disproportionality in the size
of the industries that are technically interdependent obviously makes for
breakdown and can be remedied only by deliberately organized and
planned action to establish proportionality. This statement can be made
and accepted even independently of the specific causes to which the
pernicious disproportionalities in an unregulated system may be traceable.

According to the Marxist approach, these and many related solutions are fantastic because neither the engineers nor the economists and social scientists are organized for the struggle and exercise of power, such power in the economic interpretation of history depending on a distinct function in the process of production, which in present society combines owners and nonowners, those who hold the power and those who are commissioned to seize it. Now these two, the only classes in polarized industrial society as Marxists see it, are very far apart in their outlook. The outlook of private owners is concentrated on their property; they are competitors, not cooperators; their property is theirs, and nobody else can be permitted to have a say in its management. The outlook of the propertyless employees is detached and comprehensive, their selfishness is not private but collective, not particularist but universalist, and they will use their revolutionary power accordingly. It is in this way that the ideas of proletarian socialism and of planned economy are made to coincide in the Marxian theory.

Now we have already seen that this reliance on the collective understanding and ability of the proletarian workers is only the first approach of Marxism; that, upon closer inspection, what it means to describe is the worker as he can and should be rather than the worker as he is. The worker as he can be, because there is nothing in his function in production to prevent him from acquiring that correct universalist perspective with which Marxism credits him; while the worker as he is, because of capitalist corruption, falls short of that perfection; and the gap between the two must be filled by the "vanguard," the Communist Party, the Marxist intelligentsia, in whose minds the nonexistent worker-as-he-should-be has assumed a kind of mythological reality as the goal of the education that they impose on workers-as-they-are.

But this is only another way of saying that Marxist science as such, through its students and interpreters, transforms the structure of reality and builds a new world. Marxist science alone, without the working class, could not achieve anything, naturally; it achieves what it does because it understands and explains to the workers their real interest and thus makes the power of the working class its own, Marxism's, power. But the workers alone, without Marxist science, could not achieve anything either; witness the worker-as-he-is, falling at best for trade unionism as a way to some crumbs from the table of the rich, rather than waging the total revolution against capitalism which is his historical mission. Marxist science in the world of mind is parallel to the working class in the world of matter; they are created by the same act of material history and are dependent on each other. But once more, it is Marxist science which changes the structure of reality; by presenting itself as the natural property of the working class, it changes the working class and thereby the world to be created by the working class.

Marxism was the first school of social thought to proclaim that social theory, far from merely reflecting social reality, changes it as well. Marx had programmatically announced this purpose when he proclaimed in his struggle for his emancipation from Hegelian idealism that, while "the philosophers have only interpreted the world, what matters is to change it." Not every social theory changes reality, naturally; this requires powerful thinking straight from the heart of reality to the heart of reality—"existentialist" thinking in modern parlance, of which the two mutually hostile critics of Hegel, Kierkegaard and Marx, provided the first conscious examples. In the light of Marxist theory as expounded by the Communist Party, the proletarian class struggle would acquire a new, systematized, long-range reality, which it could never acquire without such orientation and purification. In this general form the doctrine that Marxist theory is to become a decisive force in history is perfectly acceptable logically and has proved powerfully true in reality.

The strange thing is that Marxist theory restricted its own direct effect on history to the working class and assumed that its teachings would never be absorbed by the other classes, those which it dooms to be overridden by the workers' class struggle. The workers do but the other classes do not learn from Marxism (or from any other social theory for that matter). The other classes continue on their way to their appointed doom as if they had never heard of Marxism; they remain true to their purely materialistic, unenlightened existence as defined by Marxist theory. The peasants are defined as invariably stupid, dirty, un-organizable, decaying, irretrievably doomed, and completely de-pendent on the organized workers, who are to extricate them from their sub-proletarian misery by collectivizing agriculture.[13] The notion that farmers are capable of rebuilding their lives via technical modernization of their small farms and large-scale co-operatives for outside activities is considered sociologically absurd, much as it obviously is in the farmers' economic interest to do precisely this. Likewise businessmen are invariably doomed to destroy the profits of the boom by the bankruptcies of the ensuing depression, because they must continue, according to Marx, to seek maximum profits competitively in the shortest period, however much business-cycle theory and consciousness of crisis may advise them to stabilize their system via concerted action to preserve and perpetuate profits and avoid the crisis by avoiding the boom. Such higher rationality in the pursuit of their class interest is inaccessible to them, according to Marxism. But there are no sociologically intelligible reasons for this as-sumption.

What a business world confronted with the economic crisis is required to learn is a more expedient strategy but by no means a different morality. It cannot be proved, but it appears quite likely that Marx's reasons for denying the possibility of eco-nomic planning by business is a confusion between those two, expediency and morality. Economic planning by the universalist-minded working class is universalist and thus appears morally superior to economic planning by business, which is always as particularist as the private property on which the class interest of business rests. But the two are really distinguished not by morality but by the scope of the policy suggested by the class situation. The reason for the universalism of proletarian plan-ning, according to Marx, is not a religion of brotherliness, but the sober calculation by the individual worker that his private

13. For a full discussion, see the chapter "Socialism and Agriculture" in my book *Wirtschaftssysteme und Gesellschaftssysteme,* particularly pp. 105 ff. and 117 ff.—drawn together from the agricultural sections in my older book, *Communism, Fascism, or Democracy?,* 1938.

interest is best served by concerted action with all people in the same situation—that is, with everybody in a final all-proletarian world. Putting it more briefly, the reason for the universalism of proletarian planning, according to Marx, is not higher morality but the universality of the proletarian existence; once the working class becomes, through the effects of capitalism, identical with mankind, proletarian class action becomes universalist by definition.

This is dialectical materialism: it is not mind-born ideas but different economic strategies of different classes in different situations which make history. Accordingly, where the working class is still a class among other classes, not yet identical with mankind, proletarian planning is still particularist, too. The Soviet policy of the "scissors" [14] means precisely that industrial goods bought by the peasants and agricultural goods bought by the workers are so priced respectively as to raise a profit from the peasants for investment in industrial expansion—i.e., in the proletarian sector. The Soviet economists were quite frank in calling this "planned exploitation"; they comforted themselves by the consideration that, when the peasants at last had become proletarians, they would partake of the blessings thus made possible.

Hence, again, business planning would be possible in the particularist interest of business; it would so set quotas, prices, and incomes as to secure and steady the flow of production and profit by avoiding both boom and depression. That business-cycle doctrine when absorbed by the members of the business community changes their behavior and is thus condemned to run after the changing empirical reality of the business cycle without ever catching up to it is an idea as foreign to professional business-cycle specialists as to Marxists. But there is no reason why only the workers should be able to rise above a narrow short-run understanding of their class interest—"trade unionism"—to a fuller, more rational, long-range understanding. Other groups too suffer from the short-sightedness of the market and would find in the higher rationality of a long-range point of view a steadier satisfaction of their particular interests. This is

14. *Wirtschaftssysteme und Gesellschaftssysteme,* p. 35.

as true with private property as without it, and that fact leaves the Marxist theory of the "inexorable necessity" of final economic collapse pretty much in the air. The collective nature of an industrial system makes concerted, unified, long-range operation indispensable; but there is no logical necessity for the Marxist assumption that only the working class should understand this. In other words, the working class no longer has a sociologically natural monopoly on the technique of economic planning precisely because the Marxist theory has been absorbed by the whole of society.

This is not a new discovery. Rudolf Hilferding, the best of the Marxist economists, often quoted even by Lenin, in an all too brief but quite distinct paragraph [15] elongates the notion of the capitalist cartel, where independent firms submit to quotas of production and limitations of price competition for the sake of higher and steadier profit, to the idea of a "general cartel," where "all capitalist production is deliberately regulated by one instance, which determines the volumes of production in all industries" and uses purely nominal price fixation to distribute the products between the different classes. In this startling vision the technique of planning as concerted economic action is completely divorced from sociological premises and made available to any rational-minded economic regime.[16] In other words, the core of the Marxian system, the collapse of capitalism for reasons of its inherent inadequacy to the operation of a full-grown industrial world, is not logically necessary; capitalism can organize to avoid the crisis and to establish steady employment and production. Hilferding is too convinced a Marxist—or too

15. *Das Finanzkapital*, 1910, p. 295. Cf. also my *Communism, Fascism or Democracy?*, p. 193, on the "confusion of the concept of planning with the concept of equalization" and the technical feasibility of nonegalitarian planning.

16. It is interesting to note that, while Hilferding himself did not make this latter point explicit, he personally gradually moved from the radical left of the Austrian and German socialist movement to its extreme right and spent his energies during the last years of the Weimar Republic in a desperate attempt to organize the parties of the democratic government coalition for a concerted attack on the economic crisis, which then was devouring the Republic.

good a democrat—to acquiesce in this conclusion. If capitalism does not collapse for economic reasons, he says, it is the more sure to collapse for social and political reasons, in the revolt of the oppressed masses against the control of every phase of life by the general cartel. But revolt against effective control is something totally different from automatic collapse; Hilferding has clearly been led by his fearless logic outside the philosophy of materialism (and has quite deservedly been bitterly attacked for it by Marxists ever since).

It would not be correct to say that what Hilferding called general cartel is today known as capitalist planned economy. Hilferding's understanding of planned economy—so planned as to prevent collapse and to secure smooth operation—was as little developed as everybody else's before the First World War. In the absence of the test of reality, everybody understood a planned economy to be the extreme opposite of the extreme notion of a completely free market, the marketless household against the unregulated market. Both the primitive theory of socialist planned economy and Hilferding's general cartel are of this extreme and exclusive nature, totalitarian planned economies different from each other in the nature and objectives of the controlling power. Meanwhile, after the great crash of 1929–1933, nontotalitarian planning has become the object of much experimenting in practice and much study in theory. In it, elements of planning are precisely combined with elements of the market, setting certain fixities and goals as data for the calculation on which private decisions in the market rest; using in the planned sectors the market technique of deliberate monopolistic changes in supply or demand rather than the bureaucratic technique of overriding the market; and having the whole set of measures carried by the joint authority of government and business, where labor may or may not have a strong voice in government and, more generally, the strategy of the whole enterprise will be established or modified according to the political traditions or decisions of the country concerned. This is not the place to describe the integrated structure; the important thing for this discussion is that planning need be neither proletarian-totalitarian, as Marx believed, nor totalitarian of any other political and social kind, as Hilferding believed and as the die-hard liberals—the neo-liberals—staunchly maintain even today. Hilferding himself, after emancipating himself from dogma by way of his theory of the general cartel, seems to have more and more developed a pragmatic understanding of the interplay of planning and market factors; the long-overdue posthumous publication of his papers is likely to become an important contribution to such understanding. And the whole development of thought from the breakthrough in the theory of the general cartel can only be characterized as a return to sanity, or maybe to platitudinous common sense, after the excesses of exclusive planning driven by logic to totalitarian savagery and of the exclusive free market driven by logic to collapse.

Dialectic of Religion

Atheist Theocracy

Atheism as Religion

THE Soviet form of government is most easily understood as a kind of theocracy resting on the atheist religion of salvation which is Marxism. These are not analogies, they are definitions. They require explanation.

Theocracy is the accepted term for absolute government conducted by priests in the name of their deity, where the structures of state and church merge into one and the recipients of revelation and inspiration are in absolute control of every phase of life —in totalitarian control. The difference between a Christian theocracy and the atheist theocracy of Marxism lies, of course, in the kind of revelation received. Cromwell, theocratic ruler though he was, was a deeply devout man who humbled himself in prayer, thus mitigating, at least for Englishmen, the rigor of his rule. But there was no one before whom Lenin and Stalin could humble themselves. Their very religion of materialism taught them that inexorable historical necessity was driving toward the final and supreme form of reason in man's life, and made them the responsible executors of that grand design. Representing as they did "reason" incarnate, they could not permit themselves humility or moderation, nor was it possible for them to see in such qualities anything but despicable weakness. As collectivists, they could have no concern for the fate of individuals whose misfortune it was to be placed by history in the wrong sociological camp and thus to be marked out for destruction. All this was implicit in their religion, atheism.[1]

Atheism is integral to all Marxist thought and is, in a way, its climax and the test of its perfection. For as collective man in

1. *Freedom and Order* (New York, 1947), p. 282.

scientific communism seizes full control of his life in all its facets, he learns that there is no inscrutable power outside or above him, ruling the world by mysterious laws to which we have to submit unquestioningly precisely because they appear absurd to our human minds. Problems can be solved and questions answered; to do this is the achievement of reason in the human mind. This very argument, however, implies not only the final irrelevance of religion, but also its earlier power as the fantastic answer to the real problems of man. In other words, religion is a phenomenon in history and, under the dialectical law of history, has its preliminary necessity and function, just as its final disappearance is necessary.

But this final disappearance, as with everything that is dialectically necessary, is not for this reason achieved without struggle; all the interests and passions of man are involved. Being a kind of "erroneous science" (Sumner)—the wrong answer to the crucial questions of our existence—it has had the most tremendous power in disciplining people into meekly accepting the structures which private interests and their developing private rationality have chosen to impose on them. Class divisions and market fluctuations, according to the ideologists of the ruling powers, are inherent in the mysterious order of creation as willed by the Creator to test our patience and obedience, for which we shall be rewarded in eternity. Religion thus is the most formidable defense of private property, the supreme form of the alienation which is grounded in private property, the projection into heaven of man's material and mental powerlessness and misery. But by the same token, as rationality and criticism advance and finally hit upon the machine, the "heteronomy" of religion, the "alien law" which sanctions alienation, must yield to the autonomy of human rationality and human collective self-rule in communism. This is the atheist turn in "scientific socialism," linking religion with the alienation which is life under private property and atheism with the self-realization of man under communism.[2]

2. For a lucid presentation, see the section on Feuerbach and Marx in the brilliant book by Henri de Lubac, *The Drama of Atheist Humanism*, New York, 1950 (translation from the French original, 1948).

Atheism is counterreligion, and that in a double sense. It is the doctrine hostile to religion and designed to end it. But counterreligion that it is, it also is religion—the religion against religion; the rival religion. If it were not that, it could not offer itself as a substitute for religion; mere science is no possible substitute because it would leave a psychic vacuum where religion had formerly filled the soul. Nor can atheism be proved by way of scientific verification; it remains dogma, however much recommended by the claim of scientific reason to explain everything—a purely dogmatic, unverifiable claim in itself. The ambition of atheist humanism to be strictly unreligious—rather than counterreligious—founders on the facts of the nature of man, whom Edmund Burke in his struggle against the atheist rationalism of the French Revolution defined as the religious animal. Communism is the second example in modern history—maybe the third if Comte's purely academic religion of positivism is counted as the second—to seek religious sanction for its allegedly scientific rule and lift its "scientific" rulers to the rank of guardians of conscience.

The Biblical Form of Marxist Thought

That Marxism is a religion would be furiously denied by Lenin, Stalin, and all the faithful; they contend that it is science. This was, in fact, the claim by which Marx and Engels made themselves supreme masters of the socialist movement in a scientific age. But Marxist doctrine is not scientific, despite all the ingenious sociological analyses it includes. In terms of method, Marxism as a whole is strictly dogmatic—that is, it cannot be verified or refuted by scientific methods. It is religious in the dual sense that it appeals to souls searching for a faith, and that it makes this appeal by teaching a coherent, all-inclusive, objective structure of the world and of man's mission in it—a suprarational interpretation of man's position in the whole of life. Yet religion though it is, it can be accepted by the foes of traditional religion because, far from coming in religious garb, it presents itself as pure science—the only pure science, the full scientific truth. This claim is accepted by the faithful because they are unable to judge it. Wonderful are the twists of the human mind.[3]

The concern with pure and complete science is not peculiar to Marxism; it is shared by all modern social sciences. What does distinguish Marxism is the extravagance of its claim to represent science—such extravagance strengthening, of course, the hidden religious appeal. To those who deny the possibility of pure science and see all scientific endeavor as dependent on more or less hidden dogmatic propositions beyond the reach of science— because they believe that man cannot think otherwise—there is nothing objectionable in Marxism's use of dogmatic premises; to them, what is controversial is not the principle of dogma but the choice of the particular dogma and the denial that it is dogma at all. If dogma is the form taken by a proposition that is beyond scientific verification or refutation, then the dogmatic use of factual propositions which are accessible to scientific verification or refutation is clearly illicit. Of course, not any and every dogmatic proposition constitutes a religion; dogma is the stuff of which religion is built, but whether what is built is a religion depends on the two criteria mentioned above.

But the principal question is that of validity. There may be and are many religions, but there can be only one truth. If man is the religious animal and all his thoughts and actions stem from his faith—in other words, if religion is ubiquitous—then all man's purposes and aspirations culminate in the religious dimension, and there they are confronted with one another in spiritual battles mirroring those that are physical. Hence in claiming a religious or pseudoreligious nature for Marxism we are not bringing it closer to traditional religion, as some atheists continue to suspect. In order to fight each other, Marxism and traditional religion must stand on common ground, as do al-

3. The religious style of Marxism has often been discussed, most impressively in early writings of Paul Tillich and in his book *Die Sozialistische Entscheidung*, 1933 (reprinted 1948). Other books worth reading are: Theodor Steinbüchel, *Der Sozialismus als sittliche Idee*, 1921; Alexander Miller, *The Christian Importance of Karl Marx*, 1946; W. Banning, *Der Kommunismus als Politische-Soziale Weltreligion*, 1953 (translation from the Dutch original).

ternative scientific theories, and this common ground is precisely what makes them irreconcilable alternatives.

Marxism takes over from traditional Western Judeo-Christian religion the form, the style of thinking, and fills this with the contents of its own categories. It is these massive categories that Western peoples notice and study; they unquestioningly accept the form of the thought because they are in the same tradition. Being a religion of salvation, Marxism is clearly a flattened and watered-down version of Biblical eschatology; more particularly, it is a secularized version of the Book of Revelation. For it is the teaching of the Bible, and of the Bible alone among all the religious documents of mankind, that history has a purpose and that all actions and events are positively or negatively related to that purpose. The Old Testament is the narrative of the heroic struggle of the prophets to decipher God's will as it is revealed to His people, although shrouded in the mysterious language of thunder in history; and the New Testament brings the story to its climax, from the first to the second coming of Christ. The Christian creed in all its versions is a recital of historical events, beginning "under Pontius Pilate," a minor provincial administrator in Roman history. Hegel made a blasphemous attempt to describe the dialectical progress of history as the gradual approximation to God's will by means of the step-by-step reconciliation of opposing forces. To Marx, however, history was not progress through reconciliation but progress through cataclysm—a view much closer than Hegel's to the Biblical theme—leading up to the final terrible battle that finishes the work of redemption and beats down rebellion forever. Then the state, the agency of organized physical force, will "wither away" for lack of function, as the heavenly Jerusalem, whose gates are always open, comes down from the sky. "Behold, I make everything new."

Redemption through history, even though finally beyond history, is an idea that would have been scandalous to Greek thinking, where man's mind rose above history, out of history, into the pure light of ideas, which were the sole reality and of which history was only a shadow. Greek patriotism produced great historians, but their theme was the tragedy of the greatness and decline of their cities—the only dignified part of a barbarous, totally irrelevant world, an island of sense that emerged from the ocean of nonsense and then was gradually swallowed back into it. A god who would use his enemies as the rod to chastise his people into obedience to their covenant with him; one who would finally despair of that covenant in its original form and embark upon the great work of redemption by a roundabout way, through the Gentiles—such a god no Greek mind could ever have imagined. Still less could he have been the god of any of the nonwhite civilizations, which generally understand salvation as the path to a mystical union of love that burns away the suffering of individuation experienced as separation.

Hence the Marxist message of salvation through and in history is typically in the Judeo-Christian tradition, where history is related to ultimate meaning, decision, and destiny. The proposition that history is related to meaning, positively or negatively, is not the result of scientific investigation but the premise on which such investigation is based. This premise, however, is so completely taken for granted by Marxists that they never wonder about it or question it. It is not dogma to them, but what science calls an axiom; a proposition that precedes reasoning, makes it possible, and appears to need no proof because the inquiring mind finds it among the supposedly natural elements of its thinking. It is not the epistemologist but the student of intellectual history who challenges the axiomatic validity of the Marxist premise.

The Marxist does not simply relate history to meaning. He finds meaning fully realized or "materialized" in the process of history, which he sees as developing from the primitive quasi-instinctive realization of man's life in the community, through self-alienation by the different stages of private property—which is, at the same time, the unfolding of the rational faculties in the service of private property—to the resolution of the drama in the full self-realization of man on the basis of rational collectivism. It makes little difference whether we call this process the dialectical growth of meaning through history—thus claiming rationality for the process as a whole and derivative rationality for each stage of it—or describe it as a strictly causal, morally blind sequence of events following one another "with the strictness of natural law" (of which historical law is a part), and then say that history "jumps," in the transition from the last cause to the last effect, "from the realm of necessity to the realm of liberty"—that is, from meaninglessness to meaning. In either case we are confronted by the question of the origin of meaning in history, the origin of a causally necessary process which happens to lead to mankind's salvation from all its ills—to the final, full, and enduring realization of the true meaning of man's life.

A causally necessary process which culminates in this supreme moral effect cannot be the result of mere chance; it has been planned that way, as the whole that it is and for the sake of the moral goal. The objective was implanted in the first set of conditions from which the process started and in the law of motion under which it started; another final objective would have required another initial arrangement to lead to a different goal with equal causal strictness. Just as Marx predicted the Communist future as the inescapable outcome of the capitalist transformation, so a Marxist in feudal times could have predicted the same final result as the outcome of the capitalism which would have to supersede feudalism. We control the effect by controlling the cause, and further back the cause of the cause, in infinite regression.

It is true that Hegel, who claimed to decipher God's design, conceded to human limitedness that it can look ahead by only one step, and that the final denouement can be predicted only from the vantage point of the last-but-one stage; as he put it, the owl of Minerva—the sacred bird of the goddess of wisdom—begins to fly only at dusk. For in Hegel the process is not thought of as causally necessary and scientifically controllable; it is not materialistic. And Marx, proudly announcing that he had reversed Hegel—merely reversed him, we may say—thereby took over this element of Hegel's thought, as he did the others. In both cases the growth of the human mind is part—the essential part—of the dialectical history and becomes the decisive instrument in its final step. But the pattern of the dialectic, whether or not discovered late, has been at work all the time, according to dialectical materialism more than to dialectical idealism; and if the human mind is necessarily late in discovering and appropriating it, the mystery or miracle of its origin and operation is thereby only reinforced. How was the law of the dialectic instituted? That question is what sometimes caused Marx, the Hegelian, to call himself an agnostic rather than an atheist. He was too good a thinker not to realize that the problem was unsolved.

Engels, less profound and still more presuming, "solved" the problem by "discovering" a law according to which matter produces its own form. This was obviously a purely verbal solution, dictated by the logical necessity for eliminating from his materialistic system the principle of form; indeed, it was a quasi solution, for it merely replaced the problem of the principle of form by the absurd "problem" of how form can be produced by matter. But these weaknesses of Engels' doctrine proved to be no obstacle to incorporating it in the official Soviet philosophy; on the contrary, the more mysterious or dogmatic or even absurd it was, the more it appealed to the yearning in man's soul for something which could command his awe and reverence and in which he himself could be a humble partner. Nor should it be overlooked that this psychological effect is far from being limited to Marxist scholars. It also operates, dimly and vaguely, in the minds of all true believers, who can understand the absurd no more than the scholars, but take it for granted because they believe that the scholars do understand it—a strange but effective form of *credo quia absurdum*.[4]

Origin and Conquest of Sin

We turn now from the form to the content of the process. According to Marxism, salvation issues from the growth of industry. Human work remained technologically individual through-

4. Addition 1961: Soviet philosophy calls itself Dialectical Materialism, which name is chosen to suggest the broadening of the original Marxian economic dialectic, a theory of history, into the all-embracing natural dialectic of Engels and Lenin.

out many ages, but large-scale industry now collectivizes it and thereby collectivizes the experiences, aspirations, and minds of the workers who are the base of the ever widening industrial pyramid. In the upper part of the pyramid, on the other hand, the organizing principle of private property is emasculated, losing its age-old significance as ownership of personal things— tools and workshop, plow and field, home and garden, factory and manorial estate—and is superseded by functionalized, formalized, depersonalized ownership of securities, industrial stocks and bonds, apartments, and mortgages, which have commercial but no personal value. This development, described by Marx, Hilferding, Schumpeter, Berle and Means, and others, makes it easier for the effective control of property to become concentrated in the hands of men or groups who do not actually own it—thus further emasculating the meaning of "private property." Finally, the private, piecemeal management of separate properties becomes spectacularly inoperative during an economic crisis, for then it clashes with the growing machinery's even more urgent need for over-all regulation and integration— that is, for unified planned management. It is at this point that economic development converges with social development, the growth of the proletarian class in number and weight legalizing and completing the collective nature of man and society in the proletarian dictatorship after the social revolution.

What is thereby achieved is that the distortion of perspective and the corruption of vision which inevitably go with private property are overcome. The new man, partner in a world-wide enterprise both as co-owner and as co-worker, understands what no private owner can understand; that there is no private avenue to his private welfare, but only the avenue through the welfare of everybody else; that individual aspirations must be merged in the common interest; that spontaneity and differentiation contain the germs of "contradiction" and must be eliminated by collective rationality and homogeneity. The particular and its personalized spontaneity disappear; they are absorbed in the universal. In the greatest figures of individuation, men like Leonardo and Goethe, the universal is absorbed in the particular, the person is enlarged to reflect in his individual form the whole world. In Marxism the rationalist extinction of the particular in the universal assures the extinction of "contradiction" and guarantees the frictionless operation of the world-wide social process. In other words, rationality and goodness coincide in the concept of man's life as social process. In this light the new man of the proletarian utopia is the man who, instead of an individual mind, has in himself the collective mind; this by definition ensures peace and harmony forever and solves the problem of history. When this point is combined with the preceding point on method, the solution emerges with the inexorable necessity of dialectical causality from the prearranged process of history.

The moral interpretation of history, as taken over by Marxism, via Hegel, from traditional religion, divides history into three periods: a golden age of primitive innocence and undeveloped faculties; the age of alienation of man from man and of man from himself through private property; and the final age of the self-realization of man and all his fully developed faculties. The age of history in the strict sense—of dialectical conflict, change, and advance—is of course the second period, although Marx himself, looking at this period from the vantage point of the goal, designated it as prehistory. The motor power that drives man through this age of alienation is the craftiness which accrues to him, perfecting his skill, his intelligence, and finally his science in the service of his private property. Thus the real problem is how private property originated in the world of primitive innocence, to corrupt the original goodness of man and thereby to start him on his dual career of creativeness and destructiveness.

All this exactly parallels the Biblical story of the Fall and and the ensuing statement that it was Cain, not Abel, who became the builder of cities and the father of craftsmen. There is not much difference between saying with Marxism that this is a world of injustice and exploitation, and saying with the Bible that it is a fallen world. But the Biblical interpretation of human sin as disobedience to God is at least plausible, though it is not and is not meant to be an explanation of the mystery, whereas the Fall is neither explained nor made plausible by the materialistic Marxist story of the world of primitive innocence giving birth to the private property which disrupts it.

More important in Marxism than the analysis of the origin of sin is the analysis of its nature and its end. The initial parallel between the Marxist and the Biblical versions is striking. In both the Old and the New Testaments the word "injustice" is frequently used, and the difference from Marxism is chiefly that the word means something more comprehensive and profound in its religious use, where the core of the concept is disobedience to God and the social behavior is a consequence and manifestation, than in the purely moral-social use by Marxism. In any case an analysis of the world as ruled by injustice cannot be objected to by Christians in principle. This is especially true since even the New Testament puts the case in unmistakably sociological terms, for example when it says that a camel can more easily go through a needle's eye than a rich man can enter the Kingdom of God (Matthew 19:24), because a man's heart will be where his treasure is (Matthew 6:12)—thus referring to the corruption of the mind and will by sociological factors precisely as Marx does—not to mention such passages as Mary's Magnificat (Luke 1:52–53) or the Epistle of St. James 5:4–6. The power of social institutions over the souls of the men living in them is nothing strange to Biblical realism.

However, the difference between the authentic religious dimension of the Biblical "injustice" and the purely social dimension of the Marxist "injustice" cannot fail to have practical consequences. According to Marx, private property, whose origin remains a mystery in logical terms, is the seat and source of injustice. As the progressive rational usefulness of private property culminates and exhausts itself in the introduction of large-scale industry, whose consistent organization is beyond its reach, private property becomes irrational as well as unjust. It is significant that injustice is finally overcome not because it is injustice but because it also becomes irrationality. It follows that the final rational organization is also just, indeed restores justice on a higher plane. The two coincide because private property develops the means to economic well-being only gropingly and piecemeal, and has to abdicate when the very operation of developed means to well-being requires generalization of well-being. At that point economic rationality becomes dependent on social justice; in other words, social justice becomes powerful and victorious when economic rationality, for its own sake, demands it. Until that moment social justice—or equality, if we use it in the Marxist sense—is impotent. No one can doubt the truth in this construction of the general relationship between social justice and economic expediency.

But this is also the point at which the narrowness of the Marxist conception asserts itself adversely. In the underlying materialism, spiritual principles appear exclusively in institutional forms or reflect them. Communist property is distinguished from private property by being beyond the dialectical change, because there is no more inherent conflict when "all become one"—that is, when the particular is extinguished in the homogeneous universal. In the Marxist utopia this union is not a process of mystical love, as it frequently is in Oriental religious speculation and sometimes in Christian speculation, but is the result of rational progress in economic expediency and efficiency. This is the Marxist "proof" for the end of the dialectic —a sociological proof in line with the logic of materialism. Translated into human terms it means that, as private property was the cause of alienation (even though it was indispensable as the vessel of the historical dialectic and progress), so now Communist property is the guarantee of peace and harmony forever.[5]

At this point the parallel with Biblical teaching ends. Immediately following the Bible's awesome words about the needle's eye there is a brief exchange (Matthew 19:25) which makes it clear that everyone is comparable to the rich young man, for everyone has some mundane treasure which controls and distorts his mind and will (Matthew 6:12); or, in sociological terms, there is no institution without inherent temptation,

5. Properly speaking, the idea of justice, which assumes the existence of rights belonging to different persons and groups, is no longer applicable under conditions of the collective, the higher unit in which they have been absorbed. Christian love, by contrast, does not extinguish the person but fortifies and completes him and his liberty. Hence justice is always an integral part of Christian love. See *Freedom and Order*, p. 332; see also below, Chapter VIII.

moral danger, and corrupting influence, none without a vested interest of one kind or another. That is why there is, according to the New Testament, no moral or rational way to salvation, and man is entirely dependent on God's loving grace. The New Testament naturally contents itself with merely stating the religious principle and its negative implication that institutions, however indispensable for man's life in the world, can never bring him salvation. The application of this religious principle to concrete sociological situations is simple enough, however, and it appears, consciously or unconsciously, in any critical analysis of institutions, including the Church itself. But what matters here is the application of the religious principle to Communist property, precisely because Communist property is declared to be exempt from the verdict, with the corollary that religion is obsolescent.

Communist property is the property of the proletarian collective, which has no natural organs through which to think, will, or act. Every group of men singles out some of its members to act as its functionaries or representatives; so does the proletarian collective, but with a multiplied intensity corresponding to its multiplied density and power over its members. The "dictatorship of the proletariat" is not, as many have believed and some still believe it should be, a dictatorship of the many, which would be a contradiction in terms; as a dictatorship, it must be dictatorship by very few (even though they supposedly rule in the name of the many whose thought and will they have, as it were, absorbed into their own), with the huge administrative apparatus at their disposal to provide them with information for their decisions and to carry out the decisions promptly and accurately. That is, there is a steep gradation of power, from the dazzling heights at the top down through the lower echelons, none of which is without some modest prestige value, some real authority to tell others what to do, and perhaps even a slightly higher income than that of the common citizen. These small distinctions reflect, in a modest way, the splendor of the top ranks, and make the incumbents feel that they are partners in the gigantic venture. In short, the dictatorship of the proletariat substitutes for private property another form of power over men and things—a form which is new and different but is no less conspicuous sociologically and psychologically; accordingly, it cannot fail to establish its own vested interests and personal and group ambitions.

This result is logically necessary from the definition of the collective, which is supposed to be in dictatorial control. In other words, the Soviet dictatorship does not represent a betrayal of the Marxist program by Lenin or Stalin; its character has always been implicit in the Marxist program itself. If the characteristic features of Marxist dictatorship were not evident before Lenin and Stalin came to power, this was simply because they were the first who were called upon to translate the program from the phraseology of intellectuals and the utopia of prophecy into the hard language of power. The fact that the phraseology was used (in the name of Marx and Engels) to oppose the Bolshevist line of action, both outside and inside Russia—used by such distinguished Marxists as Rosa Luxemburg and later Trotsky—is more than natural among intellectuals but does not refute the argument. The fact that the social democrats, beginning with Karl Kautsky himself, ignored and suppressed the entire doctrine of the dictatorship—even though no positive doctrine of liberty filled the gap, since they continued to stress the economic phases of the Marxist system—confirms the collective implications of the original Marxist doctrine. Sociologically, then, the system culminates in a hierarchy of unchecked and uninhibited power.

Marxism itself would never admit this. It is prevented from doing so by its definition of power as derived from private property alone. Under capitalism a nonowner, such as a highly placed executive, is simply a lackey of private property, and whatever power he may hold or abuse reflects the power of private ownership, in whose name he functions. By definition, then, where there is no private property there is no power that can be abused; for the functionaries of the collective, not owning anything privately, are members of the collective like everyone else and are personally interested only in adding to their own welfare by increasing the productivity and welfare of all. The extraordinary naïveté of Communist reasoning on this point, which contrasts so strikingly with its sharp-eyed (though unfair) realism in analyzing the non-Communist world, is the naïveté of a purely economic interpretation of history. Such an interpretation sees power only as a means to private property, rather than the other way around. In the latter view, private property is but one among various roads to power; it carries psychological as well as material benefits and may be sought for any one or more of many motives, such as achievement, enjoyment, vanity, or humiliation of others. Even in purely economic terms the Communist reasoning is untenable, when we consider that the high officials and functionaries of a collectivist order receive, in addition to salary, various material perquisites such as elegant cars, interesting travel, and comfortable accommodations. In any economic interpretation of human motives, such perquisites of office are far from irrelevant in explaining the individual's interest in obtaining and keeping a governmental position.

Vested interest is unavoidable in any structure of power, and it becomes more inevitable as power grows unchecked for dogmatic reasons. Once dogma has equated private interest with private property, however, the proposition that the austere Soviet rulers are not rulers at all because they are not private owners or responsible to private owners, is a powerful support to the ideological structure which props up the worship and quasi deification of these rulers as pure vessels of light in a still-dark world.

The Marxist Priesthood

The role of the Communist Party—its significance, its responsibility, its dignity, its claim to exclusive power—cannot be overemphasized. For who is to decide where the interest of the working class lies and what should be done to protect it? As a collective, the proletarian class must develop its own dictatorial organs to ascertain and interpret its class interest. But this is less than half of the Marxist argument. The empirical proletarian class interest, as was shown in the preceding chapter, is not translated directly into proletarian class action but appears only in its purified, elongated, idealized form, of which the Communist Party is in charge.

Hence the proletarian class interest is not an empirical sociological category; no one can even pretend that it is found in the real proletarians; it is admittedly a "corrected" interpretation of the empirical reality. It is not a theory which would be measured against or modified or refuted by reality; in its admitted conflict with a direct, unpurified sociological reality, it is the reality which is overruled and the theory which emerges unrefuted and irrefutable. The workers will accept it as the "correct" interpretation of their interests once they are adequately educated; but its truth does not depend on this belated approval and hence is not affected if approval is withheld, temporarily or permanently, by unenlightened, stupid, or treasonable workers. The empirical test is never accepted as final; unfavorable facts are always explained as merely regrettable time lags. In due course empirical reality will confirm the anticipated theory regarding it, and meanwhile political action must proceed on the basis of truth rather than of reality. The Communist Party is thus the priestly caste bearing the holy flame and watching over the purity of the faith. The faith is grounded in common experience but transcends it, rising into the clear light of necessity in which supposedly inexorable trends of sociological transformation, even though delayed in their effect, merge with the final objective long taught by the theory.

Nonbelievers will naturally find it hard to accept a sociological theory superior in principle to the reality which it is to explain. Instead, they will give a sociological interpretation to the claims of the Marxist intelligentsia itself. What claims to be the administration of the final truth about society to a hesitant working class and a refractory world is, in more sober language, the highly ingenious, highly pretentious rationalization of the group interest of this intelligentsia. Their moral, political, social, and even economic ambitions are established beyond criticism, and they claim that the world, in order to be saved, must by whatever means be made over by them, the trustees of truth and of the future. They would unite in their own hands all political and economic power, receiving only modest wealth for their private use. They would exert this unlimited power in the interest of the proletariat, as they understand it; but the proletariat would not appoint them and would not be able to recall them. To assert that this doctrine expresses proletarian class interest, as the Marxist intelligentsia in naïve self-admiration does, is less than accurate. But at least Marxism is frank about the role assigned to these guardians.

Lest the reader acquiesce, however, in the cheap triumph of "unmasking" the Marxist intelligentsia's ambitions, it should be immediately added that no argument from cynical material- ism can be exhaustive. The Marxist argument—that the party leadership is above temptation because it does not own private capital—is fatuous. But it still is a fact that, group interests apart, these men and women have often demonstrated an al- together admirable idealism in identifying themselves with the cause of the downtrodden, not only in war, persecution, and underground, where they established their high moral repu- tation, but also in influential governmental and administrative positions now. Time and again American reporters have com- mented on the enthusiasm and driving power displayed in the work of social reconstruction in Poland, in Yugoslavia, and in Russia itself. A man of deeply Christian mind like Hromadka and a profound skeptic like Thomas Mann agree, contrasting the callousness of the reveling and fattening bourgeoisie in Italy and West Germany with the sincerity and warmth of the social concern which permeates much of life in East Germany and the Slavic countries. These men decide in favor of the latter alternative, despite the greater material advances in the coun- tries in which reconstruction goes forward under capitalistic auspices.

We cannot follow them; no moral or pragmatic considera- tion can be decisive when men literally claim to supersede God and make their fellow-men over in their own image as the model of perfection. Moral virtues and pragmatic achieve- ments do not contradict this judgment; on the contrary, they give to the horrible ambition the good conscience and the preliminary semblance of right and victory without which that ambition would be nothing but ridiculous. It is the preliminary good on which the ultimately bad flourishes. As the great Pascal inimitably expressed it three hundred years ago: "Man is neither angel nor beast, and the trouble is that whoever tries to act the angel does act the beast." [6] But however true this be, it does not suffice to justify every opposition to communism; if the bad recommends itself by much virtue and achievement in its service, how can the good establish its superior right but by virtue and achievement? The goodness of our cause alone will not save us if we are unprofitable servants. For, from the fact that one partner to a conflict is basically wrong, it does not follow at all that his opponent must be right; they may both be wrong in different ways, and certainly the lukewarm cannot be right (Revelation 3:16). This should never be forgotten when we criticize communism.

The rule of the guardians is theocracy. The classific form of succession in theocracy is the law of "apostolic succession," signifying that the Lord of the Church handed the key to his first apostle, from whose hands it has passed into those of his successors down the ages. (The pope does not, of course, appoint his successor; this would elevate him to a rank equal to that of his Lord. The teaching is that the election of the pope by the cardinals, who themselves are appointed by the pope or his predecessor, is guided by the Holy Ghost.) There is no official law of succession in the Soviet Union, of course, because this would conflict with the elaborately staged elections and in general with the democratic trimmings of the constitution. The succession must appear to be on a strictly rational basis. The right people, however, always happen to be elected. Marxists might say that this outcome, while it is not provided for in the Soviet constitution, is entirely rational because the guardians of the class interest must and do see to it that no unworthy person is elected. Accordingly, the only agencies permitted to nominate candidates for election are those controlled in various ways by the Communist Party and its affiliates; or nominations are "planted," as private suggestions to individual voters, who

6. Cf. *Freedom and Order,* p. 282.

are only too glad to appear as initiators of a popular motion. The elections invariably confirm these choices.

But the really decisive positions are those in the leadership of the Communist Party, and these are not filled by elections; the party was organized from the top down along strictly bureaucratic—that is, military—lines by Lenin himself, as far back as 1903. For many years of his rule, Stalin was officially nothing but the secretary of the Communist Party, remote even from the party members, let alone the voters. He was appointed to official positions in the government and the army only many years after he had been acclaimed as the man nearest to Lenin and Lenin's personal choice to succeed him. Whether he actually was may remain in doubt, but the question is irrelevant for the present issue; what matters is the assertion that he was— that is, the claim to inspired leadership by virtue of apostolic succession.

It follows that Stalin's dictatorship, contrary to popular belief in this country, was not a personal one; his whims and "intuitions" were not the law of the land as Hitler's were. Stalin's rule was rather the dictatorship of a sacred book through its priests; or, in the official ideology, the rule of reason as evolved through the ages and finally incorporated in a learned treatise and explained by its authorized interpreters. That is, the dictator must adhere to strict rules and pursue a specific objective; he himself believes in the rules and the objective, and he thinks in the categories taught by them. But he cannot change them even if he wishes to, because he is not alone; he has powerful co-dictators—Marx, Engels, and Lenin—and he cannot, without grave risk to himself and to the entire structure of power, run into open conflict with their learned spokesmen. Whatever he does must be related to the doctrine and justified in terms of it; although interpretation is elastic regarding any intermediate questions, it is fixed where the supreme principle is concerned. The dictatorship of the proletariat, as long as the proletariat is not considered mature enough to understand its own real interest, is dictatorship by the Marxist intelligentsia, and in view of the nature of their doctrine it assumes the form of theocracy.

Marxist Theocracy and Russian Caesaropapism

Only one objection, it seems to me, might be raised against this interpretation: the suggestion that the Soviet Union may represent a form of caesaropapism rather than a theocracy. Caesaropapism has been traditional in Russia since the end of the Byzantine empire; the fact that Moscow, after the fall of Byzantium to the infidels, accepted the designation (offered by the monk Philotheus) of "the third Rome and the second Byzantium" made the continuity official. The distinction between theocracy and caesaropapism is, of course, not sharp; it depends on whether the spiritual authority or the political authority appears to have been originally constitutive of the power in question. Judea at the time of the lawgivers and judges was unmistakably theocratic; Byzantium was caesaropapist because it was the emperor who Christianized his dominions in the attempt to consolidate them and who reflected his own supreme authority on the metropolitan, the head of the Eastern church. But by this test, too, the theocratic nature of the rule of Lenin and Stalin appears indisputable if we accept the definition of the Communist Party as the moral guardian of the working class, and observe how the two men led in the articulation and codification (including the vulgarization) of the atheist faith. The reverent adulation which greeted their every utterance is further proof.

It does not appear at all impossible, however, that the Soviet Union may again cross the thin line from Marxist theocracy to Russian caesaropapism, for the state church is now firmly established and the main qualification for leadership in a difficult world is political rather than doctrinal. On the other hand, such a development might conceivably imperil the controlling position of Moscow in the intellectual world of communism. For China's Mao once more represents the classical type of Marxist theocrat, whose overwhelming authority rests on undisputed mastery in the study, interpretation, and application of Marxist doctrine. Although not trained in Moscow—in which he is unlike the Marxist leaders in Indochina, India, and most other countries—he is far superior in ambitions and intellectual prestige to Stalin's more modest successors, and he may thereby be able to secure for his giant country the hegemony in the Communist world and beyond it.[7]

Finally, it is irrelevant to the interpretation given here whether the Soviet rulers did or did not tolerate the Christian church during various phases of their regime; their attitude has been a mere matter of changing strategy, not one of principle. The principle remains the same: the counterreligion is irreconcilably hostile to the religion. But changes in strategy are dictated by dialectical changes in the situation. Because Christianity is regarded as representing and sanctioning the worst

7. The following letter from the present author, dated August 18, 1958, and published in *The New York Times* of August 22, suggests some conclusions from the above:

Ever since Stalin's death it has been clear (and was said) that the greatest authority among the living Marxists and hence the potentially greatest political power in the Communist world is Mao Tse-tung.

None of Stalin's successors in Russia can raise any such claim; they are politicians whose careers and fate depend on their luck in maneuvering for positions in the game of power. Mao is also respected as a poet.

Despite much strain, China seems to be rapidly gaining in economic and military strength. A government like Mao's, technically and organizationally progressive and morally callous for doctrinal reasons, has the most enviable job in the world in a highly intelligent but neglected country. It brings the people hospitals and schools and machines and other fascinating things and can hardly fail to be successful for the time being.

Hence public discussion in this country need not be surprised at Mao's emergence on the international scene as the powerful figure that he is. Nor does it suffice to discuss the ups and downs of individual persons in the Communist hierarchy, such as now Mao's victory over Khrushchev in the matter of the "summit" and earlier in the matter of Titoism. We should rather be interested in the motivations of these men and the policies to be expected as they gain in strength.

This writer has no access to Chinese literature or to any source of inside information. But one does not need any to understand that Mao is our most implacable enemy.

The United States refuses to recognize his government because such legal recognition not only requires effective control but seems increasingly to imply political or moral connotations.

The result is that the most numerous, most ancient, and potentially most powerful nation of the world, hardly less than one-fourth of mankind,

form of man's alienation from himself—his submission to heteronomous, irrational rule—it must be fought tooth and nail as long as alienation persists in the ultimately determining economic substratum of society—that is, in the form of private property. Religion, symbolizing as it does man's dependence on a power beyond his reach, is viewed as the strongest bulwark of private property.

But as the economic foundation of atheism, common property, is securely laid and built upon, collective man seizes power over every phase of his own life, thus proving to himself his complete autonomy; and the ideological superstructure of private property, religious heteronomy, is deprived of support and is sure to collapse in due course. As man saves himself here and now, he learns that there is no God on whom his salvation depends. Thus religion can be tolerated as a transi-

---

does not exist for United States diplomacy and is barred from membership in the world parliament.

Mao seemed at first to be as favorably impressed by Tito as was Khrushchev, but abruptly turned about to violent polemic, thus encouraging all old-line Stalinists and putting such pressure on Khrushchev that he too had to retract. The original sympathy may have been with Tito's doctrine of administrative and economic decentralization.

The fierce hatred, however, must be due to Tito's quite central doctrine of internationalism, according to which all major countries are now safely embarked on the course to "socialism" defined as "workers' democracy," each country out of its own tradition and in its own way, the United States no less than the USSR (and Yugoslavia more advanced than both, of course), so that it is absurd to speak of two camps.

The implied rapprochement between the United States and Russia, as long as China is not recognized, would have left her as the pariah among nations.

The maneuvering between the United States and Russia for favorable positions in the start of negotiations for atomic disarmament runs head on into the same objection. We seek an agreement with Soviet Russia, but China cannot be included because she does not exist. Russia, however, has forcefully been warned that China must not be left out; nay, she must now equip China with atomic weapons.

Whether we can have atomic disarmament and a relaxation of world tension if China is first recognized I do not know. But we certainly cannot have them if our policy at this advanced hour implies the attempt to lure Russia away from China.

tional pastime for immature children, in the same category as folk dancing and the much vaunted ethnical autonomy—which no longer count. The concession means nothing to the government and a great deal to the people; it removes friction and strengthens the belief in the government's wisdom and benevolence. It even taps the source of political loyalty that exists in the Byzantine Christian tradition itself—providing, of course, that the re-established Church is unquestionably loyal, as there can be no doubt that it is.[8]

All of which suggests that, however orthodox the Soviet application of Marxist dialectical principles may be, it cannot be understood without understanding the conditions to which these principles are applied. Or in other words, while Soviet atrocities and Soviet achievements must be explained in terms of underlying Marxism, the power that makes them effective is Russia's power. Marxism gives them the direction, Russia gives them the power. The merger of the two is a historical accident; one could imagine that Marxism had conquered some other country. But there must have been some mysterious convergence if more than a century ago, before Marxism existed, such profound minds as Tocqueville and Donoso Cortez sensed that the enormous potential power of Russia might actualize one day in the direction which Marxism has since given it. Karl Marx, too, has a suggestion to this effect.[9]

8. Even so, it took almost twenty years for the Soviet government to understand its new chance vis-à-vis the Russian Church. And these twenty years of bitter persecution seem to have left a remarkable result: the invigoration of the Church. There are a number of witnesses to bear this out. If it is true that the number of priests had melted from seventy or eighty thousand before the Revolution to ten thousand and now amounts to forty thousand, this means that the Church is incomparably stronger than before the Revolution. A further corroborating fact would be that simultaneous membership in the Communist Party and in the Church is now prohibited by both sides.

9. There is a growing tendency among modern social scientists to regard the study of history including intellectual history as antiquated. In the light of our earlier methodological discussion in Chapter III, this is easily understood. The "behavioral sciences," as they are characteristically rechristened, use "the scientific method," as it is modestly called, rather than historical studies. "The scientific method" consists in the clever and

Eastern and Western Spirituality

Russian history begins, long before Russia herself was born, with the transferral of Roman imperial power to Byzantium, which thus became the rival of Rome at the very moment when the declining Roman empire called on despised and persecuted Christianity for its own spiritual reintegration. So Christendom was divided many centuries before the schism between Rome

---

carefully thought through use of sampling procedures developed by psychology, sociology, and anthropology to ascertain the behavior of people and their reactions to various influences; all the results of history, inasmuch as they are relevant to the present and future, must have entered into people's present behavior, thus leaving to history itself only an antiquarian interest. If we know people's behavior we can predict and, by adequate propaganda, control their actions.

There is no quarrel, of course, with the most accurate possible descriptive sociology, including the statistical proportions of the investigated phenomena; it is a great gain, a now indispensable preparation for scholarly work. But its substitution for scholarly work is an altogether different matter; it produces the most astounding results. Take as an example a writer on Soviet matters—an intelligent, conscientious, highly trained, and well-read researcher, and a generous person, a respected member of one of the world's great universities—who, after years of research, in a carefully documented book widely acclaimed by reviewers, had this to say about Russia: "The power of the population to influence the policy of the Communist Party is about equal to the power of a balky mule to influence its driver." The author and his reviewers have overlooked two sets of facts. On the one hand, twice under the Soviet regime prior to the Second World War, Russia passed through civil war, with millions of dead, nobody can say how many; and in both cases the result was far-reaching concessions by the regime, which in collective agriculture have persisted now for more than twenty years despite repeated attempts to rescind them. Other concessions, notably on the length of the calendar week—which the Soviet wanted to shorten in order to destroy the Christian Sunday—and on general education in patriotic history, were gained by the people without revolt, but certainly not without resistance. On the other hand, this same "balky" people fought the greatest war in history, of which they had to bear the brunt; mules do not win wars. These two considerations suggest the dual inquiry in this section into the convergence between Russia and Marxism, on the one hand, and the limits of their cooperation on the other hand.

That flippant remark on the Russian people would hardly be re-

and Constantinople became official, and Eastern Christendom had it own capital city, its own head, its own history, and its own splendor. It is well to remember that the central building of the Eastern Church, the Church of the Holy Wisdom, is a thousand years older than St. Peter's in its present form and that it was built by the emperor, not the patriarch; the cathedral in Kiev is older than that of Chartres. All this has a bearing on Russian history, for when Byzantium fell and the unity of

---

peated today, still less be approved by reviewers. Huge research projects have been devoted to the exploration of the Russian character and its reaction to Marxism; all Russian individuals available in the West, particularly the thousands of refugees, were interviewed elaborately and with all methodical precautions; and the results were processed by sociologists, anthropologists, psychologists, clinical psychologists, economists, etc. The emerging picture is that of a strongly emotional psychic life with a pendular movement between high spirits and contrition. It is true that we have long known this because we have read our Tolstoi and our Dostoevski. But those too have read them, and we are taught that we all really know it now only because only now has it been proved scientifically. We think, on the contrary, that the great poets in the midst of their people are reliable messengers of the truth about their people, and that our Western researchers and their largely Westernized witnesses are under the spell of the poets like ourselves and would have been in despair if their researches had produced a different result.

But this is not all. The two poles of present-day Russian life, Marxism and the Orthodox Church, are outside the domain of studies by these researchers. Inasmuch as they still know Marxism, they reduce it to their psychological, psychopathological, and social-psychological categories; ignorant as they are of what religion is, they must ingore pseudo religion as well. Still less, however, do they know of Greek orthodoxy, beyond the statement that it has something to do with the Russian consciousness of sin. The inadequacy of the entire method manifests itself most clearly at this point. Regularity and predictability are the underlying assumptions; the hundreds of lavishly financed research projects are designed to provide a reliable factual basis for American foreign policy. But regularity and predictability—including the regularity of the fluctuation between high spirits and contrition—move on the observable surface; they deny the existence of the slumbering liberty which may emerge from the depths of the religious sources. People can never know in advance what they will be capable of in extreme situations; and the negators of liberty and religion cannot get at it by their questions. For man is not exhausted by "behaving" in some way. This is the center of our argument once more.

Eastern Christendom broke up into different national churches
—Greek, Bulgarian, Rumanian, etc.—the seat of the largest and
most powerful of these churches, Moscow, became a natural
center of gravitation for them all. Merged with the political
cleavage between East and West is the age-old schism of Christianity. It is only natural that church history should set the
framework of political history.

The schism, of course, was not simply organizational but
spiritual. If one is very careful in hedging about such dangerous slogans, one may be able to say that the prevailing interest of Western Christendom has been moral and political,
that of Eastern Christendom speculative and social. The two
opposite local traditions in this respect were powerfully reinforced by subsequent history. For centuries Rome had been the
center of authority for the harassed people to rally around.
tradition of this local genius continued when the imperial government was suddenly removed from Rome; it had to continue
the more strongly as the turmoil of the great migrations, beginning soon thereafter, absorbed much of the attention of
Byzantium and imperatively demanded in Italy and the West a
center of authority for the harassed people to rally around.
Thus political authority and its vigorous tradition and practice
accrued to the spiritual authority of the great Roman bishops,
and Christian ethics was worked out, in later centuries, almost
in analogy to the casuistry of a code of law.

Contrariwise, Byzantium, the ancient city in the Greek prov-
ince of the Roman empire, had long been one of the centers of
Greek cultural life, and the metaphysical speculation which
loomed large in it now received new impulse and new material
from the Christian Scriptures, notably on the Incarnation and
on the Holy Spirit, Who in all Western interpretations strangely
remains in the shadow of the two other persons of the Holy
Trinity. In particular, Protestantism with its emphasis on
justification "by faith alone" is today criticized for neglecting
love, which after all is the real object of faith. In this connection some Eastern Church fathers, including Basil the Great,
taught a spiritually quite distinct although institutionally vague
Christian socialism for the Christian community after the model

of the primitive community. But this is without any political implications. Nobody could doubt the God-given authority of the emperor (or later of the czar), who had Christianized the empire and continued to protect the church in the midst of all the dangers of the world (Romans 13:1–4), whose power and splendor were reflected on the "right belief" of the Greek Church and served to promote it against the heretically political ambitions of the Western Church (later churches) so that only under the imperial shield could the metropolitan of Byzantium (or Moscow) ever hope to cope with his Western rival, precisely because the church-state relationship in Byzantium (or Moscow) made him a kind of house chaplain at the imperial court. This is the origin of contrasting developments which seem to reach a climax of conflict in our own day.

For the peculiar tradition of Rome and the papal history of the subsequent centuries logically led to the gradual emergence of the doctrine of spiritual supremacy over political authority, as proclaimed by the great Hildebrand and the mighty Innocent. Indeed, the only safe way for princes and governors to discharge their responsibilities before God was to consult and comply with the advice of Christ's vicar, the guardian of the Christian conscience and supreme administrator of the earthly structure of salvation. That is, the pope became the spiritual overlord of all the mundane lords, the judge of their motives and actions, the supreme political authority. It is true that the papacy repeatedly succumbed to degeneration and outright corruption because of the temptations of such an exalted position, to the point where Cluny in the tenth century and St. Bernard in the twelfth became the true representatives of the Christian conscience as trustees for the legally constituted but ineffective authority of the pope. And it is even more true that the abuses of papal power finally produced the great explosion which destroyed the organizational and doctrinal unity of Western Christendom. But the principle of spiritual supremacy over political power had taken so firm a root that no shock could affect it. In different degrees, in different doctrinal and legal forms, and with different temptations to their spirituality and integrity, all Western churches—not to mention the sects—

agree that the Christian conscience has, in extreme situations, to "obey God rather than men" (Acts 5:29), much as more normal conditions demand obedience to the authorities because they are "ordained of God" as means to preserve peace in society (Romans 13:1–4). The Christian mistrust of man includes government and is at the basis of all constitutional limitation and division of power.[10]

Confronted as we are with an atheist theocracy for which the people had been educated by a thousand years of caesaropapism and which is now immeasurably reinforced by the most unscrupulous use of all modern techniques of control and manipulation, it is impossible to overemphasize the sublime Western achievement of spiritual supremacy over political power. It is the West's most precious possession, unknown and more or less unintelligible in all other parts of the globe. It has been abused over and over again, first by the Roman Church, then by its

10. The greatest theorist of the constitutional division of powers, Montesquieu, was an atheist in the eighteenth-century French tradition. But this does not invalidate our argument. For he uses as his principal example—somewhat overstating his case—the governmental structure of England, which has never been divorced from Christian teachings. After Montesquieu, the two main architects of the American Constitution, Hamilton and Madison, were both Christians of the eighteenth-century brand. Contrariwise, the typical French trust in purely secular reason, where not mitigated by the equally typical French skepticism, easily carries totalitarian connotations, as one can see in the two most influential thinkers of this group, Rousseau and Comte.

Mistrust of men, including men in government, is not the whole story regarding Christian teachings, however. Too often it has been mistaken for the whole story or at least for the main part of the story, even by great thinkers such as Augustine and Luther, with the result of serious error on the side of authoritarianism. No government, however unrestricted in power, could establish order and peace in society if there were not in man, for all his corruption and selfishness, a residual element of order, community, and justice. The proper balance is found in Reinhold Niebuhr's proposition that "man's capacity for justice makes democracy possible, and man's inclination to injustice makes democracy necessary" (*Children of Light and Children of Darkness*, p. xiii). In terms of our discussion in the text, this means that the government and the people limit each other's power—so there is above both a superior spiritual principle. Nothing of this kind had ever been known in Greece.

Protestant critics; it is unavoidably accompanied by its shadow, clericalism—the corrupting confusion between the spiritual power and the mundane power of its representatives. But this is how the Western world lives, constantly overreaching itself, demanding of itself the humanly impossible, falling short of it because of such presumption, humbled by its failure into more modestly redefining its place, falling back into complacency because of such overmodesty, humbled by this failure into once more redefining to itself the far-off sublimity of the divine commandment—an unending cycle of struggle and failure and new struggle. Where would we be without the spiritual power pulling us beyond our own reach and judging our inadequacy to reach it?

But it is no wonder that this spectacle of the ever new and ever frustrated endeavor to give reality to the vision of the prophets should disgust outsiders and should be interpreted by them as lack of sincerity. They count the failures rather than the victories; they do not count the endeavor itself as a victory. They cannot fail to see the emptiness of the Western dynamic once the pulling power of its spiritual goal is removed and the dynamic habit finds its satisfaction in what Spengler admiringly and approvingly calls the mysticism of the machine as an end in itself, or of the political and military power which the machine produces, without spiritual ambition or justification. They cannot fail to interpret this as the long-overdue punishment for the West's Luciferic presumption, the final refutation of its spiritual arrogance. This is Eastern Christianity's always correct and always unfair verdict on our failures; the more correct, the more the spirituality which produced the dynamic is lost and denounced by its heirs as an illusion. Unencumbered by ambitions of realization, the Eastern vision of the mystical community left the world of power behind and beneath and soared into the pure air of the spirit.

The warm and joyous sacramentalism which gives the Eastern Christian a home in his church; the sense of community and brotherliness in sin and redemption; the joy of participation in the life of the spirit; the simplicity of Christian life and the appreciation of the simple virtues of the unambitious common people; the piety which preserves unadorned the atmosphere of sanctity in the holy places in Palestine, inasmuch as they are in the custody of Eastern churches, in contrast to the pomp with which Western churches there use the holiness of the places under their own custody as a pretext for the display of their imperial splendor—all these and many others are the fruits of the resignation or the flight of temptation. They are great Christian achievements; in a real sense one may be able to say that there is between Eastern and Western Christendom a division of labor in achievements and shortcomings. But ultimately a simplicity and purity of spirit which is bought at the expense of responsibility is neither simple nor pure. What appears objectionable to a Westerner is not the absence of ultimate simplicity and purity but the illusion of their presence where temptation and responsibility are shunned.[11]

They are. This is what Byzantine and Russian caesaropapism comes down to: the protection of the purity of the church by the caesar—the czar—who, in exact reversal of Western individualism, thus becomes by indirection the spiritual head of the church. It is the Christian genius of the Russian people which

---

11. There is, however, one great exception—Greece, which drew from its early war of liberation from Turkish rule a special moral and spiritual upsurge. Something similar has again taken place after the Second World War, which had brought the small country, after heroic resistance, years of Italian and German occupation and finally, as a sequel to all these sufferings, several years of civil war. A "Christian Union of Academians," a community of study and work on a strictly theological basis, found in this group more than one thousand signatures for its manifesto on Christian culture; and a declaration of approval signed by more than two hundred leading scholars confirmed, from their experiences in research and instruction, the logical indispensability of the Christian foundation. The group publishes a monthly *Aktines* and has crowned its literary work by a voluminous book, which advances from religious principles into all details of political and social ethics and is, to my knowledge, without parallel anywhere in the world. The author is the professor of law at Athens, A. N. Tsirintanes. The book has been made accessible in English: *Toward a Christian Civilization: A Draft Issued by the Christian Union of Professional Men of Greece,* 1950. The mere fact of such a development on the basis of Eastern Christendom may have unimaginable significance for such efforts at union as that represented by the World Council of Churches.

ennobled this relationship in a way never known to Byzantium. No other nation has ever bestowed on its land the by-name of "holy." To the Westerner, the "Holy Land" is a faraway country, to which he traces his spiritual, not his national, history. The constant use of the phrase "Holy Russia" suggests an aspect of national history that gives it a dignity all its own. It does not mean the pagan deification of the land, as in the case of the National Socialists, but, on the contrary, the Christian penetration and inspiration of the land. The czar himself became the "little father" of his people, something that all other absolute monarchs had always pretended to be but could never become in fact; and he was typically excused from responsibility for misery and exploitation in the village on the ground that "Russia is large and the Czar is far away." The formerly "terrible" and now acceptable Ivan IV, a man of considerable intellectual ability, counted among his responsibilities as a Christian ruler the saving of souls; this is certainly an extreme statement. The picture was disturbed by Peter the Great, the "Westernizer," who wanted to be a Western "enlightened" despot, hated and despised the Russian Church, transferred his capital from Russian Moscow to his new western city of St. Petersburg, and did succeed, by Westernization of administration, army, and technology, in making Russia impregnable to invasion from the West,[12] but at the price of driving a wedge between the monarchy and the people, reinforcing the antagonism to everything the West had to offer. The parallel to Bolshevism is startling, except that the new rulers, when their furious attacks on patriotic history, family life, and church life rebounded on them, proved more flexible than Peter and sought the reconciliation which permitted them to benefit by the traditional Russian loyalty to political authority and by the age-old rivalry of the Russian "Orthodox" Church with the heretical Western churches. Whether still remaining a theocracy in Lenin's and Stalin's manner or reverting to the more traditional caesaropapism, the Soviet regime and its strength can be understood only from a national history where the faith kept

12. This has now impressively been discussed by Toynbee in the first of six chapters of his booklet, "The World and the West."

its primitive spirituality intact under the shield of the supreme political power.

Marxist Socialism and Russian Socialism

This leaves the question of socialism for discussion. Russian spirituality in the Eastern Christian tradition, if emphatically unpolitical, is not unsocial at all. The third person of the Trinity has always been more important to Eastern than to Western piety, and the sense of brotherly community accordingly stronger. We know from the great novels that a drunkard or criminal to the Russian is not in the first place a drunkard or criminal but a brother, a fellow in sin and redemption. Likewise a highly placed person is less venerable to this spirituality than to the Western mind; nay, the nobles often feel embarrassed by their privileges and strive violently to get rid of them. Compare such tame reformers as the aristocratic Montesquieu and Mirabeau with Prince Mikhail Bakunin, the firebrand of revolutionary and sometimes bomb-throwing anarchism; or Prince Peter Kropotkin, who was convinced that, while ruling classes are cruel by tradition and habit, the people are kind-hearted and their revolutions would be little sanguinary and would establish a free society of mutual aid; or the great Tolstoi himself, whose despair over a life without Christian humility overwhelmed him in the end so he ran away from his lordly estate and family in order at least to die among the people in Christian poverty.

In the Western world everything is narrow, accurately circumscribed, and rigidly institutionalized; in Russia everything is wide, undefined, shapeless, open—this is how Russians and foreigners describe the Russian country and the Russian soul. Hence Russian socialism, approximately as old as Western socialism,[13] is something altogether different from the latter. Socialism in the West is directed against bourgeois capitalism, from which it follows in the Marxian or some other way; Russian socialism is directed against the materialism common to

13. Karl Marx began to study Russian in order to read the Russian socialist literature!

both capitalism and socialism in the West. It is a social, not an economic program; a human, not an institutional effort; it is neither industrial nor proletarian, but rural-agrarian, more often than not Christian, although sometimes atheist and anarchistic; in brief, it is the authentic outgrowth of the Russian sense of brotherhood in the traditional framework of Russian life. But the most important point, implied in all the foregoing, is that this Russian socialism had been discussed during fifty years before Lenin as the alternative to Western bourgeois and industrial development rather than as the consequence to be drawn therefrom. That is, the Russian problem was and had long been how to avoid the dreaded Westernization and preserve and develop the specific Russian virtues. It was an essentially conservative and defensive program; it could turn aggressive if the Christian Russian nation appeared as the crusader to re-Christianize the apostate West. No one can present this with a greater power of learning and a more profound and devoted faith than Berdyaev, to whom our own sketch is most deeply indebted. And nowhere has even he summarized the contrast more strikingly than in the words that Russia is far more socialized and less collectivized than the West: "socialization," according to the root and meaning of the word, denotes community-building; collectivization denotes mechanization, depersonalization, materialization. Who in the West has or could ever have developed the contrast? It is not Berdyaev but in him Russia's genius that does it.

There is no doubt that the entire idea badly underrated the explosive power of Western capitalism and industry, as Peter's adversaries had underrated it. Even Karl Marx had done it when his main argument, from the *Manifesto* on, had been that the "productive forces" released by capitalist emancipation now turned against capitalism because it increasingly "fettered" them in the interest of private property; so socialism had to step in to rescue the development of the productive forces. One could have argued from this Marxian proposition that, as Western industrialism ran into that blind alley, Russia no longer needed to bother about adopting industrialism. But Marx proved to be quite wrong; and now it is hard to see how

Russia, this time as two hundred years earlier, could have survived without a considerable measure of Westernization, which today means industrialization, although this certainly would not have been necessary either under capitalist or under Communist leadership—there now are alternatives, which might also have permitted the adaptation of Russian socialism. For if anything, socialism without collectivism—the alternative to collectivism—has only become more urgent with the constantly increasing collectivizing power of industrial capitalism and industrial communism.

But all this now is the measure of the tragedy which communism has brought to Russia and the world. Berdyaev is aware of it, and one of his most illuminating observations is that it is precisely communism which may paradoxically introduce the bourgeois spirit to Russia. But he ultimately believes that Russia may have to pass through communism as a necessary phase on her way to her own socialist form of life; so he ultimately sides with the Soviet against the West. A non-Russian mind cannot draw this conclusion, much as it must be impressed by the convergence of the different ways in which Russia was prepared for Soviet rule: caesaropapism and Russian socialism. For if Lenin inherited from a long and rich discussion the problem of how Russia could skip from precapitalism right into socialism, he at the same time perverted the social and moral meaning of this problem by substituting Western industrial collectivism, the heir and continuation of the bourgeois spirit, for Russian spiritual socialism, the adversary of the bourgeois spirit and all its derivatives. Lenin, of course, was fully aware of what he did, and his dialectic taught him how to use the most diverse and fluctuating currents and tendencies to build up Soviet power by changing strategies; he must have been convinced that his Marxism was the only way of giving reality to those childish dreams, since what ultimately mattered was forces of production alone. But if his personal honesty is not in doubt, there is no doubt either that the use of Russian socialism as a stepping stone to Marxist collectivism was a perversion, a gigantic fraud.

But again Berdyaev is right: this need not and may not be

the last word. We do not know; nobody knows at this point; the perversion may be mutual, the fraud may rebound. The Russians, without the sense of institutions that distinguishes the West's legal propensities, may take Soviet institutions for a preliminary incorporation of Russian spirituality, even of Russian Christian spirituality, and may make of them something that they were never intended to become. The spiritual ambivalence of economic institutions is something outside the reach of the Marxist economic interpretation of history, and even the machine itself, on which it stakes everything, has been interpreted by Spengler as dynamic power of mystical irrationality, dealing with man as it pleases, the symbol of fascism as the climax of Western spirituality. How Russia's spirituality may appropriate the machine, brought her by the climactic form of Western rationalism, no Westerner can dare to guess. But his hope certainly will be that the creativity of the Russian spirit may find a way.

VII

Dialectic of Liberty

Necessity as Liberty

Historical Necessity of Liberty

MARXISM'S conception of liberty was implicitly, and sometimes explicitly, considered in our discussion of the fate of individual liberty at the hands of the social sciences. It was found that the regularity on which scientific generalizations are predicated, and the techniques of control at which they aim, leave no room for individual liberty; nay, that the social sciences themselves are active agents in discouraging such "irregularities" and "irrationalities" as extrascientific extravaganzas or prescientific illusions. All this holds true of Marxism as of the other branches of knowledge and schools of thought.

Nevertheless a more specific discussion of the place of liberty in the structure of Marxist thought appears indicated. For while most scientific efforts in this age of positivism are reticent on liberty and democracy and extol them only by way of afterthought; while Auguste Comte had little use for them; while Max Weber suffered from the tragic fate which, he found, befalls liberty in the present tendencies of society; while the professorial planners of the type of which Mannheim is representative saw the future of liberty as depending on their own getting into power so as to provide an asylum for it in an otherwise fully planned system—Marx and Engels are, in contradistinction, exuberant in their claim that the course of events charted out by them will bring mankind to the point where it can and must finally achieve the "jump from the realm of necessity to the realm of liberty," where "the free development of everyone will be the condition for the free development of all," etc. And this is not an afterthought, it is the fulfillment of the promise with which Marx had set out in his youthful struggle for his emancipation from Hegel. For—contrary to Hegel, for whom the content of history is the self-liberation of the human spirit achieved "behind the backs" of the acting persons and groups—Marx had felt that the task was not "reinterpretation but change of reality" and that the reality to be changed centered in the organization of man's work. We had even seen the startling announcement that socialism—unlike capitalist private property, which "alienates" man from his work—should restore to the worker his mastery over his work and life by "restoring individual property" in the framework of "common posession of the earth and the means of production." This is the promised change of reality, the promised self-realization of man after the long march through the desert of alienation. The weight of the issue of liberty in the Marxian system cannot be overrated, and it is probably correct to say that the passionate enthusiasm in the Marx-inspired masses—at least on its ideal side—is primarily due to this emphasis on liberty interpreted quite vaguely but also most comprehensively as a kind of religion, as salvation from alienation and all its ills, in the manner discussed in the preceding chapter. Hence the general analysis of the issue of liberty as offered in Chapter III will here be supplemented by a special analysis of the meaning of liberty in the Marxist structure of thought.

Now we have attempted to show, in the preceding chapters, that there is in this system really no room for the promised liberty. Marxism is rational collectivism. Collectivism that it is, it absorbs the person and his freedom into the collective as the higher value. But again, Marxism is not simply and not in the first place collectivism; it is rational collectivism or, as it chooses to call itself with a synonymous phrase, "scientific socialism." That is, this collectivism acts under strictly ascertainable scientific law, rationally explored by rational minds and leading finally to full rationality in man and society. This law is called "historical necessity." The questions that demand clarification, then, are first, the nature of that historical necessity which leads to the great climax, the jump from necessity to freedom. For while in this latter proposition necessity and freedom are as clearly as possibly opposed to each other, it nevertheless remains true that the jump into freedom itself, produced as it is by inexorable historical necessity, is still necessary. In the second and more important place, we will then have to discuss the nature of that realm of freedom as which the classless society of communism is presented and which is defined as full collective rationality. What is meant by calling this collective rationality "freedom"?

"Historical necessity" is a notion that comes under the general heading of the scientific procedure discussed in our methodological chapter (III). There is here, however, a terminological difficulty that may need a word of comment. If it is the aim of social science to state scientific "regularities" in the positivistic terminology now preferred, then Marx's historical necessity does not fit in because what it means is a unique development, not a statistical regularity. In point of fact, the uniqueness of every phase in history and of its contribution to the final happy ending is one of the essential things in the Marxist dialectic—a conception of history that, we found, makes Marxism far superior to the conventional sciences and their lack of historical perspective. But this does not in any way make our general analysis of modern scientific procedures inapplicable to the case of Marxism. The reason is that Marxism, true to the concept of science proclaimed as final in its own day—as our social scientists proclaim their "scientific method" to be final— is strictly predicated on the law of causality, which, if anything, is more rigorously exclusive of the concept of liberty than even the present-day "scientific method." The "historical necessity" of the dialectic, says Marx, works within the framework of the laws of nature and with their strictness—an unmistakable proposition. And as all modern science culminates in practical application designed to control and manipulate reality in the short run, so does Marxism even in the long run, and with that exorbitant confidence in the unshakable certainty of its results which enables it to "correct" the reality where it does not run true to scientific form. However vast the difference between Marx's "historical necessity" and modern scientific regularity may be in other respects, neither one leaves room for liberty.

In the "realm of necessity," naturally, there is no liberty—

only its opposite, inescapable alienation, the iron rule of a law of motion alien to man. But as in our own day we are approaching the end of alienation, the nearness of the "realm of liberty" gives a completely new freedom to those who live in that realm by way of anticipation and receive their motives from there: the Marxists. Precisely because they know the "historical necessity," they are no longer controlled by it; they become, as it were, its masters. Wherever possible, they strive for the power that will permit them to speed up the course of necessary events by forceful action rather than wait for the forces of spontaneous development to lead there much more slowly. Nay, their knowledge of "historical necessity" and of the direction it must take even enables them, as it were, to save "historical necessity" from the accidents of historical contingency, if this latter term has any place in Marxian thought; that is, it enables them to prevent or undo any deviation of the development from the course it must take according to their prediction.[1] Predicting as they do future history, they make themselves the masters of present history and force it to

1. In *Communism, Fascism, or Democracy?* (1938), the writer had still been of the opinion that a correctly understood Marxism, because it lifts the process of history to the supreme position, would bow to it should the process of history lead to a result different from the predicted one, as in point of fact it does. Thus the Marxist method would lead to an open pluralist democracy. The Bolsheviks' anticipation of the all-proletarian goal of history would then imply a violation of autonomous spontaneous history. One may pose the question in this form: Who is wiser, history or the Bolsheviks? But this opinion does not adequately account for the fact that Marx himself did not leave the result of the process of history open at all but did formulate about it very precise and far-reaching propositions. The "jump from the realm of necessity to the realm of freedom," which will be analyzed later in this chapter, can be performed in the intended way only by a fully proletarian mankind, where all individuals are rid of personal incentives and have become homogeneous parts of the whole. Only then do all carry in themselves the one rational law; only then, hence, can the state wither away. The process of history is the supreme power, not because it is the process of history but because it is rational and in the end acknowledges full rationality by producing the machine and through it its creature, rational, homogeneous, de-individualized man. This is not Lenin but Marx. Cf. once more the theory of the correctly understood class interest.

fulfill their prediction; anticipating in themselves, through the power of the Marxian prediction, the rationality which "historical necessity" will produce in the man of Communist society, they make use of the freedom of action which, according to Marx, is implied in full rationality. This gives us a clue for our later discussion of liberty in the final fully rationalized society: Is that freedom of action liberty?

Relapse into Barbarity?

But for the time being it is those contingencies which claim our attention because they have recently been given something like legitimate standing in Marxian thought, although this obviously infringes upon the inexorability of the "inexorable historical necessity." It has become fashionable, since 1933, to deny the essential determinism of the system by referring to Marx's own phrase to the effect that the alternative to the success of the social revolution is relapse into primitive barbarity. So there is an alternative, a choice, a responsibility. In point of fact, no serious student of Marxism could ever have doubted the existence of a Marxist ethic. If it does not show up in the general philosophy of history, it certainly does in the many passages on the social psychology of revolution, where Marx never tires of warning his followers that the fate of mankind depends on their courage, ruthlessness, and devotion. "Historical necessity," in this view, is to be strictly distinguished from causal, natural necessity; it means the direction in which action must be sought in order to avoid the otherwise necessary relapse into primitive, unorganized society; it means an intellectual and moral, not a blind, causal necessity. (We referred to this distinction, which occasionally shows up in Marxian writings and is predominant in the early writings, in Chapter IV.)

But the argument carries far less weight than the apologists would have it; for the alternative is no real alternative. No one in his senses can recommend it, if for no other reason then surely because it would mean the loss of nine-tenths of man's productivity and the doom of the larger part of Western mankind. Far from opening up a new vista, the argument is in reality designed to prove that there is no way out, that there is no alternative to communism. This proof, it is true, is in itself an appeal for intelligent action rather than thoughtless drifting under necessity.

For the danger arises from the fact that, while "historical necessity" is rational, being oriented toward the final full rationalization of man, man under its rule is not yet fully rational. He is rational only in the limited sense of striving for his maximum welfare within given conditions, not in the fuller sense of aiming beyond those limiting conditions. Private ownership, according to Marxian mythology, broke through the conservatism of primitive harmony and happiness and introduced alienation but progress, progress but alienation. It introduced progress in the methods of operating the property and making it profitable—a vast opportunity. But being alienation, it cannot develop production in the framework of that property to the point where its organization might conflict with the special prerogatives which constitute the property. Various successive forms of private property serve as preliminary forms of economic rationality and explore and exploit all the possibilities of profitable progress within their reach, but they prove incapable—each one of them—of jumping across their own shadow once they reach their limits.

The Marxist examples are the windmill as representative of feudal property and the steel mill as representative of capitalist property. Feudal owners, caught in their ideology of their system being sanctioned by religious revelation, were unable to proceed to scientific technology as this transition became possible and necessary. They were prevented from doing it by the instinct of self-preservation, which warned them that, once unbiased rational thinking was released to reorganize production, their own highly irrational prerogatives would not remain immune to rational scrutiny. Likewise capitalist owners, caught in their ideology of private ownership being the rational principle of organization for production and society, are unable to proceed to the now required all-inclusive planned cooperation. (The flaw in the latter argument has been discussed in Chapter V.) This is what Marx expresses in the often recurring phrase that private property turns into a "fetter of production"; clinging to its prerogatives, it threatens to sacrifice for them production and society altogether and reduce them to "primitive barbarity."

But at this point, naturally, Marx does not conclude that an appeal for intelligent action must save mankind—which would be an argument in the manner of the despised "utopian socialists." He does argue that the hostile power is broken by its own lack of logic in coping with the dynamics of a new situation. For, he argues, conservative feudal properties cannot stand up to the superior competition of dynamic technological capitalist properties. And still more impressively, capitalist enterprise by its superior competition ruins small plants and their owners; it increases the army of propertyless, the "gravediggers of capitalism," and thus undermines its own power precisely by enhancing it; while the inadequacy of piecemeal management by private owners finally produces the crash of the industrial structure of capitalism and routs its remaining beneficiaries, thus clearing the field for communism to move in and take over. Only on this "material basis" does the Marxist appeal for intelligent action make sense. There is no appeal to capitalists—they would be deaf to it, they are not free. The appeal is only to the working class and their vanguard, and their expected action is prescribed by events, although these need "correct interpretation." The strictly harmonious plan of world history sees to it that the gravediggers stand ready when the mortal sickness strikes. Mankind, says Marx, never sets itself a task which it cannot perform.

Marxist "anthropology" thus leaves no room for that creative response to the challenge of danger which is the true test of freedom. Man essentially is, and will become in future reality, the vessel of economic reason, capable of and driving to highest achievement. But the growth of reason in history proceeds in spurts, which are determined and limited sociologically. The dominant types which succeed one another in history each make their distinct contributions to the unfolding of economic reason but reach their own inherent limits where their potentialities are exhausted. So new groups must stand ready to take over; and they do, by virtue of the harmonious plan of history. The whole process of discontinuities within rational continuity, then, can be likened to a succession of several generations in a family, the following generation carrying on in its own way where the preceding one left off, until the second gives way to the third, etc. The vitalities of the several generations are limited, and there is a hiatus between every two of them; but the vitality of the family is not limited and continues through them all, uninterrupted. That is, economic reason runs its appointed dialectical course through distinct successive phases under its preordained and predictable rational plan to full rationalization of man and society.

The logical possibility of rebarbarization exists because nature and reason, however close to each other in Marxism, do not simply coincide. An adding machine may indeed fail its rational job if its breaks down mechanically. But if it does, this is not proof of freedom; it is mere contingency. In the absence of this improbable contingency, the preordained result of the adding operation cannot be slow in appearing. Likewise the logical possibility of rebarbarization does not prove that communism is a product of man's creative freedom; communism is, in Marx's own presentation, the fulfillment of the law of rationality, predictable and predicted, "inexorable" and "necessary" unless reason is thrown out of gear by a mechanical breakdown of its human vessel. Socialism is either scientific or libertarian; it cannot be both.

Activism as Liberty

The course of history which is the actualization of man's potential and essential rationality is necessary—that is, preordained in the very concept of reason. It is the unfolding of what has been there potentially all the time. To observers groping in the night of ignorance, the successive achievements could appear as independent mysterious creations out of nothing. A Marxist observer, however, knows that ultimately there never was and certainly will never in future be an invention; there are only discoveries. To replace the chance event of invention by discovery of that which must be there is the nature of science. An astronomer knows where a certain star will be a thousand years from now; and a Marxist, writing a thousand years ago, should have predicted the rise of communism pursuant upon that of capitalism in our own day. In this sense communism, the perfect, fully developed rationality of man's genuine life, has been waiting to be overtaken and discovered by man's historically growing reason. The creative response to the challenge sets something that was not there before and could not have been predicted, as a work of art cannot be predicted; but communism, far from setting a new beginning, only fulfills and thereby ends the preordained development.

This is not to deny that rationality can make plenty of new discoveries, step by step, and thus achieve more welfare under communism. But progress in welfare, however desirable up to a more or less distinct point of saturation (discussed in Chapters I and IX), is not a test of creative freedom. To build more machines, to improve the machines in efficiency and enlarge them in size, even to "invent" quite new kinds of machines, are not acts of inventive creativity at all, although they were that in the beginnings of modern industry, when creative imagination, in the mysterious mental process which characterizes imagination, hit upon such finds piecemeal, as personal achievements of real greatness.

Meanwhile, however, it has become quite clear that what was inaugurated as heroic achievement and everything that followed from that pioneering step could not have escaped discovery if the field had been rationally explored and all logically possible combinations and permutations of the elements in the field systematically tried out. Schumpeter more than forty years ago pointed out that the pioneering achievement which characterized the heroic youth of capitalist industry was being superseded by bureaucratized systematic exploration of all logically and technically possible solutions to the problem at hand. Progress is now the work of the biggest corporations, not because they are led by geniuses but because their financial power makes it possible for them to build huge laboratories and hire hundreds of highly trained and highly paid physicists and chemists whose strictly planned teamwork does not require ideas but diligence and patience. There cannot fail to be a result if progress is so carefully organized and financed. But it can be so organized only because what is sought is the best possible combination of elements, the most efficient of all technically possible constructions of the machine—among the thousands, one must be the best. The solution of a difficult and practically important problem in arithmetic is highly welcome, but it has nothing to do with creativity and freedom.

The mental quality required for such progress may be properly called activism, to distinguish it from creativity and freedom. Rationalism as understood in this book is highly activistic by definition, pushing from "invention" to "invention" because critical examination of the most recent invention reveals its remaining inadequacies and thereby suggests the avenue of further advance. Rationalism is, and has proved to be in political as in technological history, a fanatically progressive, activistic force. In its name and under its guidance the revolutionary transition from absolute monarchy to bourgeois society has been achieved; and again in its name the further revolutionary transition from bourgeois society to proletarian society is sought—nay, has been predicted by Marx, more than a hundred years ago, as strictly necessary. Hence, also, the Communist leadership is under sacred obligation to industrial activism in the widest meaning of such a program; nothing can be closer to their hearts if it is the machine whose ubiquity and power is expected to produce the final rational-collective type of man. And the more backward the Communist-dominated country is, the more does it invite activism to fill all the irrational gaps and use all the unused opportunities for a demonstration of its program and the enhancement of its own power and prestige. But activism by definition is altogether different from creative freedom. What it discovers and realizes can be discovered and realized only because it is potentially there, as the solution of an unsolved problem in arithmetic is potentially there. If evidence is needed, it is provided by the fact that the hydrogen bomb has been "invented" in two countries independently and simultaneously. Progress can be organized (this is Schumpeter's thesis); creativity cannot because freedom cannot.

Statelessness as Liberty

Hence what historical necessity produces is not liberty but rational activism, where everything is known in principle and full certainty of knowledge precludes dissension and conflict and gives life an uncontroversial basis of concerted action. This is the eternal bliss symbolized by the powerful theory of the withering away of the state. Whatever else this may mean, it means full and eternal liberty, inasmuch as the logical opposite of liberty—coercion—and the agency in charge of coercion—the state—disappear for lack of function. As in the Jeffersonian utopia of individual democracy that state would be best that "governs least," so in the still more utopian Marxist vision no state has a function because all the people are united in interests, knowledge, and actions flowing therefrom. Nobody can advocate actions resulting from the hypothesis that two and two make five in a society whose members are fully rational—that is, where the problems of life have found their scientific solution and the truth is known not in esoteric form but in a generally accessible or at least generally accepted form. If the absence of coercion is the criterion of liberty, this is the promised libertarian society indeed.

But there are several questions arising. The first of them concerns the end of the dialectic, which, according to Marx, coincides with the beginning of the Communist classless society. Be it recalled that the driving force in dialectical motion, according to Marx, is class conflict, as between feudal owners and the bourgeoisie, so later between the latter and the working class; the classless society after the final revolution is then undialectical by definition. If so, then the dialectic is the law of motion of historical necessity, and liberty is undialectical. All this appears quite logical and simple.

But it also serves to illustrate the Marxian result, to confirm the unauthentic nature of this liberty. The end of the dialectic, we saw, need not be the end of progress at all; but the progress it permits is not progress toward or in liberty, if liberty has anything to do with spontaneity. It is the very opposite of spontaneity. It is the freedom to solve problems in applied arithmetic without inhibition or coercion. It is the use of the sacred name of liberty for something other than liberty because the cherished word has become dispossessed, vacant. The negative criterion, the absence of coercion, does not suffice to prove the presence of liberty if man has meanwhile been "reconstructed"—the word is Karl Mannheim's—so as to be supposedly capable of many new things but no longer capable of liberty. The state can wither away only when and because liberty has withered away beforehand, under the rule of the proletarian dictatorship with its government by kidnaping, brainwashing, and forced labor. Man has exchanged his individual soul for participation in the collective soul, whatever that be. The classless society which issues from the dictatorial phase is not society in the accepted meaning of spontaneous association; it is the product of applied science, of technology as the organizing principle, of rational homogeneity as the goal of all manipulation.[2]

Now the whole argument rests on an unreal hypothesis: the state of communism shows no tendency to wither away, not even a possibility of doing so. It would be unfair, of course, to de-

2. Emil Lederer's posthumously published book *The State of the Masses: The Threat of the Classless Society* (New York, Norton, 1940) is an impressive presentation of a related proposition, in which, however, the disintegrated, societyless masses of rationalist Bolshevism and of irrationalist fascism are not differentiated and are both subsumed under the category of crowds constituted and whipped up over and over again by violent emotions—Fascist rather than Communist. The theory of Marxism seems to point in a different direction, and reports about life in Russia seem to suggest an orderly bureaucratic state rather than one organizing periodic convulsions in order to rule the masses and keep them busy, as in the Fascist countries. The word "class," of course, means something far vaguer and also far more numerous in American parlance than in Marxian with its dogma of the two dialectically related classes only, and the "classless society" in the sense of one with no private owners confronting the workers need not be "classless" in the American sense. Lederer knew this, of course, but nevertheless Goetz Briefs (in a review) is right in holding it against the book.

mand that it do so before external conditions permit it; in a world-wide state of tension they certainly do not. In Marx's own presentation, the state would wither away in a world where the rule of communism—that is, the rule of reason—was no longer in doubt; Marx's error had been his overoptimism on the nearness of that happy day. But supposing for the sake of argument that day had arrived, the state still could not wither away, because the technological change from which both Marx and Lenin expected the withering away of the state—true to their technological-economic interpretation of history—is not visible even on the horizon, as was pointed out in Chapter V. If the state withered away, everybody would become a participant in the work of planning, and the dictatorial bureaucratic setup would resolve itself into a universal cooperative economy, the dreamland of faithful socialists. As the state does not wither and the directive functions are moving away from simplicity and transparence, the perfection of planning necessarily entails the continued ascendancy of the planners over the planned-for.

This is not a matter of property relations in the Marxian sense of the word; it need not even be—although it is—a matter of higher incomes. In order to become the source of a new class division, it suffices to have a differentiation of functions which gives one group command over the activities of the other because their professional skill is inaccessible, irreplaceable, and indispensable. If the absence of private property permits Marxists to classify the planners as proletarians and to deny the existence of a new "contradiction" in this society, they are given the lie by the power with which the new vested interest is already busy entrenching itself in education and social life.

Marx's and Lenin's emphasis on the rotation of functions should make clear that in the absence of such rotation there is precisely no democratic equality in the Marxist sense; and therefore no liberty either, if liberty requires that a person do not have to obey other persons, that there be nobody in position to push other persons around. The more strongly the new ruling elite of planners and bureaucrats entrenches itself, the more will the control be accentuated, and it is well within the range of imaginable developments that history may substitute for the withering away of this ruling class their removal by revolutionary action on the part of the people. This would be an act of freedom indeed. The trouble is only that we cannot know whether it is still technically feasible at a time when totalitarian ambitions are equipped with all the mental and physical means of control which the diligence and acumen of our social scientists put at their disposal.

Despite all this, however, we may be sure that even an unwithered, fully bureaucratized Soviet state would lay claim to the sacred name of liberty, as it does today in point of fact. For in the absence of private property the planners and other functionaries are only delegates and representatives of the united people, the organs through which the collective rules itself and must rule itself if it is not to be deaf mute. The ideology of the complete identification of the planners and bureaucrats with the common people (and of the complete unity of the common people's rational interests and aspirations) would then not be put to the test of "withering away"—that is, of withdrawal with good grace; but it would not need this test either because surrender of our own power of decision to these functionaries for administration in our behalf cannot be "alienation."

Acceptance of Necessity as Liberty

It is something entirely different. We can easily subsume it under the Marx-Engels definition of liberty, presented in Engels' polemic against Dühring, to which Marx had explicitly given his full approval and which is the most nearly complete presentation of the system in its entirety by its founders. There Engels credits Hegel with having been "the first to discover that liberty is nothing but the acceptance of necessity." The phrase obviously means something different in the context of Hegel's system from what it means in Marxism, because Hegel's spiritualism was far removed from the scientific causality of Marx's inexorable historical necessity within the framework of the laws of nature. For Marxism, anyway, the significance of the phrase is not in doubt, nor should it be belittled. Animals live under

202 Reason and Faith in Modern Society

strict necessity, driven by it, drifting with it, unredeemed,
dumb. Man alone, being an animal but also more than an
animal, can explore, understand, and accept the necessity under
which he too must spend his life. He can accept it because his
mind enables him to view himself and the necessity under which
he lives, as it were, from without and thus to free himself
mentally from enslavement to it and make it his own intellectual property. Animals do not know the necessity under
which they live; they are not free. Man, in discovering the
natural necessities under which he lives, understands that they
live in him, as his nature, of which his understanding mind is
a part; and living according to his fully understood nature, he
affirms it and becomes free. This, then, is the "jump from the
realm of necessity to the realm of freedom": the jump from a
life blindly drifting under the laws of necessity, like an animal,
to the appreciative acceptance of those laws as our own.

Combining this with the reflections in the preceding section,
we may put it in the following words. Liberty, being a formal
concept, receives its content from that which is freely to be
exerted—that is, from the nature of man as taught by the underlying doctrine of man. In Marxist philosophy man is essentially
economic rationality and ends by being so in actuality. The
last of the successive educational experiences through which
he is prepared for this destination is the proletarian dictatorship, which finally squeezes him into the mold of collective
rationality and substitutes rational normality for everything
that must appear irrational in this light: homogeneity for diversity, regularity for spontaneity, uniformity for uniqueness—
in short, the liberty of collective interest for that of personal
and communal creativity. The successful accomplishment of
this "reconstruction of man" makes it possible to take the pressure away. In the absence of that pressure, people will still continue to act as they have learned to do—that is, to act with
that perfect rationality which is full insight into and acceptance
of the necessities of their lives. It is logical that this be called
liberty in a doctrine that regards man as essentially the vessel
of collective rationality.

Be it noted, also, that it is not—and cannot be—the individual person who takes the jump into liberty; it is "man," the species, or rather "mankind" collectively. This is not only the meaning but quite accurately the wording of the famous phrase. The necessity is rationally understood and appropriated by rational men, and the rational result arrived at is as common to them as is the natural procedure by which they arrive there; it is a collective process that leads them collectively to the appreciative, rational acceptance of necessity. The jump, then, does not land "man" in the realm of that creative liberty which transcends necessity but in the realm of rationally appreciated necessity and science-guided activism.

Hence, finally, it does not make much difference whether the state has already withered away or not; we are in the realm of liberty anyway. For what the planners and other functionaries of government and administration suggest that we do is the rational application to the problems at hand of their scientific insights. They only spell out the necessities of the situation; and they can do it because on the one hand theirs is the professional skill which the job demands and which has not yet been generalized, and on the other hand, not being private owners or dependent on private owners, they are completely identified with all of us and are our real deputies in ascertaining and executing the truth, which is binding on all of us. In other words, if we did not have them to lead us that way, we would have to go exactly the same way, give ourselves the same plan and the same laws, and follow the same policies (provided we knew how to do all this). United with them in the truth as we are, we may very well accept from them such details of the truth as are beyond our technical knowledge to spell out. In sum, our liberty consists in appreciatively "accepting" their advice as incorporating "necessity"; we "accept necessity" from their hands instead of exploring it ourselves—the same necessity.

A striking coincidence has it that German professors in the First World War, in their frantic efforts to discourage Western libertarian ideas, hit upon the same definition of freedom-as-submissiveness as did Engels. It is indeed a good Germanic phrase, a perfect epitome of political Hegelianism, whether of the right or of the left. It makes mockery of the dialectic, the noblest instrument of both Greek and Christian thinking. Man's freedom, in point of fact, is never absolute, unconditioned, unlimited; it always is surrounded and limited by necessity and cannot even be thought of without this dialectical opposition. To repeat it, the sculptor's art, e.g., is bound to the physical necessities of the marble, the hammer, the sculptor's hand. It does not exhaust itself, however, in such obedience but rises above it to the spiritual achievement of new form-giving. If this opposition is dialectical, it still is opposition; it is neither coincidence nor surrender, as the Hegelians would have it. Precisely for this reason, however, this doctrine of freedom-as-submissiveness served the Bismarckian empire as faithfully as it has since served that empire's Marxist counterpart. It is the satire accompanying the tragedy. But there is no redeeming humor in the satire.[3]

Hegel had employed a mythological expression to characterize the climax and end of his system; only at dusk, he said, does the owl of Minerva—the sacred bird of the goddess of wisdom—begin its flight. That is, only as history approaches its end and goal do we fully recognize and understand its course toward that goal; the fact that we do proves that the end is near. If this is true of Hegel's system, where the constitutive concept of spirit actualizes itself in an overwhelming wealth of forms, how much truer is it of Marxism, where the creative spirit is reduced—Marx says "reversed"—to economic rationality exclusively and the dialectic is explicitly said to stop because the driving force, the tension between interests of opposite groups, has been resolved once and for all in the supreme

3. Another much quoted passage in Marx and Engels is usually misinterpreted to prove the democratic and libertarian character of the Marxist program. In *The Communist Manifesto* the two authors say: "In place of the old bourgeois society with its classes and class antagonism, we shall have an association in which the free development of each is the condition for the free development of all." "Free development" here obviously means a development unhindered by class barriers; a person gifted for a musical or a professional career will be given the necessary education, free of charge. But this has nothing to do with "free development" of spontaneous unguided thinking, creative imagination, and critical faculties; in one word, with spiritual freedom.

homogeneity which is communism. The state can wither away because personal liberty has withered away. It is not far from the vision of this Marxist paradise to Nietzsche's scornful vision of the last man, "who only still winks." It is the end indeed.[4]

4. Marx's explicit statement that the historical dialectic stops upon reaching communism has come, in recent years, to be a thorn in the flesh of East German communism in its contest with Western libertarian ideas. It is now said that the dialectic, far from stopping, only changes its form; no longer does it proceed in spurts through conflict—which has become impossible in universal homogeneity—but it assumes the form of wave-like movements within the homogeneous society. The reinterpretation is proudly displayed to demonstrate the scientific character of Marxism, which, far from being doctrinaire, does not shrink from criticizing and correcting errors of its founding father. In point of fact, what the re-interpretation does prove is something totally different. Marx, who was a thinker, fearlessly formulated the logically necessary conclusion of his system of thought; present-day Marxists no longer understand what think-ing is and believe it sufficient to formulate some arbitrary proposition convenient in the political struggle, without bothering about the logic of the argument, without caring to refute Marx, nay, without reasoning at all.

Lest there be any misunderstanding about the subject of the contro-versy, it should be clear that there may very well be material progress in a completely homogeneous society, and that it may take the form of wave-like expansion from the center, as in a pond into which a stone is thrown. The subject of the controversy is not the possibility of such undialectical movement but the continuation or discontinuation of the dialectic—that is, the unity of opposites, the movement through opposites. This move-ment, says Marx, comes to an end if his premises hold. He is right, and it will not do to bestow the name of "dialectic" upon a patently undialectical movement in order to be able to say that the dialectical logic of history is preserved in the future as in the past. What we hold against Marx is not the logic of his argument but the falsity of his premises. The dialectic con-tinues, contrary to Marx's proposition, for reasons to be discussed presently in the text. See also *Freedom and Order*, p. 165.

A much more interesting attempt to solve the Marxist difficulty can be found in Sidney Hook's *Toward the Understanding of Karl Marx*, 1935, p. 98. The dialectic is lifted, he says, from the social plane to the "indi-vidual and personal" plane, from "the problems of social existence" to "the more significant problems of personal development," from "the ma-terial problems of subsistence" to "the problems which arise in the course of the individual's intellectual, emotional and spiritual development." But the dialectic has always been working on that level too, so its continuing to do so does not mean a continuation of dialectical history in changed form. It still is the end of history.

Among educated and thinking critics of Marxism it has become customary to reprove Marxism for its utopianism (in the
sense of misjudging the nature of man and overrating its possibilities by overrating the scope and power of reason in man).
This point of view recommends itself particularly to Christian
critics; Marxism then appears as a kind of Christian heresy. For
it is the typical heresy to believe that Christ's saving love has
retroactively undone the Fall and returned to man the perfection with which he had originally emerged from the creator's
hands. For then he is no longer in need of the divine grace because he no longer sins, and he is no longer in need of the state
because he does not want anything but harmony. This belief
was more or less dominant in the sects of the thirteenth century
and the Reformation period, and remains dominant to this day;
and Marxism seems to come close to it.[5] But if our presentation
is correct, Marxism should not be called utopian. For it is a real
possibility that man may be so completely emasculated by
mechanization that he can no longer sin because he can no
longer create. There may very well be more activity than ever,
but it still would be the end of man.[6]

5. Cf. *Freedom and Order,* pp. 395 ff. To my knowledge William
Temple was the first to see it that way.
6. This "fourth man" has been opposed to the "third man," the man
of our civilization since Greece and Christianity by the eighty-five-year-old
Alfred Weber in a book of impressive constructive power and wealth of
ideas; his hope for the future of the third type is attached to a fuller unfolding of the tendencies which he sees reach beyond traditional religion
as "immanent transcendency" (Alfred Weber, *Der Dritte oder der Vierte
Mensch, Vom Sinn des geschichtlichen Daseins,* 1953). Among the descrip-
tions of the fourth type George Orwell's *1984* is now rightly world famous.
The present writer met this type first in Ernst Junger's glorifying book
Der Arbeiter.

PART THREE

The Person in the Community

* VIII *

Rationality, Irrationality,
and Suprarationality[1]

Rational Society and Christian Dogma

THE CONFLICT in the rationalist unity of the present world has been described in Parts One and Two. In the very beginning of the discussion the mutual criticisms of the two systems were summarized—and trivialized—as a too radical social rationality in the one system and a too hesitant and inhibited rationality in the other. The two opposing systems are connected in systematic logic, as it unfolds itself in history.

1. One cannot warn too urgently against the misuse—frequent in Germany—of the word "irrational." The fondness for this word—that is, for oneself—covers a bad lack of discernment. It shrouds in sentimentality the damp and sultry corners of the soul which need above all illumination and ventilation; it lifts the senseless to the position of supreme value, as e.g. in fascism. It goes so far as to comprehend under the "irrational" even religion, which teaches an objectively valid meaning of life, even if we can understand it only incompletely and express it still more incompletely. (Thus one may comprehend genius and criminality under the name of "anormality" but would cause nothing but confusion through such a nomenclature outside a strictly circumscribed purpose.) That which is beyond rational illumination is not holy for this reason, and the holy is desecrated if one hallows "the irrational" as such. It does not follow, however, that we now must accommodate under "rationality" everything that should not be called "irrational": a Mozartian melodious line or Lutheran theology, etc. The official Roman Catholic theology, indeed, is rational and means to be so, but Protestant theology is not (and is rejected by Catholics for this reason). The distinction between the rational and the irrational, hence, must obviously be supplemented by adding the "suprarational," the objectively valid but not rationally derivable. Or one may conclude that one does not do full justice to the irrational either if one approaches it too closely to the merely confused. In this case it would appear that the dangerous word is best shunned altogether.

But while the program of the modern world is rationality crystallized in science, the reality looks different, in Russia no less than in the West. Frequently, from the introduction on, our presentation has referred to surviving forces of prerational Christian tradition under the surface of the rationalist institutions, both in the discussion of Russia, where they are stronger, and in that of the West. It is quite possible that the Christian tradition will in fact evaporate; but this, far from proving its irrelevance, would reveal its vital significance even to the blind, if it is true that it is this very tradition which accounts for the remaining cohesion in our strife-torn society and that without it there would be complete and final disintegration.

The first contention—by no means original—of this book has been that rationalist society has lived on the surviving wholesome forces of its Christian inheritance, while criticizing the latter for the destructive effects of its degeneration, and that it is coming to its own end as that source of its spiritual vitality is exhausted by rationalist criticism. The tragedy started from the discreditable account which Christendom had given of itself in many respects during the last phase of the Middle Ages. Christianity was naturally judged by the achievements and failures of its representatives, and was made responsible for much superstition which rising reason would not tolerate, for the degenerating feudal organization of society to which it seemed to be wedded, and finally, after the religious revival through Reformation and Counterreformation, for the religious wars. In the light of this record, rationalism—in the sense of the supremacy of rationality in society—was not only a plausible reaction; its humanism was a noble attempt to rebuild the life of Western man on the basis of God-given reason. Reason, as understood at that time, did not preclude but did reinterpret Christianity so as to permit the tremendous achievements in social and spiritual life which bear witness to the glory of reason. It not only produced enormous strides ahead in every realm of social, intellectual, and spiritual life, but incorporated itself, as it were, in a new, generous, delicate, and highly educated type of man, such as has ever since been found in all Western countries.

There was a moment in history when Western mankind

seemed to benefit from a perfect balance between religion and reason, from both the continuing moral tradition of Christianity and the creative power of unfettered reason. No wonder man decided he could continue to live in this way and perfect his earthly existence. It was not seen that this was a fleeting moment, as declining religion and rising rationality crossed their paths at that point but would immediately continue their opposite movements to ever stronger unbalance. It was not seen, in other words, that rationality, put in the supreme position, lives on that which it criticizes and criticizes that on which it lives, and that that first phase was therefore only a short-lived transition, inaugurating as it did a highly dynamic process, which enhanced reason and corroded Christianity.

What is a Christian society? Certainly it is not a society in which people live according to the precepts of the Gospel. Such a society is precluded by the fundamental doctrine of Christianity itself, according to which man is a sinner.[2] Nature drives man, and reason directs him to his natural objectives and teaches him the means to the ends. In the choice of their means and the pursuit of their ends people always go to the limit; the question is where that limit is. It is given in a climate which permeates the minds and actions of men without being consciously present all the time to the individuals; certain things can be done, others cannot. The limit naturally changes in history. The otherworldly goal of Christianity, for so long as it was taken seriously, put a limit on the operation of natural drives and mitigated their fury by reminding man that his earthly objectives were not what mattered ultimately; and that, however offensive the other man and his actions may appear to me, he still is my brother, my fellow in despair and hope, in sin and redemption.

The first phase of the Age of Reason, the humanist phase described above, did not change, and did not mean to change,

2. However, "man is not bad, he is only sinful" (V. A. Demant, "The Tragedy of War and the Hope of Peace," in *The Universal Church and the World of Nations,* 1937, p. 174). Or, as H. J. Iwand puts it (in a private letter), "From the fact that we are sinners it must not be inferred that we are criminals."

that moral climate; it even reinforced it. For if God is the supreme mind and Christ is identified with wisdom—as in the Greek stream of thinking, which had been integrated into the Christian tradition by the Fourth Gospel—then the spiritual and moral principles of the preceding phase were not discarded; the opportunity of reconciling the new belief in reason with the Christian religion was eagerly seized. After all, man, though corrupted by the Fall, is still created in the image of God; witness thereof is the reason which man alone among all creatures has been given and which enables him to explore and admire the miracles of the laws and structures of nature. It is the proud and heroic sense of the dignity of man as an ethical and aesthetic program which permeates early humanism. That is, the Christian system of virtues was preserved, although transformed intellectually; it was preserved precisely by such transformation.

Only very slowly did reason move into a position of contrast to and conflict with religious dogma, and the war in the name of reason against everything dogmatic began. "Dogmatic" now comes to mean "unreal." Spiritual existence as such, without physical evidence, now is suspected of unreality—of being an illusion, an erroneous reflection of physical needs. Can one prove that there is such a thing as truth? The logical positivists tell us that it is a dogma; and indeed it is, emanating from the dogma of the one Maker making the one world which is represented by the one truth; there cannot be several conflicting sets of truth if our system of science is to make sense. Our scientific knowledge of the world does not refute the dogma, although it does not prove it either. If it could be proved it would not be dogma; it cannot be proved because it precedes every proof. The fact that it is dogma does not invalidate it, on the other hand, as soon as we become aware of the limited nature of scientific knowledge because of the limiting conditions on which it rests; this is precisely what we have learned from the logical positivists.

Naturally, a dogma—if it is to be a real dogma rather than arbitrary nonsense, namely an attempt to formulate a truth about a reality beyond the grip of science—must not conflict with logic. Dogma that it is, it is not on safe ground if it assumes that because the regularities of nature have so far worked reliably the way the physical sciences have described them to us, therefore they must continue to work that particular way forever; the logical positivists are quite right in pointing out that this does not follow. But this refutation, on the other hand, does not imply that nature is mere contingency and anarchy; the facts of nature's order and durability do not permit such an interpretation. The correct conclusion from the detection of that logical flaw is that, as we do not have scientific knowledge of the essence and source of the observed regularities in nature on which we rest our technology, so those regularities may change one day, now or in a billion years. The laws of nature may change. But a change of such laws of coherence would not be any less lawful than the absence of such change, or any less indicative of an ordering authority. If our limited experience certainly does not permit us to say that the present laws of nature are eternal, it does permit us to say that there is order and coherence rather than contingency and anarchy. And the religious dogma turns out to be the axiom of our thinking; the structure of our mind does not enable us to think otherwise.

Justice, too, is a scientifically untenable dogma, despite some frantic efforts by social science to justify it before its own tribunal. The Maker has instituted the commandment of one justice for His one world in order that His creatures can live out their destiny in peace. But this is an idea to which nothing in experience corresponds; we know it because it has been revealed to us, because we cannot think or act without presupposing the validity of the commandment of justice, much as we may argue it away or deliberately violate it. Once critical reason is all set to ferret out and destroy dogma, nothing is left for man to live on. This is logically inevitable, however long it may be concealed by the fact that the dogmas of truth and justice, constituting as they do nothing less than the essence of the human mind itself, appear to the mind as its very nature, exempt from its own rational criticism. The self-destruction of the Western mind has taken a few centuries.

This result, logical and historical, may be summarized in different words. The structure of the human mind—or of the Western mind—includes the knowledge of the law of oneness and of the derived commandments of truth and justice; reason can and must explore them but cannot replace them. A Christian society is one which is conscious of all this and in which the moral effort required to live up to those commandments is generally recognized as basic to the life of society. Again, this is far from pretending that a Christian society realizes justice; it does not. But from this it does not follow that society can give up the belief in divine justice without destroying its own cohesion—that is, its life. Rational society, however, claims to find in human nature and reason a purely immanent basis for its life. This is what we have called social rationalism.

While religion had made it its task to keep man's natural drives under control—frequently in forms that would not be accepted today—the doctrine of man's self-realization by the wise pursuit of his self-interest was now developed to sustain these drives and give them moral and quasi-religious sanction. If and when the latter doctrine is recognized as the correct interpretation of "humanism," of man's "autonomy," religion naturally becomes "heteronomy," a violation of man's sacrosanct nature. But this reliance on man's unfettered natural drive as the element and guarantee of ordered social life—whose social effects we studied in Chapter II—reduces man to mere nature and thus is guilty of either one of two errors which converge in the result. The nature of which man is a part and is now to be nothing but a part is an ordered, coherent whole, which by its very existence and durability proves the handiwork of a sustaining power. One may analyze it by abstracting from this ground of its being but certainly errs when forgetting the abstraction and concluding that there is order without an ordering authority. At the same time, in thus making of man an element of mere nature in order that he may partake of the authorityless harmony of nature, his freedom from and over nature (including his own nature) is denied and left without guidance and direction to run into anarchy and chaos. It took a few centuries to bring these consequences into the open, but they were implied from the very beginning.

Eighteenth-Century Humanism

How slowly social rationalism, however, unfolded its own inherent tendencies can be seen from illustrious documents of liberal democracy in the three leading countries, as late as the second half of the eighteenth century. Adam Smith, who is generally recognized as the father of laissez-faire, interpreted the nature of man's mind to include sympathy; nay, he and the school of Scots philosophers of which he was a member rested the life of society on such sympathy between the citizens—taking the word not in the sense of friendship but in the linguistically literal sense of awareness of the feelings in others—"feeling with" them—no matter whether "sympathetic" to us or not.

On this naturalistic-psychological foundation he erected a complete system of sociology, under the characteristic title *Theory of Moral Sentiments,* which the numerous commentators generally accept as a kind of introduction to his great economic work, *The Wealth of Nations,* or at least as easily compatible with it. The bridge between the two is in Smith's highly skeptical judgments on the blessings of wealth and the rationality of striving for it. Our real motive, he says, is our "sympathetic" attitude toward men of greater influence and authority, not only because we erroneously believe them to be happier but because they are superior and therefore can organize peace, order, and security, which everybody desires, and in the longer run that progress of civilization which is the real content of history. Such admiration then leads to imitation; we accept their achievement and attempt to emulate it. More generally, sympathy leads to understanding and approval for other people's value judgments and thus imposes on all members of society a tissue of unified sentiments, cooperation, and neutrality, where everybody according to his best judgment gives away something for the benefit of others and receives back the equivalent.[3]

3. This is an example of that antirationalistic psychological empiricism whose greatest representative was Smith's older friend Hume, and which in our introduction we nevertheless combined with rationalism as the rational autonomy opposed to the religious attitude.

Now all this would be a rather poor foundation for laissez-faire. But on the one hand, according to Smith, the work of "sympathy" does not exhaust itself in the "sympathetic" knowledge of the reactions of others to our activities; the harm we may possibly do them cannot remain hidden from us. This possibility is very familiar to Smith the economist. Over and over again he fulminates against the "shameful avarice of businessmen," goes so far as to say that every intervention of the government in favor of labor is likely to have justice on its side, and presents as the guarantee of the common good not the freedom of enterprise, which would include monopoly, but solely the pressure of competition on the free enterprisers. Accordingly, Smith the social psychologist, too, is far from considering fairness in mutuality a natural fact. If self-interest, which includes self-responsibility, is an indispensable virtue, it still cannot be the sole or supreme virtue because Smith takes the "feeling with others" seriously and hence has the "respectable virtues" culminate in justice, the "lovable virtues" in loving-kindness—both are necessary for social life. Thus only the argument from mutuality in the market can be completed: the fury of the pursuit of interest is mitigated by "feeling with others"—that is, by the desire for their respect—and an atmosphere is created that puts limits to the conflict of interests and shields the cohesion of society. This Smith had indeed not made explicit, but he needed not do it because it was taken as matter of course in his circle.[4]

Adam Smith, of course, lived two hundred years nearer the Christian Age than we do, and his society was a small-scale society, where a man had to deal with his neighbors; whereas in modern large-scale society the partners or adversaries in a deal

4. Smith's teacher, Francis Hutcheson, who seems to have influenced Smith's thinking more than any other person, makes the following surprising statement on the intertwining of sympathy and self-interest (*An Inquiry into the Original of our Ideas of Beauty and Virtue*, II, pp. 127–129): "Reason and calm reflection may recommend to us, from self-interest, those actions which at first view our moral sense determines us to admire without considering this interest. . . . While we are only intending the good of others, we are undesignedly promoting our own greater private good."

are far away and personally unknown to one another and they can appear to the mind as economic or statistical magnitudes rather than as human beings. It makes a difference whether we must expect to meet those harmed by us or are immune to such exposure. This explains why "feeling with others" was a social force in Adam Smith's society, and made it possible for him to believe that such "sympathy" was a natural ingredient of enlightened self-interest. It does not refute but rather confirms our point that Adam Smith's humanism, far from repudiating the Christian inheritance, drew on it by interpreting as natural to man's reason what has since proved to be a historical Christian virtue, which evaporates from social life. But because he mistook it for natural, Smith did not care to cultivate and perpetuate it by deliberate recommendations. Equipped with Christian virtue or at least a reminiscence of it, though duly reinterpreting it, rationalist society seemed to be viable.

Jefferson was one degree wiser than Smith in explicitly recognizing his debt to the inheritance of Protestant education, without which, he admitted, his society of free individuals would not possess the necessary earnestness, conscientiousness, and sobriety. But he also was too deeply steeped in the belief in automatic progress to infer that he had to do something in order to preserve and renew the precious tradition; he too seems to have been convinced that, once mankind had acquired those essential qualities, they had become part of human nature. At least there is in the Declaration of Independence no reference whatever to any social virtue, however diluted or reinterpreted. Of the three documents here discussed, Jefferson's text no doubt is the most exclusively individualistic, and so has the culture of his country been to this day, with all the glory but also with all the dangers implied in this fact.

Now Jefferson's text is of very early origin, from the same year (1776) as Adam Smith's great book, when there was not yet an industrial technical development worthy of the name. This helps to explain why in the Declaration, despite Jefferson's strong egalitarian convictions, no limitation of liberty in favor of equality is discussed. For in a pretechnical, predominantly rural economy such as Jefferson had in mind, liberty and equality, at least insofar as economic life is concerned, are far easier to reconcile than in the explosively dynamic economy of the industrial revolution. When this began to become manifest, Jefferson remained characteristically skeptical vis-à-vis industry for the sake of democratic equality, while his great adversary Hamilton rejected equality and democracy for the sake of industrial growth. The tension between industry and democracy was familiar to both men. Thus Hamilton became the principal architect of America's industrial power, as Jefferson became the prophet of the "American dream." But without America's wealth and power the American dream could never have conquered half the world—one of the great paradoxes of history. If we pay due attention, therefore, to the historical conditions in which Jefferson wrote, what strikes the eye is that his individualism is not the familiar explosive individualism in an explosively dynamic society, but, if we may put it that way, the individualism of the common man who is proud of his independence earned by hard work; who is neither the boss nor the competitor nor the creditor of his neighbors but simply their neighbor, an equal among equals who through their cooperatives defend and strengthen their individual independence; briefly, one of those of whom in the same tradition Lincoln said that God must love the common people since He made so many of them. This individualism of the common man is not the dialectical opposite of collectivism, leading up to it and tipping over into it, but simply its opposite—wherever it is not overbalanced by big industry.[5]

In addition, it would be unfair to forget that what the Declaration of Independence aims at is a strictly circumscribed purpose, national independence; one would not be justified in expecting a complete constitutional program. But in popular consciousness the monumental second paragraph has more and more assumed the significance of such a constitutional program, as the original end has been attained and become a routine property so as to vanish from the living reality of the problems. So much the more the original purpose and occasion have become a living reality among the peoples of Asia as they emerge from colonial rule and receive the Jeffersonian message from

5. Cf. *Wirtschaftssysteme und Gesellschaftssysteme*, p. 103.

the Hamiltonian power. The original conditions of the message, naturally, cannot be understood there; it now appears again as national and social program in one, and now even more emphatically detached from the Western religious presuppositions, which are not explicit in the deistic wording but from which the author himself derived the democratic virtues.

The most interesting of the three documents, from the point of view of our inquiry, is the French revolutionary program of liberty, equality, fraternity. Liberty is here balanced by equality and arched over by fraternity—only in the brotherly city can liberty prosper and liberty and equality coexist side by side. Now fraternity in the ideology of the French Revolution certainly was not related to Christianity. The third link in the triad was not there from the beginning; it was added only in a revision of the program a few years later, which makes it only the more fascinating. Its origin does not seem to be particularly marked; it reflects a frequent reference to solidarity among citizens in the social philosophy of French Enlightenment. Its ultimate root was in ancient philosophy, in Stoicism and, further back, in Aristotle, who taught that friendship among the citizens—in the small Greek town—was fundamental to the state, and brotherly friendship—that is, friendship between equals—to the republic.

It is a hardly credible tragic fact that the French revolutionary program should have been accepted as anti-Christian by both atheists and Christians for a century and a half. Speaking in terms of intellectual history, Aristotle was not only the source from which classical thought flowed down the ages through Stoicism and the Renaissance to French atheistic Enlightenment, but also the main philosophical inspiration of Christian political theory throughout the Middle Ages and beyond; the two trends of thought were closely related in their origin and meaning. Liberty and equality in the brotherly city—could there be a more genuinely Christian program than this? And still it was under this flag that French democracy, and much of continental democracy in general, fought against Christianity because Christendom seemed to be wedded to predemocratic structures and interests, and denounced democracy as un-Christian. Thus the real source of brotherliness was denied French democracy, and more generally, modern free society stripped away precisely that element from its program which was designed to safeguard it against degenerating into a free-for-all, particularly since equality without the rule of brotherliness must fall prey to liberty. On the other hand, it required only an unbiased and profoundly Christian mind—that of Jacques Maritain—to discover the Christian message in the revolutionary program, reveal the absurdity of the conventional division between the two camps, and breach the wall so as to lead the Christian forces into their democratic home. But this is another story, part of a new chapter; it could be written and heard only when the conventional animosity had all but wrecked the democratic structure.[6]

The Deadlock and Fascism

Rationalist liberty without sympathy, without Christian education, without equality and fraternity, is unbalanced; there is nothing to limit the fury with which self-interest now asserts itself against others and against the community as a whole. As the dogmas of humanism—truth and justice—were gradually overcome and the inhibitions of the Christian tradition and memories were eliminated, the program of individualist rationality began to reveal its self-defeating nature, the frustration of individuality, the degradation of community, the tendency to positivistic thinking toward collectivism, as discussed in our first three chapters; and the transition to the rationalist collectivism of Marxism, as presented in Chapter IV.

We have argued, however, that the two systems of individual and collective rationality, of bourgeois liberty and proletarian equality, while indeed parallel and inversely related in their beginnings, did not continue that way (Chapter IV). The first

6. The decision of the U. S. Supreme Court against racial segregation in public schools in 1954 made this manifest in a domain which has long and badly been lagging behind other fields such as labor relations. Most recent developments, with mostly smooth progress despite some outrageous setbacks, may be slower than one might have hoped but do not necessitate a change in the above text.

of the two systems of rationality produced the second as its mirror and negative replica, a hundred years ago; and the second has since grown and has actualized its possibilities so as to make its inverse relationship to its origin almost mathematically pure —rather than find a progressive dialectic. But precisely under the impact of the second system, the first embarked on a progressive dialectic, incorporating more equality in its institutions of liberty, more respect for the spirit of community in its individualism. The symmetry of the picture is seriously disturbed.

But Marxism can never admit this. Its own unprogressive dialectic rests on the exclusive and paramount premise that individualism is once and for all prevented, by the supremacy of the rule of private profit, from reforming itself. To Marxism, then, constitutional democracy is and remains still capitalism. And Marxism is helped in this assertion by the slowness with which the new spirit of responsibility spreads in constitutional democracy from domestic problems to those which are most visible to the awakening masses outside the white world: the problems of racialism and colonialism, which rightly or wrongly are identified with capitalism in popular consciousness because they certainly appear in symbiosis with it.[7] Colonial and post-colonial capitalism in the new Asian states, furthermore, is still of the predatory variety, to which the new democratic governments in their formative years find it very hard, naturally, to catch up. If all this is not surprising, what is surprising is that the newly reformed countries of old capitalism should consent, under the pressure of their capitalist interests, to identify themselves as capitalist and should trace their newly acquired virtues to capitalism rather than to their dialectical reaction to Marxism.

The result is that the intellectual and moral contest of our days is being fought on the terms of Marxism, approved by our die-hard liberals, rather than on our own terms. The two related and antagonistic systems seemed to stand side by side, engaged in heated controversy, hardening in the conflict, and each drawing strength from the defects of the other. If this obviously ex-

7. Cf. my "Schumpeter and the Problems of Imperialism," *Social Research,* June 1952; also *Wirtschaftssysteme und Gesellschaftssysteme,* Chapter VII.

hausts the possibilities of rationality as the principle of social organization, then this very principle now appears refuted by its consequences, and men turn against reason with exactly the same psychologically inevitable logic with which a few centuries earlier the split in Christendom had turned minds against Christianity: the representatives of the cause are responsible for the cause. Modern society has run its course.

Nay, the antirational protest easily becomes antispiritual protest, because rational life is a product of Western spirituality and is praised by its representatives as the highest and ultimate form of that tradition. The antirational and antispiritual protest of fascism made the divisive forces of blind nature supreme after thousands of years of the belief in oneness and spiritual unity.[8] Again, this is how the terrible logic of history works. After the spiritual message of peace and harmony through love had failed to unite people and dogmatic discussion over its interpretation had disrupted Western society; after the doctrine of the unifying power of human reason and science had failed and had divided the world into two dogmatically opposed camps —what now remains is the integration of the societies severally on the purely biological plane, where there cannot be dissension since spiritual and intellectual principles are stripped away; man is revealed as nature, vitality, power; and the new hierarchy of values puts the apparently divisive forces of spiritual and intellectual life under the strictly unifying control of supreme irrational power.

The rise of irrational power, contemptuous of intellectual justification and using all intellectual techniques for its own enhancement, was triumphantly described by Spengler, a few years before it materialized, as the necessary outcome of the intellectual deadlock in intellectual society. It materialized in both Italy and Germany when both nations cleft wide open in the fundamental split between bourgeois individualism and proletarian collectivism. The controversy as to whether fascism was closer to capitalism or to socialism was without substance be-

8. "Blessed be Egypt, my people, and Assyria, my handiwork, and Israel, my inheritance" (Is. 19:25).

cause what fascism rejected was precisely the belief in unifying reason which the two had in common. Hence the institutional question was not fundamental for fascism; it was free, as expediency dictated, to use technical institutions of either capitalism or socialism in the service of its own irrational ends. The antirational attempt has been smashed by an alliance of the two mutually hostile camps of rationalism. But as long as the inherent conflict of social rationalism has not been solved and the deadlock now continues on the largest international scale, a reversion to fascism in any form appears only too logical, and possible at any time.[9]

Social rationalism ends in the logically insoluble deadlock between individualism gradually reforming itself and the despotism of collective rationality. It used to live on the Christian inheritance of social cohesion. But, arising as it did as a protest against the abuse of that tradition, it mistook clericalism for Christianity and gradually superseded Christianity with scientism. In the younger generation of the United States there are many who have never seen the Bible or heard even the most external account of Biblical events, not to speak of their spiritual significance. They literally do not know what Easter, still less what Good Friday, is all about. The fear of clericalism outweighs, in the system of education, the concern for moral and social integration; this is literally called freedom of religion, since it is supplemented by a perfect freedom of religious instruction outside the public schools. The example illustrates the trend which finally cuts the tradition of Western spirituality off in the leading country of Western liberty and leaves the younger generation without fundamental orientation in the turmoil.[10] The downward spiral of the development from suprarational spirituality through the hopeless conflict of social rationalism threatens to continue until antirational reintegration is the only way out that is left to the bewildered people.

9. "Woe unto the world because of offenses! For it must needs be that offenses come; but woe to that man by whom the offense cometh" (Mt. 18:7).

10. For a most circumspect discussion of this highly complex matter, see John C. Bennett, *Christians and the State,* 1958.

Re-Christianization

But another way out is just as logical; whether it is possible in reality it is too early to say. It is a reversion, under the shock of experience, to the spiritual level of the ignored inheritance. A scientific age is never tired of proclaiming that only that which can be verified by experience is real; its folly is to believe that an experiment can never take more than a few hours or a few weeks or perhaps a few years. Science is blinded by its own dogma of tangibility, measurability, and the short period. But people may come to see again as the abysses yawn; they may begin to understand that it is the huge experiment of a life cut off from its Christian roots which has led them, over a period of a few centuries, into the impasse.

The greatest and most tragic figure of modern political history, Lincoln, knew that democracy could be saved and re-vived only as Christian democracy. In our own day, in different countries, different languages, and different theological struc-tures, the powerful pens of Karl Barth, Nicolas Berdyaev, Emil Brunner, Jacques Maritain, Reinhold Niebuhr, Eugen Rosen-stock-Huessy, William Temple, and Paul Tillich—and many others as well—teach the same lesson. And so does implicitly the Jewish prophet of our day, Martin Buber.[11]

The inheritance of Christianity is one of original and funda-mental social cohesion. The idea of community is just as strong in it as is the idea of the person; the two are like two poles of one axis. Old Christian wisdom says that one Christian is no Christian; only in the community can the person live—just as the community, in order to be a community, must consist of persons. Without the proper balance between the two they be-came atrophic or rebellious. The balance had been violated in the later Middle Ages, and the rebellious emphasis on the in-dividual conscience in the Reformation helped to produce, in

11. The above enumeration is intolerably summary. For a very careful and supremely fair critical discussion of Brunner, Hromadka, Tillich, Berdyaev, Niebuhr, Barth, and Gollwitzer, cf. Charles C. West, *Com-munism and the Theologians: Study of an Encounter,* 1958.

the countries of Protestantism, that exclusive belief in individual liberty which parallels the influence of rationalist philosophy in Italy and France. The balance has been relatively best preserved or restored in the Protestant country of Catholic tradition, England. The stronger the integration of the person in the community by the sense of responsibility and moderation, the more easily can the community respect the freedom of the person. Spiritual integration is the alternative to coercion.

That is why individualism is no viable principle, no possible foundation. It is as untenable for individual as for social life, because it rests on a faulty doctrine of man. The fundamental fact about man is that he is incomplete as an "individual," more incomplete if he makes it his aim to "realize" his individuality. The supreme power in man's life is that of love, which drags him out of the prison of his individuality and beyond himself and makes him free by forcing him to lose himself in the other. It is this experience from which he receives himself back more complete, more whole, more himself than he was before. There are many kinds of love in human life, none like the other, each with its own unique beauty and also its own problems and dangers, which the depth psychologists have richly explored; love between man and woman; between parents and children, nay, between mother and child, mother and son, mother and daughter, and again between father and children; between brothers, between sisters, between brothers and sisters; between grandparents and grandchildren; between friends of the same sex and between friends of different sexes; between teacher and pupil, etc., etc. The person is a loved and loving person, and whoever cannot love and be loved is lost.[12] Hence love is not a means to the end of the individual's self-realization; it is the end (in the sense of termination) of his individuality and the beginning of his being a person.

But by the same token, then, love in creating the person creates the community, the hanging together, the warmth in which life can grow and bloom and bear fruit, the sense of mutual

12. One of the most comforting words of the Bible is: "The lonely woman has more children than the one who has a man" (Is. 54, 1). Alice Salomon, of blessed memory, often quoted this.

obligation and devotion, which must not be mistaken, as such, for emotion, passion, and enthusiasm. As a French writer has beautifully expressed the relationship between husband and wife: "The family is the place where one learns to fulfill freely chosen duties." [13] Brothers do not freely choose each other; but no matter what I may think of my brother, he remains my brother—a unique relationship, particularly in distress. Blood relationship is not freely chosen; friendship is. There are many different kinds of friendship in accordance with the different nature of the ground on which the partners meet: neighborly relationships or mutual career and assignment, common destiny or hobbies or mutual participation in worship service or common studies. None of these normally matches the cohesive strength, durability, and readiness to sacrifice of the family relationship, but they all spread from the persons in the center with diminishing intensity in all directions of their activities and interests.

The stronger the relationship the more easily can it be misused for segregation and tendencies to domination, which monopolize all warmth of community life for members of the inner circle and present them as callous and heartless to outsiders. Marriage or family, then, are a kind of enlarged individual, and the family egoism coincides with individualism, particularly in business life, where the family head alone meets outsiders.[14] The love relationship, hence, shares the deep ambiguity of everything noble in human life, which is never secure from abuse and perversion.

Nevertheless it remains true that the social whole is composed of innumerable relationships which spread in all directions, cross and entangle one another, and overlap; where every one of us stands in the center of a limited number of relation-

13. This sentence was quoted to this author by André Philip thirty or thirty-five years ago. Unfortunately, neither one of the then interlocutors remembers the source today although it was referred to at that time.
14. Werner Sombart, who, without always taking his witty paradoxes as seriously as he expected his readers to do, did not shrink occasionally from disfiguring by them his great work, contended that the primary motive in capitalism was love.

ships, owing to our limited time and vitality, but rightly imagines that beyond his own relationships those of his friends spread farther and farther. A delicately woven fabric of innumerable threads in innumerable colors ties people into the community, where respect and affection accrue to a person not because he is more efficient than others but because he is a person, a warmhearted and active human being. The uniqueness of the person and the richness of the community are one and the same thing. Just as the person can become a person only in the community, so the community is community only as a community of persons. The person and the community are the two poles of one axis, they are set either one through the other.

The uniqueness of the person serves as a pretext or maybe as a misunderstood ground for individualism, if the dialectical unity of person and community—that is, their interdependence —is not taken into account. The misunderstanding is further made plausible by the occasional rise of the person beyond the community and in opposition to it—Peter's far-ringing proclamation that one has to obey God rather than men. Such a proposition would indeed have been unthinkable in Greece; it adds a new dimension to personal life. The relationship between person and community—as between person and person—is never static and often far removed from that secure harmony which appears to preclude change and growth. Man needs solitude as he needs community; hours for meditation, prayer, and work in solitude are provided for in the rules of the most severe monastic orders. For all this, however, it is no less true that, as Martin Buber has expressed it, man becomes an I only by saying Thou, where the Thou precedes the I; the spiritual life of man begins with his greatest work, language, the organ of communication among brothers.[15] And when the great minds and hearts appear to reach the peak of solitude and seclusion, on Mount Sinai or Mount Tabor or in the desert, they are in intercourse with the Thou that is greater than their I. The fact that man transcends even the community does not prove that he is not rooted in it.

15. Martin Buber, *I and Thou*, 1922, and Eugen Rosenstock-Huessy, *Der Atem des Geistes*, 1951.

In other words, there is essentially no such thing as either individualism or collectivism. The individual without the community is a blindly drifting atom; the aggregation of drifting atoms is a manipulatable collective. As the person emancipates himself from the community, his self-inflation is his frustration and the degradation of the community. As the collective is made supreme, both person and community are degraded. As the person and the community are interdependent, nurturing and sustaining each other, they are of equal dignity, and their proper balance—never stable under constantly varying conditions of life but always instinctively sought—is the health of man and society, beyond any calculation of expediency and efficiency. The dialectical unity of person and community, of man and society, of freedom and order is created, as is everything else, by the supreme power of love.[16]

16. That the supreme power to create—the omnipotence of God—is paradoxically identical with the supreme love, which is the complete renunciation and abnegation of power, self, and ultimately life; that the supreme love, which is the complete renunciation of power and life, is precisely the supreme power to create—this is the central dogma of Christianity. Even such humanists as are much inclined to religion—unitarians and ethicists—regard it as the great stumbling block because they imagine that in order to submit to it they would be required to give up arithmetic: how can three be one? That the central mystery of creation must be denied because the human mind cannot fully grasp it; that there cannot be anything that the human mind cannot lock up in its simple formulas of the type "two and two make four"—this is the dogma that rationalism opposes to Christian dogma. Hence the supreme power of the supreme renunciation of power does not exist. Hence love does not create the person and the community in one and the same act. Hence either the individual is, in his own interest, the creator of society, or the society is the creator of the individual. Hence we must have either individualism or communism. Q.E.D.

We are far from saying that only Christians can be good democrats: the facts would militate against this, and if it were true, then it would be disastrous in a de-Christianized world. What we do say is that non-Christians can be good democrats only because they have in themselves the Christian reminiscences; or in other words, that democracy presupposed and is derived from the bipolar unity of person and community, liberty and equality, which modern scientific thought is constitutionally unable to understand but which is implied in the Christian doctrine of love

This Judeo-Christian understanding of love as the creative and redeeming force is altogether different from that of the Oriental high civilizations, where love, as in the West, heals isolation, separation, and loneliness, but does it totally by absorbing the individual into the mystical union where all become one. Individuation in the East is considered identical with suffering, and suffering disappears only as individuality disappears in the great fire of mystical love. Love in the West is love between persons, and they become persons precisely by loving and being loved. That is why love implies liberty and justice; love can be given and received only in freedom (this is the paradoxy of a "commandment of love"), and it longs to give the loved person that which he needs and is entitled to in order to be what his maker intended him to be. Without justice—i.e., the supreme respect for the rights of the loved person, among which there is the right to liberty—there is no love between persons. That is why Christianity is the hopeful, optimistic religion, confirming and comforting life in the midst of all its troubles, the opposite of any Oriental principles of negation or abnegation, and indeed so insistent on personality as to teach the resurrection of the body and the belief in God's merciful love making us whole in spite of all our sins.

Community in the Judeo-Christian tradition is constituted by love and organized by justice in liberty, because it is community of persons. This is the shining and warming light in our life. There are no justice and liberty in the fire of mystical love, which melts individuality into union. Nor are there justice and liberty in communism, whose cold fire—solidarity born of class interest—burns personality down into collectivity. It is logical that there should be no justice nor liberty when all have identical interests, while justice and liberty are the organizing forces in the community of love which is the community of persons. Hence also is it logical that the collective which is the identity of interests should require, and produce, the homogeneity of its members which makes them and their interests identical, while the uniqueness of the person transcends regularities and is, from

supreme; and that, cut off from that root by social rationalism, democracy is in grave danger.

the point of view of the collective, nothing but "contradiction." Interest unites those who are alike, love unites those who are different. For the class interest is the stronger the more the members of the class are alike; while it is the differences between persons—between man and woman, old and young—which make each richer by his share in the life of the other and make of the diversity of unique persons the wealth of the community. The contrast between communism and Christianity is at no other point more glaring than in the homogeneity created by interest and the diversity overarched by love. We do not say that communism is not possible; we do say that it is possible only at the price of the uniqueness and diversity of persons. Is there sense in having ever more millions of copies of exactly the same specimen? A sense other than the purely mechanical sense of multiplied efficiency and power? The diversity of unique persons in the community is an abridged version of the infinite variety of finite forms in which the infinite power of the Creator manifests itself.

But man is fallen man, and the community is a structure built by fallen, unjust men. For a sociological discussion the institutions of society are in the center. Like everything in human life, they are ambivalent—necessary to sustain life and dangerous to the spontaneous growth of life—not only through their unavoidable rigidity but even more through the injustices that were built into them. Their rigidity, as Casserley has wisely remarked, is salutary and beneficial, in that it gives man the fixed rules and forms about which he need not bother when using them, for which he does not carry responsibility, whose quasi-automatic operation permits him to concentrate his limited strength and time on the things essential to him personally. Nobody is strong, free, and creative enough to build his whole life, every gesture and every word, in terms of strict personal self-expression; the institutions and conventions of society put at his disposal a limited choice of proven and accepted forms, which only an exceptional person in exceptional conditions will be able to break, while the ordinary members of the community will feel at home in them and find in the choice between them sufficient latitude for the expression of their ordinary feelings.

But by the same token they are shaped by these institutions and conventions, and it is here that the power of institutions over the souls of people becomes conspicuous. For it is not only the sustaining power of the institutions which is sociologically relevant; it is also their terrible power of distortion, their forcing on people a behavior which they would never choose of their own free will. The businessman whom an economic depression forces to dismiss his employees is sure not to enjoy it; he does it because he cannot help doing it, as he is losing his business capital. He is not immoral; the institutions are. This durability and persistence is the reason for the emphatically religious relevance of institutions. This once more is the power of the commandment of justice—that is, of just institutions—in flagrant contradiction to the sentimental interpretation of love as a purely spiritual relationship between bodiless souls, as taught by too many preachers.

It is all very well to infer that our institutions should be changed. But in the first place, they are quite likely to persist for a while. We may change something, but we shall not rebuild all institutions at once. We may clear some slums in our city, establish some playgrounds and some schools, etc., but we cannot rebuild the city wholesale; its layout, its streets, and its squares remain what our ancestors made them and will form the framework in which our successors live. And secondly, if and when the institutions are changed, the new institutions are likely to develop their corresponding shortcomings and temptations unless we come close to a miracle. For if it is true that our institutions sustain and distort us, it is also true that the reform of those institutions, inspired as it is by the commandment of justice and removing one particular incorporation of injustice, carries in it other forms of injustice. For in reacting to those institutions negatively, we are no less conditioned by them and may be inclined to overrate the avoidable bad in them and the promise of good in the reform—nay, to underrate the opposite dangers in the reform, which happen to be our own particular dangers. As we begin to realize the power of institutions over man, the severity of our judgment on our predecessors and adversaries will be mitigated, and our confidence in our own power and justice will be reduced to a modest and reasonable measure—no small contribution of Christian ethics to social cohesion and responsibility.

It should not be inferred that essentially nothing can be done, and that the commandment falls flat. This would be true only if this were a static world, if life were not life. But life is movement and aspiration, and if doubt, defeat, and frustration are part of it, so are achievement and fulfillment. Neither one is final, but either one is real for a time, and either one may turn into its opposite in due course. Nay, it is only against the background of possible frustration that it makes sense to speak of fulfillment—and the other way round. If we shall certainly not establish justice forever, this is no reason not to try to establish it for our time or for as limited a period of time as conditions permit, thus leaving to our children their hopes and aspirations, which will be their life, as their inspiration will be different from ours, even though coming from the same commandment of justice.

Liberty and Equality

There is no doubt that justice always includes a measure of equality, and that in our own time equality has come to serve as a real criterion of the justice to be established. Thus Maritain, one of the few really consistent and profound believers in progress toward equality, rests his belief on the confidence that "evangelical inspiration" is doing its "quiet work in the lay conscience," the conscience of the common people; if not in Christians because they are too timid, then in heretics and atheists, as in the French Revolution. It is true that heretics and atheists do not know whence the call comes, but they hear it and follow it. We have argued that this cannot simply be progress, that it also is tragedy because the heretics and atheists, cut off from the source, cannot understand the profundity of the call and their own need for the quickening power of its source.

But Maritain's interpretation of modern democracy in the light of the pseudo-atheist program of "liberty, equality, and fraternity" is unassailable.[17]

Everything in the institutions of democracy hinges on the reconciliation of liberty and equality, which the rationalist development has torn asunder and now locates at opposite extremes of its fateful dialectic. Liberty and equality are the two halves of democracy; equal liberty is required for democracy. But this is what rational science cannot understand; it can only prove that the two are irreconcilable. This is precisely the failure of the two wings of social rationalism, that they destroyed equality by developing liberty and lost liberty when forcing equality. And yet every true democrat believes in liberty and equality, in their union, their identity, as did Jefferson and Lincoln. If the mutually exclusive opposites of rationalist science are reconciled and united in the vision of democracy, the source of the vision can be only in the people's prerational memory, in their religious inheritance, their "evangelical inspiration."

Liberty and equality are irreconcilable in rationalist systems because men are not naturally equal: equality makes them unfree, and liberty makes them unequal. But equal they are as children of God. And free they are as children of God. For we are taught that man has been created in the image of the Creator —that is, creative himself, capable of adding to God's creation. Creativity is the supreme manifestation of freedom: man is free because he is creative. And all men are God's children, unequal in talents but equal in personal rank before Him. The children of the family are also unequal in nature, in vigor and talents, but equal in the family in the sense that oppression and exploitation of one by another are not permitted. The freedom of man created in the image of God and the brotherhood of all God's children—these are the two essentials of democracy, and they are one.

Democracy needs leaders, to be sure; but they must humbly remember that power corrupts and that, to quote Maritain again, the common people, by and large, have a chance of err-

17. *Christianisme et Démocratie*, 1945; also in an American edition.

ing a little bit less than the powerful, not because the common
people are more intelligent but because they are less tempted.[18]
It is the special glory of the French democracy to have ringingly
proclaimed that liberty and equality can be united only in the
brotherly city; but this is more profoundly true than the rationalists of the French Revolution imagined. Liberty and

18. This author knows only one other argument of equal power for
democratic equality. It is the content of Alvin Johnson's essay "The Faith
of a Skeptic," reprinted in his *Essays on Social Economics* (New York, 1954).
The author, incomparably versed in the history of human work—experienced farmer, classical philologist, economist, and economic historian—
explains how the anonymous common man in unswerving loyalty tilled the
soil throughout thousands of years and thereby preserved the continuity of
life, but invented and developed, in addition, the countless clever tricks
by which well-being and culture were made possible in different countries
in different ways, depending on the nature of climate and soil. Everything
hinges on the modesty and faith of the workingman since the higher
classes busied themselves with alternately erecting and demolishing short-
lived empires.

One may say that this is nothing new, that the socialist theory of labor
value tried to express the same idea by originally imparting value-creating
power only to hard bodily labor and directly deriving all higher culture
from the value-creating production of goods. The great difference, however, is that in socialist theory this is presented abstractly and meant
collectively: "Social labor" creates value in proportion to its quantity, and
its productivity "grows" in due course, quasi-automatically; while Alvin
Johnson presents to the reader the unending strain and inventive power
of the individual workingman as personal achievements. It is implied in
the Marxian tendency to make "social labor" the active person, as it were,
and extinguish the active person; in Johnson's presentation the real person appears with his real virtues, where "social labor" is nothing and the
active person is everything. In this way only can one arrive at the anti-
totalitarian democratic equality of persons. The tradition in which this
argument is conceived, in other words, is not that of Marxism but of
Jefferson and Lincoln.

Among political theoreticians, Carl J. Friedrich, in *The New Image
of the Common Man* (1950—second edition of a slightly differently titled
book of 1942), seems to be the only one who pursues the problem of the
common man's abilities and worthiness in terms of principle and tries to
draw therefrom lessons for the constitutional setup of democracy. His contention that the common man is superior to the experts and elitists, not by
intelligence but very much by character, come close to the position of
Maritain.

equality, irreconcilable in rationalist argument and torn asunder by the two systems of rationalist organization, are one in the vision of the Kingdom of God. And the less possible it is to realize liberty and equality in perfect and perennial institutions, the more it is vital for democracy to seek always a new orientation toward the vision of man's ultimate destiny. The inherent, quasi-deterministic dialectic of rationalism drives forth and back between individual rationality and collective rationality, inordinate liberty and tyrannical equality. The terrible logic of this movement between opposites cannot be broken on its own plane; it can only be transcended to the higher plane, where reason accepts and explores spiritual meaning instead of pretending to substitute itself for it.

Social rationalism ends in defeat because it has set itself a task too big for scientific reason. Our system of social knowledge has to be rebuilt on a new foundation and in a new framework. This implies, however, that the fall of social rationalism is not the end of rational endeavor. On the contrary, once freed from the impossible task of determining its own objectives, rational endeavor acquires a purpose and a meaning once more. If rational endeavor enlightens us on how to establish or re-establish justice in social life, how to reconcile liberty and equality in changing human institutions, how far the two can so be reconciled, what is possible and what is impossible of achievement by way of such institutional incorporation, and how to change institutions in order to preserve their supreme meaning under changing circumstances, then rational endeavor is worthy of the highest ambition.

Nor does such a change of scientific structure invalidate the honest and ingenious efforts of past and present generations. When the Copernican system superseded the Ptolemaic one, the teachings had to be translated, as it were, into a new language; but they were thereby preserved, not lost. It is true that social techniques taught without genuine spiritual orientation produce spiritual anarchy and lend themselves to use and abuse by clever manipulators. But these same techniques are indispensable for substantiating, materializing, incorporating, and thereby validating spiritual meaning. Christianity is incarnation. The unity of liberty and equality is the Christian meaning of democracy; but democracy is not a doctrine of meaning, it is a system of meaningful institutions. Institutions, however, are not revealed, they require rational building. In a system of Christian social thought, scientific endeavor finds its supreme validation.

It is perfectly true, and most fortunate, that other continents have other traditions, symbols, and beliefs, which may converge with ours. This is the hope of the world. But it also is emphatically true that the Western community cannot be revitalized and reorganized out of Chinese or Indian wisdom, much as this wisdom may occasionally inspire individual Western students. A community lives on its own cultural tradition and can find its inspiration only in the quiet work of that atmosphere. We do not know whether Maritain's trust in the growth of Christian conscience in the Western world is justified. But at any rate, if democracy is to live, it can live in the future only as Christian democracy. For the belief in democracy presupposes a belief in things higher than democracy.

The "New Birth of Freedom"

There is a serious religious objection to the foregoing. The religious commandment, in its Mosaic or prophetic form or in that of the great commandment of the New Testament, is always an appeal to man's essential freedom. But religion is at the same time the doctrine of man's fall, which is his enslavement to sin and which makes the commandment rebound impotent. We came close to this central conflict—but avoided it for the time being—in the discussion of the compulsory power of institutions and their built-in injustices over the soul of man; the special institutional setting seems to determine man's actions. Engaged as we were in the exploration of the religious commandment, we contented ourselves with the conclusion that it is precisely their formidable power which makes the institutions relevant to religious ethics or, in other words, makes the commandment of social justice an integral element in Christian piety. We did not yet face the question of how the power of institutions over men shall be broken by men subject to that power.

In a way, our discussion so far has been on the plane of the Old Testament. There is nothing wrong with this, and many readers whose religious interests center in ethics will find such a discussion conclusive. But it is incomplete, as the Old Testament is indispensable but incomplete. The commandment is to give us guidance in the use of our freedom so as to keep it from straying and abuse—but where in this discussion is the place of human corruption? The Old Testament introduces man from the very beginning as created in the image of his Creator—that is, as creative himself—and with increasing clarity also strives to orient fallen man's freedom toward loving-kindness and justice as the criterion of restored partnership in God's work. It is as if the Old Testament refused to recognize the fact of the Fall and tried to undo it by ever more moving appeals. But "the good that I would do I do not and the evil that I would not do that I do—wretched man that I am" (Romans 7:19–20). The New Testament accepts the fact and understands that it cannot be undone but must be overcome by an altogether new dispensation: salvation in spite of the Fall. This is continuation but climax—a climax which could never have come without the preparation but nevertheless does not follow logically from that preparation. What of religious ethics on this plane?

Be it understood that there is a world of difference between the "impossible possibility" (Reinhold Niebuhr) for fallen man to follow God's call, and the absolute impossibility for a creature of nature to step outside the rules of his life; the question is whether man is under God or under nature alone. Not that nature is not God's; but the man "created in God's image" is not exhaustively described in terms of necessities or regularities which preclude creative freedom. In theological language, the "impossible possibility" receives its character as "possibility"— which is not necessity but freedom—from God and its "impossibility" from man's fall, which God has made possible but not necessary; while God has given nature the strict rules which preclude both freedom and sin so that a purely "natural" man, not being free, would not be able to sin. Nevertheless, the ritualists and legalists of the Pharisean type, frightened by the proclamation of the "impossible possibility," seek shelter under a strict code of behavior and institutions which should give them protection from sin by limiting their God-given freedom, just as nature's children find shelter from freedom and from sin under the inescapable strictness of nature's rule. The Old Testament introduces man's freedom, and with it the possibility of sin; the Pharisees and legalists, frightened by sin, try to undo man's creative freedom.

This tragic tangle can be resolved by referring to our earlier methodogical discussion in Chapter III. The answer to the problem of freedom in the midst of necessities was there given by introducing a power in man which is normally—"regularly"— dormant but intermittently aroused to rise above the necessities and regularities and which intermittently sets a new beginning outside and above those earlier necessities. This solution was characterized as purely formal, methodological; statistical regularity and causal necessity are not in its way, and the way is open for the scientific recognition of man's freedom and religious responsibility. But all this presupposes, of course, that the purely formal assumption of such an intermittently active power in man can be given a content, that the logical possibility can be translated into a human and historical reality.

What is called liberty in formal terminology, in the sense of unpredictability, is "rebirth" in Christian experience: the self-transcendence which denies the former self and sets a "new birth," a new beginning on a higher level of life: the "regeneration," the self-renewal, which may appear in spectacular or unspectacular form but cannot be understood from former conditions and, being itself a new spiritual creation, makes new action possible. "The wind bloweth where it listeth, and thou hearest the sound thereof but canst not tell whence it cometh and whither it goeth: so is everyone that is born of the spirit" (John 3:8). This is the rise over "the law," be "the law" understood as the ritual and legal rule in which the Pharisees and legalists sought and seek salvation, or as the natural necessities or regularities which appear as the contents of life and guarantors of harmony to our scientists: the word "the law" covers both in that it sets normalcy supreme and exclusive. Hence the New Testament is not lyrical or psychic or mystical but only exact when it promises us "the glorious freedom of the children of God" (Rom. 8:21) because "the truth shall make us free" (John 8:32): free from "the law" through "rebirth," "birth of the spirit," regeneration, self-transcendence.

The rebirth of man, then, is the work of the divine love, undeserved by fallen man, mysterious as the blowing of the wind, unpredicted and unpredictable. "God is love, and He that dwelleth in love dwelleth in God, and God in him" (1 John 4:16). What Lincoln calls "a new birth of freedom" is the work of redeeming love—it is love which makes man new, makes him free from the laws of the Pharisees and the scientists, and makes his formerly blind freedom seeing, so as not to go astray again. This is how the story of creation is brought not to its completion but rather to its beginning: by the revelation of the creative power as the power of redeeming love.

Examples were given above (Chapter III); more specific examples will be given later (Chapter X). Suffice it here to say two things. In the first place, in public discussion it makes little difference whether one uses the vaguer Old Testament terminology and speaks of a new sense of loving-kindness and justice awakening in man, or the more accurate New Testament terminology focusing on rebirth. The more accurate version, if insisted upon to the exclusion of the broader version, carries with it the danger of a new Phariseeism, which anyway is implied in every orthodoxy—whoever does not claim to be reborn cannot "dwell in love." But it is precisely the "dwelling in love" which is the true criterion for being reborn, rather than the other way round. The moral danger of the new Christology is a special case of the general moral danger to Christians in making the divine grace a matter of their personal pride. Theology is indispensable to logical minds, but it is not religion and must not be used to disrupt the community of the faithful.

In the second place, "the new birth of freedom" is not an event in merely individual or private life, as some narrow-minded pietism would have it. It is a historical event, in which we are given a new orientation and direction for the right use of our freedom by a new vision of the supreme love and justice and, derived from it, a new possibility of loving justice among men under the concrete technical and institutional conditions of the day. To repeat it, this is not a matter of absolute unselfishness, which never exists among men; it is a matter of profound anxiety, profound shock, revealing to us the flimsiness of the foundations on which we have built our life and which is about to collapse and bury us under the ruins. Repentance is part of rebirth; [19] repentance is precisely the act of regretting our past actions and demonstrating thereby that we have grown beyond and above them to a new and higher level of our life.

This analysis is implied in the famous phrase in which Toynbee describes the possibility of historical societies renewing themselves and gaining a new lease on life: the "creative response to the challenge of the emergency." The phrase is a Christian one or at any rate close to a Christian one. One cannot say, however, that Toynbee has put it to full use, since he finds his examples in different civilizations at different times, a Christian possibility in any society. The less this is objectionable in itself—*anima naturaliter Christiana*—the more urgent is the question whether this Christian possibility is not more intimately associated with Christian societies than scattered throughout the world.

Since St. Augustine it has been common knowledge of students of intellectual history that Christianity has constituted history in the concrete sense of a movement directed toward a goal, in which everything that is fragmentary will be whole, everything frustrated will be fulfilled, everything imperfect will be perfect. This goal, defined as the Kingdom of God, cannot be reached in history but is anticipated in our every judgment on events in history as creatively revealing new possibilities of life that struggle, often in vain, to come into their own. That is, Christian history is not success, as post-Christian secularists and scientists seem constantly to demand. It remains full of frustration and tragedy but still it lives on hope, is sustained by hope,[20] and is totally distinguished from events outside Christian history, which have been correctly described by pagan philosophers

19. "Reue and Wiedergeburt" is the title of a beautiful essay by Max Scheler.
20. Cf. Reinhold Niebuhr, *Faith and History*, 1949.

and historians of the pre-Christian era and again by Spengler, the pagan philosopher-historian of our own post-Christian day, as moving in the hopeless circle of nature from birth to death, without a way out, without meaning, without a goal other than death. Christian society lives in nature too, and is subject to its law of rotation, but this is not its full story. For its hope for a final perfection in God's own time is given an earnest in this life in the experience of "the new birth of freedom under God," which is always a possibility, whether realized or not. The Kingdom of God is not a historical possibility, but the new birth of freedom is.

Christian philosophy of history has been renewed by Paul Tillich in his doctrine of "Kairos." [21] "Kairos" is the destiny-filled point of time in which an entire future is concentrated, or in which this future breaks into and through the routine of life and renews life. The term "Kairos"—a Greek word to designate the right time, opposed to "Chronos," the empty mathematical-mechanical time—is employed in the New Testament and particularly by Paul to designate the decisive turn of the times which is brought by the life, death, and resurrection of Christ. For in this event the world is conquered by love; the divine in temporal, historical, unique form invades history and transmutes it. Hence Tillich speaks of the secondary "Kairoi" which are derived from the primary one, which reflect it by aiming at a fuller humanity in new forms of life, and which leave the old forms behind. On the other hand, the fact that they are "secondary" is grounded in the finiteness of their effects, which, coming in historical form, exhaust themselves in history, while the one great "Kairos" transforms history as a whole and removes it. In other words, salvation is not possible within history, but the "new birth of freedom" is. Now one may have doubts on philosophy of history because it looks for some kind of law in history. The "new birth of freedom" is certainly not subject to any law; it is rarely possible and may also be missed. But the

21. For the first time in an article under this title in the periodical *Die Tat,* 1922, reprinted in *The Protestant Era,* 1946. But this doctrine is central to Tillich's understanding of the world and is for this reason more or less explicitly developed in most of his not purely theological writings.

Reason and Faith in Modern Society

material of philosophy of history is history itself, and it teaches that the "new birth of freedom" is possible.

Lincoln's great vision is, in our own day, the vision of Jacques Maritain: the trust in "the quiet work of the evangelical inspiration in the lay consciences." But it is more than a vision in the majestic work of Eugen Rosenstock-Huessy, who has presented—against Spengler's glorification of naked imperial force driving to the death of its victims and finally to its own death—Christian history as the history of the creative achievements in which, step by step, the dangerous problems of Occidental history were solved.[22] Periodic renewals break through the cycle of nature and start history anew on the new level, even though evil, too, assumes new forms there. Christian history thus creates a unique and meaningful sequence of achievements, each of which is made imperative by the unsolved problems of the preceding phase and will likewise give rise to further dynamic urges. For a thousand years of incessant stress and strain—since the imperial and monastic revolution of the tenth century, the Gregorian revolution of the eleventh century, and the Franciscan revolution of the thirteenth century—Europe has not been broken; it has always done that which could not have been predicted, in creative response to the challenge of the emergency. It has preserved its unity and tradition throughout all revolutions by limiting each of them to its own national section and integrating its spiritual, political, and social results into reforms adopted in all other national sections so as to present a picture of an army "marching in echelons" from goal to goal. It has thus conquered new problems and created new forms of life at every step because Christianity has taught it the mystery of regeneration, the power to rise above one's past failures. All the weaknesses and vices of man, to be sure, harass him on the new level as they did on the old, and for each problem solved a new

22. *Out of Revolution, Autobiography of Modern Man*, 1938. The original version of this book, *Die Europäischen Revolutionen und der Charakter der Nationen* (1931, reissued 1951) is differently organized and uses partly different material. Cf. by the same author: *The Christian Future, or The Modern Mind Outrun*, 1946, and *Heilkraft und Wahrheit*, 1951. Most recently, *Soziologie*, 2 vols., 1958.

one emerges. There is thus no room for a utopian belief in redemption through history, but what matters is the experience that, after all, problems can be solved and new levels reached. Christianity, in other words, has taught man a new dimension of his life; it has invalidated the classical doctrine of the law of the natural cycle controlling and frustrating his aspirations; it has given him hope.

Under the pressure of the distress into which the perverted Marxist solution of the proletarian problem has plunged the world, the Western societies renew themselves even today, for all their weakened spirituality, and seek and find solutions for problems whose very existence had been denied a few decades ago.[23] Rosenstock presents this creative reaction to the threat of Marxism explicitly as a progressive dialectic, and we have followed him in this and have contrasted it with Marxism's own spurious dialectic, which, spurning creative liberty for the sake of scientific necessity, constitutes nothing but a vicious circle. To the uniqueness of the person created in the image of God and reborn of the spirit corresponds the uniqueness of the community, which renews itself out of a renewed and higher vision of its life, a new birth of its freedom.

To sum up a lengthy discussion: Liberty contains in itself no guarantee of its use in the service of the good only. Man is not a pure vessel of reason, much less a pure vessel of justice and love; and his freedom, hence, is ambiguous, being freedom for good and evil alike. That is why man, endowed by his Maker with freedom and power in order that he can creatively contribute toward the richness of God's creation, is also given the commandment, to keep him from abusing his freedom and to show him the direction in which to use it. This is the Biblical understanding of man; as it dies out, liberty degenerates into selfishness and disorder. But liberty can be born anew, as Lincoln put it; it recovers its creative dimension if it is guided by a reawakened sense of responsibility and justice—that is, if it recognizes the supremacy of justice born of love. The decisive event is the new birth of freedom, the reawakening of the sense

23. In the middle of the last century a German liberal wrote a book on "the so-called social question."

of responsibility and justice. "Reawakening" is a mysterious act beyond the power of our will; the reawakening of the sense of responsibility and justice cannot be achieved by conscious moral effort. On the contrary, the very effort is proof that the reawakening is already in the process of being achieved; that which has mysteriously become possible is now being actualized. This implies, on the other hand, that the moral effort, although not primary, is indispensable. It is man's contribution to the new birth of freedom.

IX

Socialism Versus Economism

and Statism[1]

The Circular Reasoning of Economism
and Governmentalism

WHAT the preceding chapters have tried to show can be summarized as follows: Democracy, defined as union of liberty and equality, sprang from religion and continues to draw its furtive inspiration from the moral inheritance left by religion. For potent historical reasons, however, democracy became officially severed from its religious source and ran into decline and crisis as liberty and equality proved irreconcilable on the plane of rational principle (Chapter VIII). The doctrine of liberty came more and more to lean toward rational individualism as a form in which liberty was to be realized at the expense of community and basic equality (Chapters I–II); and its opposite, Marxist socialism, originally designed to restore the balance, was driven by the same rationalist logic to reject liberty for the sake of equality, understood as uniformity, and logically ended in totalitarianism (Chapters IV–VII). The regeneration of democracy thus is a task of both spiritual and institutional reconstruction (Chapters IX and X).

In the present chapter we concentrate on the reconsideration of socialism, in both its institutional and its philosophical aspects. In its institutional program socialism must become what it was originally designed to be: the corrective for the institutional defects of liberalism rather than the alternative to liberalism. Philosophically, this presupposes the recognition of standards

---

1. For this chapter see the article "On Economic Planning," *Social Research,* Sept. 1950, reprinted in *Wirtschaftssysteme und Gesellschaftssysteme,* Chapter II.

higher than both socialism in the traditional sense of the word and liberalism; and the problem is particularly keen and grave because, being younger and more advanced in rationalist logic than liberalism, traditional socialism has come to oppose its own historical materialism to any and all spiritual claims, which, according to this doctrine, merely reflect material interests. On both counts, naturally, the discussion would be worthless if it were limited to academic speculation; on both counts, however, as throughout this book, the task is to draw together, and interpret in terms of principle, existing tendencies and movements. For it is experience—more specifically, confutation by experience—in the light of which old ideas are liable to reconsideration and revision; and it is, in our case, the appropriation of the Marxist doctrine by communism which forces liberty-loving socialists to re-examine their system of thought and institutions if they honestly believe that socialism is the road to liberty.

In the traditional and generally accepted view of socialism, the problem appears insoluble. Socialism is defined as political control of things economic, as opposed to laissez-faire, which is the autonomous financial control of things economic. The nature of the controlling power determines the goal toward which the control is oriented. In either case it is efficiency—technological efficiency as yielding profit in the one case, governmental and military efficiency in the other. In both views the dilemma is clear cut; it is between the power of the state or the government and private financial power. Inasmuch as liberty is understood as freedom from governmental control, it is sought in laissez-faire; inasmuch as laissez-faire is understood to produce undesirable social effects, justice or equality is sought in governmental control. The ultimate sanction of the power of government is in physical compulsion; the ultimate sanction of economic power, in the threat of starvation. Governmental power, if unchecked, is tyranny; financial power, if unchecked, is exploitation. Now according to the traditional view, socialism, for the sake of justice, restores that governmental control over things economic which laissez-faire had destroyed for the sake of liberty. This again is, in a way, the theme of the two first parts of this book.

If the resort to political control is not simply to be the completion of a circle—from the despotism of the absolute state through the exploitation by laissez-faire back to the new absolute state—a modification must be introduced, and the modification on which traditional socialism seems to stake its entire program lies in the democratic technique of making government representative of and dependent on the governed. In this way liberty is supposed to be added to justice. The Founding Fathers of this republic, however, were wise in not staking too much on that device of representation through election, even when the power of government was limited by economic power; they rather added to the technique of election a number of quite different devices to protect and promote political and personal liberty. Indeed, the democratic technique of making absolute government representative of and dependent on the people has not yet been found and cannot be found. In the Soviet case it has not even been sought: the government is supposed to be representative of the "true" aspirations of the people, but is not dependent on the people as long as the people do not surely understand their own "true" aspirations. Even apart from this special theory, in a renewed absolute state the disparity of power between the government and the governed would generally be such as to make the semblance of representation a farce —and this more surely and more inescapably today than ever before, because the so-called means of communication are strictly one-way affairs and confront any government with an almost irresistible temptation to increase its efficiency by manipulating and standardizing the minds of the people.

The premise of the dilemma, however, is the definition of socialism as political control of things economic, and the premise is wrong. The word "socialism" derives from society. It denotes the control of things economic by society—a thing totally different from control by the state. The use of the word "society" in socialist terminology has survived to this day, but its meaning has been lost because of the ever closer equation of society with the state; socialists have long employed the words "political control" and "control by society" interchangeably. This is due to the influence of Marxism, which has always concentrated on action of an emphatically political nature, although the original meaning of the word "socialism" proper is still preserved, in perverted form, in the final Marxist utopia of the stateless society. Oddly enough, the Communists give this final phase defined as stateless society the name "communism," while the word "socialism" itself denotes to them the preceding phase, that of all-inclusive governmental control, or dictatorship, of all things. The confusion in terminology demonstrates the loss of meaning.

Socialism means control of things economic by society; it is equally opposed to both control of things economic by the state—governmentalism—and control by the autonomous forces of economic life itself—economism. This meaning of the word is confirmed by a reflection on the historical circumstances of its origin. If the current view on socialism were right, mankind would forever be doomed to be driven around in a vicious circle between the two opposites, the excesses of state power and of economic power; socialism thus understood would not make any ultimate sense. But the early socialists were much too near in time to the excesses of the power of the absolute state to turn to this power for salvation from the economic power of capitalism. Socialism clearly is conceived as the way out of the dilemma, the third and superior alternative in a triangular relationship. The fact that some of these early socialists turned politically anarchist—notably the great Proudhon—must be traced not only to the reckless optimism on human nature which they shared with the entire liberal and democratic movement of their day but also to their insight into the nature of society as an organized and organizing force apart from and superior in principle to both government and economy.

Government and economy, in principle, are special functions of society and wield specific powers for their specific purposes. Government is in charge of public order and peace, to protect the life of society; the economy is in charge of feeding society. It has already been said that their powers are the drastic and brutal powers of constraint by the threat of physical violence and by that of starvation. Both being equipped with the most formidable powers, they are constantly tempted to emancipate themselves from control by the society which they are designed to serve and to set themselves up as supreme. In so doing they set the standards for the life of society itself, ultimately absorbing it into themselves or crushing it between them. This is the story of our age: commercialization in the West and totalitarianism in the East; the subordination even of art and learning to commercial standards guarded by art dealers, concert agencies, and publishing firms; or to standards of political expediency and legitimacy guarded by an all-controlling and uncontrolled political state. Governmentalism and economism stand in exact correspondence, and each pretends in its self-inflation to represent the whole of society.

What Is Society?

What, then, is society? It is the aggregation of smaller and larger spontaneous groupings and associations in neighborhood relations, civic activities, cooperative agencies of an egalitarian or unegalitarian nature for economic life, recreational arrangements, educational institutions, worshiping communities, and so forth. The smallest spontaneously formed group, the family, is rightly considered the cell of social life. The fabric of society is no less dense and solid for being held together by purely spiritual controls, more often than not of a subconscious nature. This is done, that isn't done: self-respect and respect by others demand compliance on the part of the members of the group. Society in all its groups and as a whole wields the power of moral injunction and prohibition. It is, on the other hand, in constant flux, subject to constant spontaneous rebuilding and renewal; new ideas emanate from individuals and groups and change the life of the whole and the character of the persons who live it. But old or new, flexible or rigid, society is organized life; it canalizes the activities of its members. Its rule is effective even more in the form of self-respect than in that of group pressure; and it is most effective by the rigorous limits which it sets to the actions of groups and individuals.

Society is held together by the spontaneous convictions of the people and by the consequent disciplines to which they spontaneously submit in the common pursuit of their spontaneously conceived common ends, as in the family or the study group or the sport club or the worshiping congregation. If moral convictions and commonly held disciplines constitute society, then the background from which society springs is the spirituality of the people. Spirituality certainly does not preclude materiality, in which spirituality is incorporated, but controls it and gears it to divergent spiritual ends. The spirituality of the people is religion; philosophy, including the autonomous ethic derived from it, is not a matter of the people but of philosophers. Philosophy and ethics seem to guide the people so long as the philosophers themselves are still permeated by the atmosphere of religion which they attempt to rationalize; or when the philosophy is inflated to a pseudo religion, which appeals to the religious needs of the people, to their sense of awe, belonging, and meaning. In both cases it is the religion behind the philosophy which makes the philosophy a historical force.

Religion, which imparts to people the sense of awe, belonging, and meaning, does not speak to them in the conceptual language of philosophers. Theology does, and must do so; the logical structure of religious experiences and teachings must be explored and systematized by those among the faithful whose business it is to think, and their service in answering doubts, establishing derivations, and interpreting the meaning of Biblical events is very great. But theology is neither religion nor a substitute for religion, it only translates religion into conceptual language. Religion itself speaks the colorful language of stories, narratives, sermons, parables, myths, songs, feasts, and customs; and it is understood by everyone according to his station and age. The child's understanding begins with Christmas, the adult's with Easter. The vast panorama unfolds only as life proceeds; its sublimity and profundity are not felt by the inexperienced. But there are those who do not ever need experience, the transported souls; and there are those who do not yet need it, the children. The spiritual and moral life in man is religion, and the power of cohesion in society is religion. More generally, then, the historical force of religion works in and through society; and what ultimately constitutes society is religion. To the religious mind it is an abomination to speak of the historical force of religion through society; how much watering down, how much abuse and perversion of the divine revelation is inevitably implied. To the social scientist the constitutive force of religion in society is the key to the understanding of the nature of society, which lies in spontaneous cohesion.

Hence, when society is strong, it keeps the separatist and imperialist aspirations of the state and of economic life in check. Neither the members of the government nor those of the business community are separated from the general flow of social life; they are members of society, delegated to those special functions but not there exempt from the general obligations of their membership in society. The stronger the society, the less can its functionaries in government and economic life afford to violate its moral principles; to do so does not even occur to them because the society is in them as in anybody else. A Christian society, e.g., cannot and need not have at its disposal a Christian state; such a thing does not exist except as a caricature. What a Christian society naturally has at its disposal is Christian statesmen, who are limited or inhibited in their freedom of action by the moral convictions in the people and in themselves. The fact that they often violate these convictions under pressure does not refute the statement; the important thing is that they often obey them. Lest the proposition about inhibitions appear too negative, it should be added that the positive actions of such men, their understanding of their own task and that of their people, will be inspired and directed by those convictions; exalted by society as they are, they can contribute to shaping and reshaping those convictions by their actions. The two greatest examples of such men in modern history are William of Orange and Abraham Lincoln.[2]

As society and the forces constitutive of it weaken, however,

2. John Courtney Murray, S.J., in several brilliantly erudite and sagacious papers conceived in the natural-law tradition of his church, proves that the state has a function all its own and is not simply a tool of the church. His reasoning can be adapted to the above distinction between state and Christian society.

the separatist and imperialist tendencies in state and business take over, push ahead, and develop the inherent logic of their special functions in a kind of slow cancerous growth. Private financial power and its twin and opposite, the power of the state, begin to develop their own pseudo religions within the framework of rationalism, which is the dissolution of the belief in the intangible suprarational values and the substitution for them of the tangible—the individual and the state—and the measurable—profits and guns. It has already been discussed how society, if understood as a means for ends pursued by individuals, may or may not appear the most expedient means in the individual case; and how society, if understood as the source of political power, is stripped of its moral essence. But these statements now appear too weak. As society weakens, its apparently irrational but real organization is destroyed and is replaced by a rationalist organization in terms of either business or the state, both of which lack essential moral authority and must increasingly depend on the efficiency of their controls.

No one has shown this in greater clarity than Karl Polanyi (*The Great Transformation,* 1944). His dramatic account of economic history from primitive society to our own day may well be said to be an inquiry into the nature and changing place of economic life in changing society. The systematic inquiry in the present chapter rests on Polanyi's historical vision. The center of his argument is that society consists of man and nature, i.e., man working in and on nature; that business in search of profit always existed at the outer fringe of society in international trade and finance but was always barred from the economic sphere of society proper, that is production, both rural and urban, which remained organized as part of society directly; that the absolute state of eighteenth-century rationalism, however, permitted the gradual absorption of man and nature into the labor and land markets organized by financial power for financial considerations; and that the resulting laissez-faire completed the dissolution of society into the all-inclusive market, the commercialized society, where man and nature are estranged from themselves, subject to foreign domination, and used as means of production. Social organization of man's life and work gives way to economic organization of society, the apparently irrational to the rational. And this result is accepted and approved by the Communist critics; their point is that the commercial organization of production is not yet rational enough and should be replaced by a governmentally imposed economic plan which absorbs both society and production into the new and absolutely rational state.

Hence, authentic socialism is to wrest economic and social life from control by economism and governmentalism and restore them to control by society. In our day that means control by democratic society. That man and society cannot live as mere means of production is revealed by the crisis of our time, which is a total crisis, a crisis of society and civilization. The fact that communism is not an answer at all, but would drive the crisis to a further head, can be seen from the diagnosis itself; it will be discussed in more detail below. Socialism, conceived as the way out, the third and superior alternative, is far from a halfway station between capitalism and communism, as even Toynbee asserts it to be; it cannot be that because a compromise between economism and governmentalism would not be a remedy to the malady represented by both: the destruction of society. To establish democratic society—that is, libertarian and equalitarian society—in control of the economic system is the clearly indicated task of socialism.

Critique of Economic Liberalism

It may be useful to delimit the case for neo-socialism from the neo-liberalism which is forcefully expanding these days, brilliantly represented in the English-speaking world by F. A. Hayek (*The Road to Serfdom*, 1944, and *Individualism and the Economic Order*, 1949) and Kenneth Boulding (*The Organizational Revolution*, 1953); and in the continental countries by such men as Walter Eucken, Alfred Müller-Armack, Wilhelm Röpke, and Alexander Rüstow. Schumpeter (*Capitalism, Socialism and Democracy*, 1942) comes close to the diagnosis given by the neo-liberals, but is separated from them by his positivistic outlook on the future. The neo-liberals too have rediscovered the vital significance for economic life of the original life of society, but they construe the relationship between society and economy in a way contrary to that of neo-socialism. They know that liberty cannot live without an order balancing and limiting it; but they locate all liberty in the free market and assert—in a way reminiscent of Adam Smith's argument from sympathy, previously discussed—that the struggle of man against man in the market is balanced and prevented from becoming disruptive by the cohesive power of a strong society. To them, hence, society is the sphere of order, whose health and vigor permit the economy to be a free-market economy without degenerating to class society and communism.

They assert, but never attempt to prove, that if society were healthy the economic crisis inherent in the free market of capitalism would be kept in tolerable bounds without deliberate regulation; combination of employment in industry with continued life and work in the countryside after the model of Switzerland is recommended as means for stability even in depression. Some of the neo-liberals advocate drastic action to break up monopoly and restore the genuine competitive order of the market. The stock objection against this proposition is that it is self-defeating because the elimination of monopoly from the market would require governmental interference of a strength and intensity incompatible with the liberal setup. This writer follows Schumpeter in regarding the monopoly issue in the dynamic flux of capitalism as grossly overrated. Incomparably more important for an honest liberalism are universal education, and the abolition of inheritance which Alexander Rüstow, following Franz Oppenheimer's social liberalism, proclaims as indispensable for equal opportunity.[3]

"The market" is not limited, however, to the production and distribution of industrial goods; it organizes, in addition, the use to be made of the original factors or production, labor

3. A keen and sagacious criticism of neo-liberal economic theory and policy on the basis of much of its literature is given by Hans Ritschl, *Die Grundlagen der Wirtschaftsordnung* (1954) in the section "Wirtschaftsordnung und Wirtschaftspolitik."

and land. The fact that the market largely fails this task and makes subsidiary measures imperative would probably be admitted by many liberals. For regulation by the market presupposes that supplies grow in response to rising price and diminish in response to falling price. But a wage reduction may force women and children to seek a supplement to the family income in the labor market; likewise a diminution of agrarian prices may lead to an expansion or intensification of agriculture; so that in both cases the evil is reinforcing itself and demands to be broken by intervention from without. The practice of economic policy has long been familiar with these problems, and so has been economic analysis for some time. But the neo-liberals talk about harmony of the market as if there were no labor market and no land market. For the market is oriented toward short-run, short-sighted efficiency but not toward long-run social effects, which demand labor protection and soil protection as well.

According to neo-socialism, the balance between freedom and order must be established within the economic organization itself, by an interlocking of market and planning agencies and by making many market agencies representative of different groups and aspirations rather than representative of the exponents of economism. According to neo-liberalism, this is the road to serfdom, because liberty is defined as the free pursuit of private ends. The strange thing in all neo-liberal writers is that they discover the significance of the autonomous life of society as a framework for a liberal economic system but steadfastly deny that the rediscovery of society could have any bearing on socialism too. The truth is that socialism derives from society and means the re-establishing of society in control of economic life. Neo-liberalism, equating as it does liberty with economism, is thereby too deeply entangled in the fatal polarity of economism and governmentalism in economic life to understand that socialism is the third alternative; it continues to define socialism as governmentalism. It merely wants to keep economism from slipping into governmentalism by tying it into the framework of society; it does not want society to "interfere"

in economic life. The brilliant performance of neo-liberal professors in Western Germany in building a highly successful
capitalism clinches the point.

It is gratifying to report, however, that the rigor of the
doctrinal position, while strictly kept to by Mises and Hayek, has
been abandoned by Röpke, Rüstow, and the younger Müller-
Armack, and has been replaced by the study of policies designed
to stop technical or social deficiencies in the operation of the
market by techniques "conforming to it" rather than overriding
it in the manner of bureaucratic fiat. A rich catalogue of measures legitimate in this light is gradually being worked out and
converging with analogous attempts in the neo-socialist camp by
the group of Karl Schiller and H. D. Ortlieb. The pertinent
writings of the present writer for more than thirty years have
had as their one goal the proof that "the market" is quite flexible
and can be used in the service of rather far-reaching reconstruction by monopolistic techniques on the demand side or the
supply side. In other words, what was characteristically called
"market socialism" from the 1920's on—to distinguish it from
the socialism of the equation system—has been consciously in
search of forms "conforming to the market." It would be instructive to study the points of agreement and the remaining
areas of disagreement between the two schools of thought.[4]

4. Even so, it would be highly unfair, in however brief a survey of the
debate on neo-liberalism, to leave unmentioned the fact that after the collapse of the National Socialist "command economy" and in the ensuing
general economic paralysis, of which liberalism seemed to be the only
logical beneficiary, Edgar Salin alone (in a number of articles in the Swiss
international periodical, *Kyklos,* founded by him) asserted the dignity of
genuine, historically trained scholarship and the realistic insight into the
political conditions of any economic system. He did that during the years
before the socialist critique, which seemed to be drawn into the collapse
of national socialism, formed itself anew. If anybody asks for the contribution of scholarship in this phase of history, he will here find the
answer demonstrated to him. The writer of these lines has not always
subscribed to the political conditions of economic life as formulated by
Salin in pre-Hitler days. For further corroboration a word on the Anglo-
Saxon critique of liberalism might be useful. A man of Herman Finer's
great gifts discredits even his legitimate objections by his rancor—what a
miserable, purely polemical title is his *Way to Reaction* if compared with

The controversy, then, centers in what we have here called "economism," which we have described in Part One of this book and have defined as the power of "economic life" to impose, through "the market," the rule of efficiency and profit upon society, forcing society to adjust itself to the rapidly changing requirements of a rapidly developing technology and commercialization. Efficiency and profit are the inherent goals of an economic management exempted from social obligations and moral inhibitions, and the fabulous success of economic activities so organized in raising living and health standards and strengthening political and military power is traceable to this single-minded concentration of all energy on one point.

But according to the neo-liberal theory, the free market operated by private property is the sole and infallible guarantor of personal and political liberty, while any tampering with it, any attempt to doctor its results for the sake of welfare or justice, would start us on the "road to serfdom."

We have criticized this line of thought in Chapter I from the point of view of social psychology and have shown that life-long, strenuous, and hazardous striving for material means makes that which is logically nothing but means into the final end of life, and the efficiency-minded individual into the dominant type. This is no theory: it is the experience of our time, and the ignominious, nowhere-else-to-be-found aspect of the industrial cities built in Europe and America in the nineteenth century makes the facts visible even to the blind.

In addition, the far too idyllic concept of the market, such as liberalism forms in its apologetic zeal, misjudges not only on the negative but also on the positive side, making it appear much too innocuous and much too trivial and thus seducing the critics too to condemn it on moral grounds and accept its achievements as if they were a matter of course. No critique of capitalism can be correct that does not recognize the formidable failure as the price that had to be paid for this tremendous

Hayek's *The Road to Serfdom*. Barbara Wootton's little book *Freedom Under Planning* (1945) is excellent as far as it goes but limited in its layout. And the wise John Maurice Clark in his *Alternative to Serfdom* (1945) hardly came to grips with the practical problems.

achievement. Capitalism cannot be judged in simple terms of
morality; it is tragedy on a heroic scale. It is more than doubtful
whether the unique development of productivity—i.e., of standards of living and health—which everybody wants, could have
been had without that unique concentration of all mental
energies on efficiency, which nobody wants.[5]

Nay, even the blessing of productivity turns into a curse
as the mere means multiply, as it were, automatically and without relation to human needs, so that finally our problem is no
longer the production of goods for an unsatisfied demand but
the production of a demand for goods. In the present chapter
we are concerned with this structure of production. If ever
increasing productivity gets us into trouble morally and internationally, as we have maintained, why then do we not stop
it? The answer is that we cannot do that—even if we wanted
to do it—because the "free economy" does not permit it. Industrial expansion had originally freely been chosen by free
individuals in the free market with brilliant results, but it has
now become compulsory: the compulsion to expansion has been
built into the physical structure of industry.

The autonomous structure of capitalism is characterized by
a most spectacular development of the steel and related industries, for purely market reasons and disregarding even the extra-
economic factor of armaments. It is those industries which have
to build machines for all industries, both to replace used-up
machines and to add new ones, either of the same kind or
heavier and costlier—quantitative and qualitative expansion.
Considering that five or six generations ago there were no industries worthy of the name, the steel industry has had to build,
within an amazingly short period of time, the entire tremendous
machine equipment of modern industrial society. In the process
of providing for such a staggering and constantly increasing
material expansion, the steel industry itself was forced to assume

5. Sombart is quite right in saying that nobody has ever praised
capitalism the way Karl Marx has done it. In this lies Marx's greatness, not
attained by any of his followers or by any of his critics. Tillich has coined
the concept of the demonic, to describe the transmoral achievement and
destructiveness of such great phases of history as capitalism.

Socialism Versus Economism and Statism 259

a corresponding size. Hence a steel industry of that size, in order to be fully and steadily employed, is now dependent on an undiminished pace of further industrial development and expansion. Our industrial system cannot live unless it expands because its central industry, in charge of providing the means of expansion, would be stricken by crisis and unemployment if expansion slowed down.[6]

The dynamics of capitalism is usually and rightly attributed to the rule of profit. Without profit, no production; hence progress of production for the sake of profit. But however correct this is, expansion is forced on us not only by social psychology but also by the physical structure of the industrial system itself. So little is the market the place of freedom.[7]

6. Kenneth Boulding, who is not only recognized as a leading economist but is appealed to as an authority for the Christian evaluation of economic life by official Protestant agencies in America, writes (in the volume *Religious Perspectives of College Teaching*, the Edward Hazen Foundation): "Economics is not primarily interested in human behavior as such, it is interested in the 'behavior of commodities.' The world of commodities is regarded as following its own laws of motion, like the planets of the solar system; the men who move them are not the focus of interests, any more than the angels, if any, who move the planets, are a focus of interest of the astronomer. . . . If human behavior is regular enough it can be neglected, just as the astronomers can neglect angels." This is exactly what Karl Marx has called the "fetishism of commodities." But Boulding continues undisturbedly: "Wicksteed established economics firmly as a general theory of choice under conditions of limited resources, and the student who has read his illustrations of the theory of value in terms of how much one should shorten family prayers in order to speed a parting guest to the train, or how high a cliff one should jump off to save a mother-in-law will have little doubt of the generality of economic principles. It is evident from the above also that economics cannot be accused of being materialistic. Economics clearly recognizes that all material objects are intermediate goods, mere means which serve the end of increasing that ultimate spiritual product known technically as 'utility.'" Hence economics now is the theory of free choice, and the market is the place of free choice. If this is Christianity, what then is utilitarianism?

7. A quite different approach, not in physical but in monetary terms, leads to the same result. Since Keynes, the main threat to the stability of the system is found in the growing saving quota, as briefly discussed in Chapter I. Out of too low incomes nothing can be saved; rising income will gradually make saving possible and more and more desirable; sav-

We resent it if people suspect us of materialism. Yet we must make ourselves richer. Marxist theory, of course, has an answer to the problem of surplus productivity in laissez-faire: growing international tension, armaments, and war. But even disregarding this possibility—and who can disregard it these days?—our economic position in a world that is one cannot be judged as if we were alone. Next to war, the world's gravest fear is that of a recession in the United States, which with 6 per cent of the globe's population produces 50 per cent of the world's goods and uses up most of the raw materials exported by the poorer countries. A recession in the United States would mean famine in the raw-material-producing countries.

We are confident that the pragmatic spirit of this country will not again permit a serious depression to develop; a number of governmental and semigovernmental institutions stand ready to step up expenditures should this be needed for stability. The trouble is only that this expedient does not come near the fundamental structural problem, that of the compulsory expansion by which the dreaded recession would be avoided. Reconstruction so as to extricate us from the compulsion to expand—which is mistaken for freedom—can be achieved only by putting the structure and its operation under a different law, by gearing it to specific ends and establishing corresponding long-range controls. We must in the first place find a level of income which we regard as satisfactory and intend to preserve by and large— upward adjustments will be included. Certain technical phases of the problem will be governmental, but the whole is a moral problem if there ever was one—that is, one of long-range, far-sighted education for and insight into spiritual and aesthetic

---

ing will grow more than in proportion to income. The other side of this observation is that consumption will grow less than in proportion to income; there will be a growing gap between rising income and lagging demand for goods. But goods can be produced only if demanded—hence the threat to employment from growing savings out of growing income. In order to fill the gap of employment, the system depends on technical progress, which forces every participant in the market to order heavier, costlier, more efficient machine equipment. Simple expansion of production will not do; it becomes impossible in the presence of a lagging demand for goods. Growing mechanization again is the way out.

questions, something that can be produced only by consensus codified in some basic governmental action. The structural change thereby made possible would then consist in the transference of supernumerary equipment from the steel and other expansionist industries to those concerned with consumers' goods and services. Further gains in productivity would easily be translated into still shorter work hours—provided the gain in leisure could once more be made meaningful for personal life. The entire program is one of long-range planned reorganization and re-education.[8]

The liberals are quite right, therefore, in saying that planning implies common ends. But they are grievously wrong in saying that the unguided market leaves everybody free to make his private decisions on his private ends. The free market subjects everybody to the despotic rule of efficiency sole and supreme, and in this way builds an industrial structure which can live only if it goes on expanding. In the past this fabulous expansion has proved a blessing to living and health standards. Projected into the future, it becomes absurd and offensive, a mockery to the organic balance of the human soul and to international standards of decency. Hence what Western mankind will have to do is switch from the now empty dynamics of efficiency supreme, incorporated in laissez-faire, to social and moral controls, which are the definition of a newly conceived socialism.

We are not utopian-minded enough to believe that such a dual program is easy of achievement or about to be achieved. All we say is that it is the logical way out of the structurally,

8. All this already in *Freedom and Order*, 1947, pp. 72 ff., although at that time—immediately after the war—not yet with equal urgency. More recently, the problem has been discussed in several articles, beginning with "The Economy of Abundance," *Social Action*, January 1957, reprinted as a pamphlet by the Calvin K. Kazanjian Economics Foundation of Westport, Conn.; "The Affluent Society," *Kyklos*, 1959, No. 2; several German articles; and relatively most fully, "Après le Succès du Capitalisme—Òu Allons-Nous?" *Economic Appliquée*, 1959, No. 1-2. The problem will be one of the focal points in *Social Theory of Economic Systems*, on which I am working. The well-known and deserving book by Galbraith, *The Affluent Society*, ignores the structural problem.

morally, and internationally untenable position into which laissez-faire—allegedly nothing but the freedom of private choice —has maneuvered us. We cannot overemphasize the structural nature of the impasse, which demands a structural remedy, a structural reconstruction. This is why a purely pragmatic approach in the best tradition of American philosophy—though far superior to the dogmatic despotism of laissez-faire—appears to us inadequate. The problem is not one of piecemeal difficulties to be handled piecemeal, but of a rigid structure geared the wrong way. The glory of constitutional democracy (as discussed in Chapter IV) is that it has broken the dogmatic rule of economic efficiency erected over society by capitalism and continued by communism. The new socialism—which has nothing to do with class war, common property, and the other implements of governmentalism, but everything to do with moral ends to control efficiency run wild—must reorganize the industrial structure itself under the representation of the various moral and social ends.

Note on the World Congress of Churches at Evanston

The World Council of Churches, which in powerful manifestoes in Oxford (1937) and in Amsterdam (1948) had spoken the language of the alarmed prophetic conscience, did not find the prophetic word on the structural problems of modern economic society in its seventeen-day conference at Evanston in August, 1954. (The WCC has indeed spoken with admirable power in its general message and in its decisions on evangelism and racial problems, but not in those about the "responsible society" and about international affairs; the decision on faith and order in the Church stands outside this appraisal, due to its special nature.) Reading the preparatory documents (in the volume *The Christian Hope*) and the Evanston decisions themselves, it is easy to discern what happened. The preparatory report on the responsible society gives a brief, good survey on the development of economic and social thought in the postwar years, which have largely realized, in the Western world, the programs of the social reformers (and of the WCC), but have thereby deprived the social reformers of their program.

Inasmuch as the reforms have been realized, experiences not only of a positive but also of a negative kind were gathered; the reforms did not fulfill all hopes nor refute all warnings. For we are never quite so good or intelligent as we believe, and our adversaries never so bad or stupid as we believe. It is this situation out of which the Evanston decision must be explained. It is predominantly retrospective—a kind of account, item by item, done with exemplary precision and conscientiousness. It weighs the tasks and limits of government; the advantages and disadvantages of governmental intervention and of free enterprise, of egalitarian income distribution and the incentive to productivity provided by unequal income, of private property and public property. Everything that it says is correct and on most things it has something to say. (But the inflationary pressure of the wage and price increases which big businesses and labor unions use to enrich themselves at the expense of the consumers, and which in the period of "countervailing power" [9] become overwhelmingly dangerous, seem to have been completely forgotten—a strange omission.) This is pragmatism at its best: evaluation item by item instead of by a rigid principle.

But the piecemeal pragmatic approach fails irretrievably vis-à-vis a closed "structure," a "system," a "Gestalt." If the blind compulsion to expand is built into the economic order by the mere size of the steel industry, how nonsensical is it then to preach: "The tendencies to create limitless wants, to overaccentuate the material values, to appeal to arrogance, envy, and covetousness and to stimulate them through irresponsible selling tricks and advertisements, are dangerous and must be curbed." Nothing has done more harm to the authority of the Church than incompetent sermons on morality.

All this, however, is doubly enigmatic if one consults the study *Christian Values and Economic Life*,[10] published at the

9. John Kenneth Galbraith, *American Capitalism: The Concept of Countervailing Power,* 1952. The book is a pioneering achievement, but overoptimistic.

10. John C. Bennett, Howard Bowen, William Adams Brown, Jr.,

same moment by John Bennett, one of the two chairmen of
the Commission on the Responsible Society in the preparations
for Evanston and at Evanston itself. After the central problem
has been discussed with characteristic lucidity, circumspection,
and fairness, one arrives at the last paragraph and reads there:

"Nay, one of the most penetrating objections against capitalism—even in its present form, which has overcome many of
the injustices of nineteenth-century capitalism—is to the effect
that this seems to be a structure in which particular habits of
compulsion are forced on the people and the world by the
requirements of the system of production itself."

This indeed is the opposite of the moralizing exhortation
of Evanston: the recognition that it is the system of production itself which enforces the immoral habits of consumption,
thus making senseless any pragmatic separation of the judgment
on the system of production and the habits of compulsion. But
as the reader is not introduced to the argument behind that
surprising turn of the picture and is not referred to a source for
his own instruction, the mere statement does not help him.
Moreover, Bennett continues:

"To a certain extent we may be forced to consume what
we do not need, merely to keep the system of production
going. Should this be the only way to preserve an economic
order favorable to political and cultural freedom, we may have
to accept it. But then we must recognize one thing: if in this way
the choice of goods and of standards of value in our society are
to a large extent determined by the mere weight of this dynamic
system of production, the price paid would be high."

If one is to take literally this far too brief (and perhaps
hastily written?) paragraph, it would amount to the proposition
that Christian responsibility must abdicate vis-à-vis the compulsion to expand built into the sizes of the industries of an
economic system abandoned to itself (its "autonomy," its "freedom"). Since the expansion, however, is not one limited act but

---

and G. Bromley Oxnam, *Christian Values and Economic Life,* New York,
1954. Copyright © 1954 by Harper & Brothers. Quoted by permission of
the publisher.

an urge directed toward the infinite, the proposition would become unimaginable.

At this point can be seen the limit of the pragmatic approach, which Reinhold Niebuhr has connected with Christian ethics because of its freedom from rigid worldly yardsticks.[11] This approach is adequate where the forms stand loosely side by side so as to make it possible, e.g., to exchange public ownership and private ownership in individual plants as expediency advises us to do. But the pragmatic approach rebounds from the fixed framework around such a loose, decentralized organization; within the system the individual pieces can move more or less freely, but they all partake of its general form and autonomous motion. Each plant in the system abandoned to itself and oriented toward efficiency and expansion need not participate in the expansion; this is its freedom and the justification of pragmatism. But unless the whole expands in some of its parts, all of them lose their freedom and are drawn into the crisis. (Likewise the individual national economic bodies stand relatively loosely side by side, but the structure of the world economy as a whole continues to force the formerly colonial nations into a defenseless service position, which cannot be eliminated pragmatically but only by recasting the world structure, as discussed in the following chapter.)

The decision of Evanston, however, is totally determined by pragmatism. Its lack of structure becomes its structure, which does not permit it to understand the completely different structural problems of the immediate future. In the decision itself the fundamental repudiation of structural thinking is expressed by saying that "debates about 'capitalism' and 'socialism' deflect the attention from the really important problems of economic and social policy," because "either one of these two words is applied to many different social and economic systems." This sentence is dubious, in the first place, logically: all men, for all their infinitely many personal and cultural differences, fall

11. Reinhold Niebuhr, *The Children of Light and the Children of Darkness. A Justification of Democracy and a Critique of Its Conventional Defense,* 1944. Cf. my article "Niebuhr's Pragmatic Conservatism," in *Union Seminary Quarterly Review,* May, 1956.

under the notion of the species man. But in the second and more important place, the sentence is oriented, unfortunately, toward the historical circumstances of the principles rather than toward the principles themselves. Therefore it misses the fundamental distinction between an economic system abandoned to its own law of motion, in which the individual plants may indeed be differently organized but are all of them dependent on the blind expansion of the whole (and the former colonial nations remain chained to the market fluctuations in the former imperial countries—cf. below) and, on the other hand, an economic structure which—unswayed by the disastrous Marxian equation of socialism with proletarian class war and finally general state ownership—puts far-reaching goals before the economic units and directs them toward those, so that in this framework and through it freedom of motion, decentralization and individual property can exist without disturbance.

Economic Institutions of Socialism

A genuine socialist economy, then, balances freedom and order within economic life itself, after the orgy of freedom resulting in the tyranny of expanding efficiency and after the dual orgy of order, of rationalist and irrationalist political tyranny. Socialism balances freedom and order by interlocking market and planning processes in one economic system. The market presupposes that the economic units must be formally free to pursue their ends and seek their incomes. In order for this formal liberty to be filled with social content, the internal constitution of the economic units must be changed from economism to socialism. That is, they must not remain in the hands of irresponsible financial powers; irresponsible power is the very negation of democracy.

This is far from implying, however, that private property as such should be eliminated; to preserve and develop it is emphatically necessary, not as a compromise with a recalcitrant reality but as a matter of democratic principle. Private property is a legal form which permits very different sociological contents, ranging all the way from positions of command in na-

tional and international economic life to those millions of
modest properties which merely protect a man's independence
in his work—e.g., in the family farm. If it is the goal of socialism to emancipate man's work from domination by a dehuman-
izing economism, it would not make any sense to destroy the
form in which workers are free in their work. What should be
envisaged is not the destruction of small but the transmutation
of big productive properties. The line between the two must be
drawn according to judgment and expediency, but it will certainly not exclude a considerable range of moderate-sized enterprises, which cannot be suspected of irresponsible power if the
employees are protected by labor law and even more strongly
by full employment, and the consumers by competition.[12]

For the transmutation of big property, utmost importance is
accruing to the patient and pedantic work which the British
Fabians have achieved over a period of more than fifty years in
elaborating socialist method and organization. They turn in the
main to municipalities and counties as owners of local industries, to cooperatives for enterprises of a larger scale, and
to autonomous corporations like BBC in England and TVA in
this country for nationalized industries. The elaboration of
these forms in such detail is the strongest single instance of the
authentic idea of socialism surviving in the midst of all the
present confusion. As Germany re-emerges from the collapse of
the governmentalism which had risen to power out of the collapse of economism, Alexander Mitscherlich's and Alfred
Weber's manifesto *Free Socialism* gives a profound statement
of socialism as opposed to both economism and governmentalism
almost in these terms, and Gerhard Weisser's *Form und Wesen
der Einzelwirtschaften* (1947) explores the structure and operation of free planning agencies.

The many forms in which large-scale enterprises might be
reorganized include, in addition to the roster compiled by the
Fabians, the "foundation" as tried out by the Zeiss Optical

12. On the justification of individual property cf. *Communism,
Fascism or Democracy?*, pp. 38 ff. A detailed critical appraisal of private
property is given by Hans Ritschl in the second chapter of his book
Grundlagen der Wirtschaftsordnung, 1954.

Works in Jena and analyzed and modified by Robert Wilbrandt
and, more recently, by Alfred Weber; also the workers' corporation, where shares are in the form of labor rather than
money, as suggested by H. B. Parkes (*Marxism,* 1939, pp.
247 ff.); and what Lewis Corey (*The Unfinished Task,* 1942,
pp. 262 ff.) has similarly described as the "functional corporation." Rathenau's idea of the joint stock corporation buying
its own stock so as to belong to nobody may well be worth
while if its vacuum of legal obligation is filled with a new
sense and tradition of social responsibility in the managers.
But this may be too costly a procedure; the same result may be
obtainable by the widest dispersion of shares among small savers
so as to have management without their control and free to bow
to higher standards. This, however, is precisely the direction
in which many of our biggest and most powerful firms are far
advanced. Their managers do not own the firms, nor do they
depend on the "owners." There is no dearth of possibilities,
although many of them will surely overlap.

What all these forms have in common is that, in the control
of production, they replace the representatives of economism by
various groups of society and their combinations. Speaking in
economic terms, this implies that the principle of cooperation
between them and with governmental authorities is natural for
them all. There is no "rugged individualism"; there is not that
heedless chase for highest profits in the shortest possible time
which runs head-on into the crisis, and which economic theory
accepts as the axiomatic premise of all its analyses. Nor is there
that "lack of confidence," that absurd fear of doomsday, which
scares business into withdrawing from investment as public investments are stepped up to increase total investment and employment. There is, on the other hand, no governmentalism
even in nationalized industries or general agencies of over-all
planning; none of them is "the government"—they do not
legislate, they must persuade.

Now it is all very well to describe the methods and forms of
organization in the new setup. But it is not enough to say who
does the necessary things and makes the decisions; it must also
be suggested how the necessary things are to be done, and that

the whole will be a functioning, organized system. In other words, the reorganization is not only a matter of economic sociology and institutions but of economic theory as well.

The outline of the theory is simple enough. In the first place, the economic units are connected by the market, selling and buying among themselves and receiving through the pressure of cost and the lure of price and profit the needed instruction on the relative intensities of the demand for their products, ultimately from the consuming public. The relative sizes of firms and industries are thus integrated with the whole of the existing demand structure on the one hand, and with the existing supplies of natural and human resources and technological possibilities on the other hand. For what the market achieves through the interplay of prices and costs is to ascertain the demand structure (in terms of the existing distribution of purchasing power) and to allocate scarce supplies of resources for production accordingly. The market does this automatically—that is, without needing a bureaucratic apparatus, which would certainly enhance the power of government and diminish output by draining that much man power away. The fact that the results of the market process cannot be better than the economic society which uses it and sets its conditions contains no objection to the market; it is additional reason for using this invaluable instrument of orientation in an improved setup.

This is far from saying that the market should be left in exclusive control of economic activities. The time when it was in exclusive control is long past, even in the most liberal of liberal democracies, the United States. The market is short-sighted by definition, dealing with existing demands and supplies in terms of present prices and costs, but not anticipating such changes in the demand-and-supply situation as are brought about by the predictable effects of the present use of supplies. The longer the time range of technological process in production, the more indispensable becomes the principle of planned anticipation of future market situations.

Suppose we have produced and sold five million automobiles a year to fill the pent-up postwar demand—how can we continue to do that after everyone who can afford it owns a

new car? And what shall then become not only of the auto-
mobile industry but of the steel and all related industries? Will
it be possible to raise more and more potential buyers rapidly
enough to that level of income where they would actually buy
a car? Or suppose the typical case of every boom-and-bust cycle,
where the explosive demand for some far-reaching innovation
has taxed the possibilities of everything connected with the
building of machines to the peak of capacity but will then, by
the same token, fall off again. The market can do nothing but
register the change of demand after it occurs. Planning anticipates the change and prepares the exposed industries and the
entire system to meet it. It does so not by tampering with the
keen and sensitive instrument of orientation which is free price
formation in the market, but by interpreting its present results
and elongating them into the future so as to provide orientation on the foreseeable changes of the market. The long-range
problem implied in the physical structure of the American
industrial system has been discussed in the preceding section;
it is the culmination of this argument.[13]

Planning must vary from country to country. In the development of an undeveloped country, e.g., there is no market from
which to draw orientation on a not-yet-existing reality—so the
plan itself must fill the gap. How far planning goes will depend
on the stage of development and the temper of the society. In
an already developed country, where the task is to provide for
stability in further growth, planning will be delicate and conservative—that is, heedful of the existing structure of the
market, which must not be shaken but must be permitted to
absorb the results of the plan's execution. In order to slow down
an investment boom lest it run into a period of saturation and

13. Long-period orientation toward agreed binding goals instead of
short-sightedness of the market is the central idea in Carl Landauer's
Theory of National Economic Planning, 2nd edition 1947. The long-range
nature of planning, however, puts the constitutional machinery of democracy to novel tests. Carl J. Friedrich has called attention to these problems,
without plunging into a premature attempt at a solution, in a special
chapter of his book *Constitutional Government and Democracy*, revised
edition 1950, where this chapter appeared for the first time.

recession, the nationalized steel and credit agencies may very well temporarily cut salable supplies and raise the price of steel and the rate of interest; this would be planning not by overriding the market but by using it, since the new higher prices of steel and credit would be expressive of the new shorter supplies and would thus give correct orientation to potential users of steel and credit in the new situation. Technically speaking, this method of influencing a market by unified control of supply and price is known as monopoly; competing sellers cannot act that way. Planning, then, uses the technique of monopoly, thus directing the market rather than destroying it. This is, in brief outline, the economic theory of the new system which is growing under our eyes.

The Problem of Incentives

The grave unsolved problem is not economic but psychological; it is the problem of incentives in the new setup. It is true that this problem is naturally incapable of a theoretical solution in the same sense as the economic problem does permit one; it can only be tried out. But this is the point: while unquestionably much has been achieved by trial and error, and while one may trust that more can be achieved, a clear insight into the nature of the problem does not yet seem to have been attained. Yet the problem is of strategic importance. The material part of welfare depends not only on the optimum composition of the total output attainable over a sustained period of time, the optimum allocation of the total capital and labor supplies to the different industries in proportion to the desires of the consuming public—the economic problem—but also on making this total as large as possible with the present technology—the psychological problem.

The problem is one for both management and workers, and it is solved under capitalism by what is popularly known as a combination of the stick applied to the rear of a certain animal with the carrot in front of him: the combination of the threat of bankruptcy and starvation with the hope for unlimited financial gain and social advancements. This combination certainly has proved capable of overcoming much easygoing tradition and natural inertia, and of spurring people to those intense and sustained efforts which in the case of managers never acquiesce in the existing technological organization and profits therefrom derived, and which in the case of workers make full use of improved equipment for larger output. The Soviet, after the disaster of its early optimistic appeals to solidarity and good will, reintroduced the hierarchy of incomes as an indispensable incentive. Managers, of course, cannot accumulate capital for private investment but may rise to ever higher honor and power without capital ownership; the gradation of incomes themselves, steep as it is, is limited to salaries. By extraordinarily high premiums, workers are spurred on in a manner which Western trade unionism considers incompatible with working class solidarity. In both cases the threat of starvation as the ultimate sanction in the anonymous market of capitalism is replaced by the threat of the forced labor camp as the ultimate penalty.

What about experiences and attempts in free socialism? The most general observation is that, not unlike the first period in Russia, the "stick" has been removed and there is more or less exclusive reliance on the "carrot." Can that be a workable system? It is true that managers and owners are not immune from removal in case of failure. The nationalization of the British coal mines, although surely a matter of high principle for socialists, was partly motivated and vastly facilitated by the shocking inefficiency of management under laissez-faire—"let them do as they please." But it is a fact that major bankruptcies are implicitly precluded by a policy of full employment. More generally, the atmosphere, full of storm and threat to the national economy as a whole in the present turmoil, is one in which the individual feels less exposed than formerly. On the positive side, too, it is public initiative which, in the countries of democratic socialism, takes over much of the work left to individuals under laissez-faire, thus lowering the average responsibility of management and requiring less strong incentives.

For all this, however, the question of profits, and more generally of income incentives, is far from settled and will demand

a much more generous approach than traditional trade unionism is likely to accord it, if the system needs personal dynamism
on the part of managers in both the public and private sectors.
This is not to deny the possibility of major changes in the
response to incentives, such as have occurred, e.g., in the
psychology of military leaders, from the desire for booty—at
the time when generalship was a private enterprise—to that
for service and honor. Inasmuch as the basic reward in every
field lies in devotion to a responsible task and in the satisfaction
accorded by a job well done, this incentive is certainly at work
in the builders of industry under capitalism too. Nevertheless
the atmosphere in that system cannot fail to increase the desire
for private wealth, while the atmosphere under socialism stresses
cooperation and public distinction and should work in favor
of the intangible incentives. But how far, and how rapidly or
slowly, cannot even be guessed in advance.

As the danger in capitalist individualism lies in private
rapacity, so the danger in egalitarian socialism lies in the cult
of mediocrity, which would destroy material progress and discredit the very principle of democracy. The danger is vastly increased by the natural reaction to the excesses of capitalism. Far
more than their employers, the workers under capitalism are at
the mercy of forces utterly beyond their control; mass unemployment is second only to war among the anxieties which beset
modern man. Hence the overwhelming urge for security in the
job. This, however, threatens to knock the bottom out from under the system of incentives. Can a system work where a man is
immune from the consequences of his dereliction of duty?
The question should be carefully distinguished from the question of unemployment for reasons beyond a man's control,
reasons in the imperfections of the capitalist system. The latter
kind of unemployment is altogether contrary to true liberty,
which is self-responsibility and should not burden a person
with a responsibility too heavy for him to shoulder. But if
liberty does mean self-responsibility, it cannot possibly include
the liberty of being derelict in duties; it must include the
liberty of starving for reasons of personal laziness and neg-
ligence, although certainly not for reasons beyond one's control.

The difficulty here lies only in the fate of innocent families, who are to suffer for reasons beyond their control, just as they are in the case where a member is in conflict with the law, and just as they also draw benefits from the social distinction which a member may acquire. Since care for the family is the strongest of all incentives, it is in the nature of the family organization that such undeserved suffering is unavoidable to a considerable extent; it should obviously be mitigated as much as humanly possible.

Paradoxically, however, the same egalitarian philosophy which threatens to exalt mediocrity may become dynamic and serve as the great inspiration for a real social advance, a real cooperative adventure. Both tendencies are noticeable where socialist labor movements are victorious. There is the inclination to rest on the laurels of victory, the comfortable assumption that things must become easier once the dual whip of exploitation and unemployment is removed; also the ingrained ideology of the unions' class struggle, suspecting of lack of solidarity anyone who distinguishes himself among his fellows. And there is, on the other hand, the sense of mission, of the great hour, which has permeated all socialist movements from the left-wing sects in Cromwell's army to this day; which has passed into Marxism, receiving there a most spectacular pseudo-scientific cloak; but which is just as awake in democratic socialism and as ready to spring into action if it finds leadership and tasks which appeal to the imagination. Logically there is no conflict between the suspicious watch over solidarity and the social dynamics of equality. Where the latter sets the pace, individual efforts are easily absorbed into the general advance, and solidarity will spur on the inert rather than hamper the ambitious. But dynamism never becomes an inherent quality; it may arise at any time and slacken at any time. What then remains is the permanence of egalitarian inertia, the mortal threat to socialist democracy. The more clearly this is seen, the better.

The great measure of equalization is taxation. The romantic love for the spectacular and the ignoble lust for spectacular if only partial revenge never fail to praise expropriation without compensation as the true revolutionary measure and to belittle taxation as tame reformism. From a rational point of view, it does not make any sense to pick out the owners of some special industry for proletarianization and leave the others in undiminished control of their properties. If political power and expediency permit a certain advance toward equality, the only rational way is to spread it thinner but on the widest possible front. That this method is anything but ineffective can be seen even in this country, where it surely is not seriously suspect of, although vocally accused of, a socialist objective; in countries where it does serve such an objective, taxation proves a powerful instrument. As such, however, it shares in the ambiguity of the egalitarian principle. It may be harmful inasmuch as it cuts into capital accumulation in fields where public ownership is not desired. On the other hand, it is precisely the severity of the tax system—e.g., in favor of a universal health plan—which gives the people the feeling that equality is more than just a dream and that they are on their way. The ambiguity remains; there is no theoretical solution. All one can and must do is firmly envisage the opposite dangers in order to find a practicable way between them in the individual case.

Nor is this all. There is a third grave danger, less conspicuous in terms of productive efficiency and political power and therefore easily put aside as irrelevant, which makes it only more dangerous. It is the fate of the unorganized and unorganizable cultured middle class between those upper and lower millstones. The Dutch government in its plan for reconstruction, whose author is Professor Tinbergen, is wise and farsighted in emphasizing this major tax problem. But no other socialist movement seems to have grasped the question. If the society which socialism wants to put into the controlling position is to be morally and intellectually alive, nothing can be more absurd than to ruin the guardians of a cultured life, the only ones from whom one can learn what culture and education are. For there is no other way to education but through living tradition.

Liberty and the Economic Interpretation
of History

No guide to any of these practical problems can be found
in the traditional philosophy of the post-Marxian socialist movements on the continent, which is the economic interpretation
of history. They do not use it in its entirety, which would make
them Communists; they do not even know it enough to be able
to say how far they follow it. The trouble is, however, that the
lingering elements of it are sufficient to obstruct the rise of
that frankly libertarian philosophy for which socialists grope
and without which they have little chance of standing up to
communism in the long run. For the superiority of communism
in Marxist philosophy is overwhelming. So this philosophy
perverts socialism. The confrontation of the two must round
out the argument.

It is correct to say, of course, that social democracy has
long been in retreat from Marxism. But the reasons in former
years were not of the highest order; they were not elevated to
the plane of principles, as can be seen from the fact that lip
service to Marxism as the inspiration of the movement continued to be paid in all countries, and that an attack on the principles of the system was hardly tolerated before the advent of
the Hitler regime. Even so, sober realism began to doubt the
doctrine of the proletarian unification in late capitalist society,
and the vested interests of party and labor union bureaucracy
in parliament and social reform not only discouraged much
revolutionary enthusiasm but came close to the belief that,
with production taken care of by capitalism, all labor had to do
was redistribute the product through social reform. These illusions were properly refuted by the economic crisis and the
accession of Hitler to power, which they had helped to bring
about; and the re-emerging social democratic movement, steeled
by suffering, no longer denied the necessity of facing the problem which it had too long ignored. Its conflict with communism
had long been defined as one of political method exclusively.
It had been claimed that the transition to socialism could be

achieved much more smoothly with democratic approval by the people than if imposed by force—nay, that the personal liberty to be realized by socialism could be attained only by this procedure. Now it was at last realized that there was no place for liberty in a philosophy dominated by the supreme principle of rational proletarian class interest.

The economic interpretation of history seemed to be the proper theory for the socialist movement as long as one could believe that the pure logic of economic transformation—the growth of the large-scale units, the unification of propertyless masses, the aggravating disturbances of piecemeal management, and the resulting drive for unified collectivization—would make for the twin goals of social justice and full employment. Government and society were not considered to be structures in their own right, but instruments in the hands of the dominant capitalist interests; they seemed to derive from and reflect them and would give way along with them when the economic time was ripe. This doctrine was put to a severe strain when the Russians refused to wait for the promise to come true in their own backward country and used the arm of government to shape economic forces in the desired direction. But in so doing the Russians were true to the supreme meaning of the economic interpretation of history. As capitalist government is subservient to capitalist interests, so the proletarian dictatorship subserves and promotes, with all the means at its disposal, the "correctly understood" class interest of the workers which lies in the collective rationality of the industrial structure. Assuming, with the Marxist doctrine, that economic rationality is the supreme driving force and its collective consummation the supreme goal of human life, communism is the appropriate social form of that consummation. The economic forces tend toward it, and other social forces including government, unable to prevent it even if they would, should use their special powers and techniques to promote it. The Soviet government lives up to this task of government, and its initiative and leadership, far from refuting the economic interpretation of history, brings out its industrial collectivist meaning.

These ideas can now be presented in systematic form. Socialism has been defined as control of things economic by society. Its opposites are economism—laissez-faire capitalism—and that governmentalism as which socialism has too long understood itself, which is now revealed as totalitarian communism. The trouble with this distinction and confrontation is, on the one hand, that Marxism does have as its final utopia the control of things economic by (stateless) society—our definition of socialism—and on the other hand, that economism itself—control by the autonomous forces of economic life, which is our definition of capitalism—is identical with the Marxist economic interpretation of history. Marxism thus combines all three forms. Marxist economism is distinguished from bourgeois economism by having the autonomous forces of economic life drive on beyond laissez-faire, which is bourgeois rule, toward proletarian rule as the working class becomes the whole of society; proletarian economism then finds its higher form in Communist governmentalism. The difference between bourgeois economism and Marxist economism—between laissez-faire and the economic interpretation of history—is that there is only one phase, progressive but unchangeable, in the former, and there are two opposite phases in the latter. But both are at one in the assumption that economic life is controlled by autonomous economic forces and that this economic logic does and should determine economic and general social life.

In particular, Marxism's boundless optimism always equates that which *must* happen under the inexorable scientific law of the tendency which dominates history with that which *should* happen from the point of view of moral necessity. The fundamental proposition of the economic interpretation of history is dual: first, the autonomous economic forces are supreme in history, positively determining social, political, and ideological forces, or at least overriding them if they resist and replacing them by more pliable ones; and second, this is as it should be because man's reason—which is his real nature—seeks welfare and ever higher welfare and manifests itself in economic progress until it finds its own perfection in an all-inclusive system of economic rationality and disposes of the irrational as unreal. Briefly: the autonomous forces of economic life are and should be in control of history; being the seat of human reason, their growth finally redeems mankind. It is, in the Marxist dialectic, economism itself which leads up to (stateless) socialism, its opposite, and finds therein its goal. And it is again economism which, in order to attain that goal, leads through the last-but-one phase where the human vehicles of the final phase are already in control but neither uncontestably so nor themselves fully developed rationally and morally, with the effect that the proletarian dictatorship becomes imperative: governmentalism in our terminology, the reality of communism today. The extraordinary intellectual brilliance of the Marxist dialectic can most clearly be seen at this point. The three magnitudes of the triangular relationship appear here, not as mutually exclusive opposites but as successive phases of a consistent, harmonious movement in opposites, with economism in the lead, using proletarian governmentalism as its final instrument, and producing (stateless) socialism as its inherent goal.

The discussion in Part Two should have made the spurious nature of this dialectic clear. It is quite true that, as its fundamental economism and its derived governmentalism go hand in hand and are merely different successive forms of the same unfolding stuff, so this relationship is confirmed in recent history. Commercialized society has produced its logical counterpart, totalitarian society, and they are united by the belief in man's ultimately economic nature and destiny. But what Marx calls (stateless) society, being nothing but the third and final form of the very same stuff once more, has only the name in common with the society of authentic socialism and with everything really worthy of that name. Marxist stateless society is not society in the genuine sense of the word because it is released by and issues from the all-absorbing state. It is in its own image that the all-absorbing state makes this society over before releasing it; the state can "wither" into this society only because the society is the state's own enlarged form; uniform, collective, economic rationalism. In contradistinction, society proper is the realm of liberty, of spontaneity; and socialism proper is the rule of society.

But society has signed away its supremacy and liberty in the modern phase of history and has thus started economism on its career. In Chapter VIII this was discussed in terms of religious and intellectual history: the vital balance between the person and the community, between liberty and equality, was lost because that which bound them together was permitted to lapse. In the present chapter the same process was discussed in sociological terms: society, the spontaneous form of life controlled by the moral convictions of the people, was overwhelmed by economism. Polanyi has described how society literally became an appendix to economics when man became the object of the labor market and nature the object of the land market. With economism thus in the saddle in reality, it was easy to generalize this empirical observation into a scientific law of supposedly universal and perennial validity. This generalization is the economic interpretation of history represented by Harrington, Adam Smith, *The Federalist,* and most economic theorists; [14] and it is, in the far more sophisticated form of a dialectic running through three mutually opposite stages, the economism of Karl Marx. But generalization is not proof; the rule in history of a freedomless necessity and inexorable economic logic is not proved by the experience that there is no freedom of action after we have signed this freedom away. In signing it away we did use it. And socialism is the attempt to resume it.

Liberty is not a by-product of economic logic; it must be willed. Hence, the present generation, anxious lest liberty be lost in an autonomous economic development toward organized class rule, discovered democratic government as a fact of its own which could be used to shape and limit economic forces, and also discovered the moral convictions held by society as the guarantee of governmental and economic forces keeping within their bounds. The rediscovery of the moral power of society, partly embodied in democratic government but also binding it, is an event of great consequence. And it is this event in which the forces of pure secularism meet the forces coming from Christianity and searching for institutions of justice. This encounter will be discussed in the final chapter.

14. The most conspicuous exception is John Maurice Clark; see, e.g., his *Guideposts in a Time of Change,* 1950.

* X *

The Encounter Between
Religion and Democracy

Christendom and Democracy

IN the United States, Christianity and democracy have for a long time been allied or united. In most countries of the European continent, they have always been arrayed on opposite sides—antidemocratic Christianity and anti-Christian democracy fighting each other. Yet the present condition in the United States is hardly preferable to that in Europe.

The success of democracy in the United States is largely due to the religious element in it. The two greatest figures of American democracy, Jefferson and Lincoln, are eloquent witnesses to that. Jefferson praises Protestant education of the past for equipping the democratic citizen with the required moral stability and reliability; Lincoln in his classical utterances gives profound Christian interpretations of the tragedy of the Civil War and prays for a "new birth of freedom under God." Yet there is a fundamental difference between the two, in that Jefferson gives religion credit for its past performance while Lincoln speaks of the present and the future. In the history of the country Jefferson has scored over Lincoln, and whatever the part played by religion in founding the American democracy, the roles of religion and democracy in their mutual relationship have long since been reversed, and the Christian religion now at best appears as an affiliation of democracy.

Jefferson himself pointed the way by his abridged version of the New Testament, concentrating on "the life and morals of Jesus of Nazareth"—this is the title of the volume—and leaving out the dogmatic, that is, the properly religious elements. In so doing he felt he was acting as "a really good Christian," and

the honesty and warmth of heart of his successors can be doubted
as little as his own. But religion lives on dogma, and if morality
lives on religion, as Jefferson felt, then the three will and
do go down, not indeed together but with a time lag of at best
a few generations between them. Recent American history and
experience certainly do not refute this statement, which was
discussed in the preceding chapters. Meanwhile, following
Jefferson's precedent, Christianity in America has accommo-
dated itself to the climate of optimistic, pragmatic, scientific,
progressively secular life, and it owes its continued popularity
and relative influence precisely to the fact that, for all practical
purposes, it is identified with the democratic regime, just as
the old churches of Europe were identified with the ancient
regime. That is, American Protestantism now lives largely on
American democracy; democracy is in the lead in the partnership. If, for the sake of the argument, we may assume a catastrophe of democracy, it is doubtful that Christianity could extricate itself from the entanglement and preserve enough vitality
to rebuild its life on a new basis. On the other hand, democracy
in its present moral crisis certainly has no more religious reserves
at its disposal for its own renewal. Only the Roman Catholic
Church, for all its great influence on both government and
labor, stands outside the secularizing trend of American church
life and dares oppose it on such major issues as birth control.

On the continent of Europe the influence of Christianity has
always been on the conservative side, and democracy has had to
assert itself against it in a running battle, which has extended
over centuries. The split between the two has been, in a way, the
fundamental malady of Europe. No doubt Jacques Maritain is
right in saying that heretics and atheists took up the Christian
message, and that the latter lived on in them and was betrayed
by the official churches; that it is "the quiet work of the Evangelical inspiration in the world and in the conscience" which is
the really driving force in modern history. But this is tragedy
because it cuts off the forces of struggling democracy from the
source of spiritual life.

As the advance of democracy was at the expense of Christianity, democracy itself was undermined in its moral health

and spiritual power—that is, in its power of internal cohesion beyond the natural conflicts of group interests in free society. Christendom, on the other hand, spiritually strong but hardened in its resentment over the defection, ceased to be the community and became a party; the message of redeeming love was made a weapon to threaten the doubters with exclusion from redemption. While American Christendom, affiliated as it is with modern society, was gradually watered down, continental Christendom hardened and narrowed in its resistance to modern society and so lost its power of sanctification. While the danger to American democracy lies in the absence of an independent church life as a source of moral renewal, the danger to continental democracy lies in the estrangement of the two. The problem in both cases is fundamentally the same: Can Christianity deepen and emancipate itself in America and broaden itself in Europe so as to become what it is destined to be, the soul and conscience of the community? Can democracy transmute itself so as to be open for Christianity to penetrate it?

The Ethics of Democracy
Between Atheism and Clericalism

The meaning of democracy lies in the liberty and dignity of the person and the community; or one may say that it lies in their dignity, which includes their liberty.[1]

1. The idea of the liberty and dignity of man has its obvious historical root in the Biblical doctrine of creation but cannot be discussed without the darkening by the Fall. Depending on the appraisal of the Fall—as devastating in orthodox Protestantism, less so in Catholicism where the original nature intended by God still shines through, still less so in the sects and finally in religious and political liberalism—the problem is more or less difficult. In the former case the center is occupied by astonishment at the tremendous arrangements instituted by God in order to save man despite it all—so important does He appear to find him. This is the orthodox Christian foundation of the idea. But the earliest political conclusion for the freedom of religion—freedom *from* religion could not yet be conceived—was drawn on sectarian soil, in the constitutional charter of the small New England colony of Rhode Island, 1647 (Roger Williams). The Universal Declaration of Human Rights, proclaimed by the United Nations—but not yet ratified by the United States—naturally

Since, as was shown before, the dignity of the person and of the community can never be taken for granted in view of the formidable power naturally accruing to the agencies in charge of government, the problem of democracy can be said to consist in the threefold relationship between the government, the majority, and the minority. The government must not be too weak "to govern forcefully"—Alexander Hamilton's main concern in the making of the American Constitution—nor too strong to respect the dignity of the people. The widely accepted solution of the problem lies in the division and balance of powers, which obviously includes such a delimitation as to make their smooth cooperation on the higher levels of decisions both necessary and possible. Constitution-making is a great art; without strong forms and their limits the best-intentioned officials would never know how far they are expected to go. On the other hand, it is just as obvious that no constitution, however wise, can secure domestic peace if the balances thereby established are not honored and respected by those working under it. Abuse is always possible in such a delicately perched system; the lust for power can always find loopholes in the most elaborate net of institu-

---

and legitimately stands on a universalist-humanist ground; the World Council of Churches and the German Evangelical Church have commented upon the draft. Cf. the beautiful article by Ernst Wolf, "Die Freiheit und Würde des Menschen," in *Recht, Staat, Wirtschaft (Schriftenreihe für staatswissenschaftliche Fortbildung)*, Bd. IV, 1953; and for the entire complex of problems, the monumental work by M. Searle Bates, *Religious Liberty*, 1947.

In empirical reality, the dignity of man is not very well off. People are often a little funny. The reconciling and healing power of humor consists precisely in serenely accepting the little weakness and thereby turning it affirmatively, while lack of humor plunges from good-natured fun to ridicule. Human life characteristically reaches full dignity only in moments of complete self-forgetfulness, in very great happiness and in very great sadness. Lovers sometimes are given such supreme fulfillment, but it comes much more often to young mothers in the exchanges with their small children. The awe-inspiring sublimeness of deepest sadness Georg Simmel found symbolized in Rembrandt's "Man with the Golden Helmet": the helmet is something like a halo unknown to the bearer. Several drawings and sculptures by Käthe Kollwitz seem to say something similar. The fact that this can happen to man is the essence of his dignity.

tions. Political democracy cannot function unless the underlying ethic is intact.

If political democracy is the free cooperation of free citizens, it consists on this level in the indissoluble unity of two elements: majority rule and minority protection. Without the latter element the former would not be complete; nay, it would never be possible to ascertain whether it really was majority rule if the minority had not all the rights which might enable it to become the majority in a free contest for votes. What the arrangement of democratic government requires is then two things: compliance of the minority with the laws passed by the majority, and respectful toleration of the minority by this majority. What it requires, in other words, is restraint in the use of power by both the majority and the minority. In the absence of such restraint, free society would be torn to pieces by conflicting interests, and only authoritarian force could secure its physical existence, although never its freedom. Restraint in the use of liberty is the prerequisite of liberty, the alternative to authority.

This, naturally, holds not only in the case of majority-minority relationship; it holds for all group relations in democracy. Always what the freedom of free society requires is self-restraint on the part of the strong, a determination to avoid oppression of the weak and respect their freedom and dignity; and self-restraint on the part of the weak rather than sabotage and rebellion, in the confident awareness that the way to reform through peaceful change is open. It must be clearly seen that in modern technological society any strategically placed group of special interests may wield the most formidable power and can terrorize society if it chooses. The numerically weakest group may be strong in virtue of its function, for the interdependence of innumerable functions in the close-knit machinery of modern society creates many positions of technological power which lend themselves to ruthless exploitation. If every group interest goes to the limit in thus using its power, the logical end is the war of all against all and the sure substitution of authoritarian force for their common freedom.

The life of democracy, then, depends on its social ethic—on the authority of its justice, whose principle must be accepted by all even though they quarrel among themselves on how to apply it to their own particular case. But since modern democracy understands itself as the realization of human reason, this ethic must not be a religious ethic because this would make it necessary to assign a public function to Christianity. It must be an autonomous, secular, rationalist ethic, derived from man's autonomous reason. That such an ethic is a possible foundation of democracy is an optical illusion, which could prevail only because and as long as the inherited content of the religious ethic continued to live on in people's souls and was easily understood as natural ethic. Now, however, atheist democracy becomes increasingly impossible in practice as it has always been in principle; only Christian democracy can regenerate the moral reserves on which the life of democracy depends.

A Christian democracy, however, is not one in which everybody need be a Christian. The political argument does not coincide with the missionary commandment. For the sake of his own soul everybody should be converted to Christianity. For the sake of democracy this is not needed, perhaps not even desirable in an imperfect world. That it is not needed can be seen from the very fact which teaches the necessity of democracy being Christian. Even when democrats had officially cut the tie with religion, democracy was still viable and strong so long as religious content was in the atmosphere and in men's souls. What democracy requires is not the Christian dogma as such but the ethic derived therefrom. History has proved that ethic cannot live on without religion, but it also has proved that an allegedly autonomous ethic can live on if the religion does. An areligious person is, in a society of Christian tradition, far from being an immoral person; past and present experience shows, on the contrary, that the pure ethicists and humanists in a Christian climate often are the most sensitive, most delicate members of the community. They are so, as they rightly claim, precisely because none of their mental energies is spent on things behind tangible reality; they err only in inferring that the existence of an unreligious ethic in a religious environment proves the possibility of such an unreligious ethic without the religious environment. But the gifts are many and manifold, and not everybody need have a strong personal sense of religious reality. At a time when religion threatens to become an intellectual fashion without moral commitments, the integrity of nonreligious ethicists cannot be protected too carefully.

If an element of secular morality is thus perfectly compatible with the life of Christian democracy, the presence of this element may even be desirable in that it prevents the community from going clericalist. Clericalism, the abuse of spiritual authority for worldly power and worldly positions under the pretext that this benefits the soul of the community, will be an ever present danger as long as clergymen are human. The most radical way of meeting the danger, naturally, is disestablishment of religion, a complete secularization of political life. The United States has in this way effectively prevented the strife of the denominations from rending the life of the community. Republican France has kept the Catholic clergy from acquiring the sinister influence which it has long had in neighboring Spain. Even high dignitaries of the Roman Catholic Church have been farsighted and fair-minded enough to recognize that disestablishment helps the personal ethics of their clergy. No one, then, can lightly advocate the form of re-establishment which would be implied in making Christianity a public function again, primarily in the system of education. But one has to advocate it if he sees that the overwhelming danger of our day is not clericalism, which our fathers fought, but de-Christianization, which they promoted. And the danger of clericalism, always grave politically and detestable from a religious point of view, can be reduced by the presence in the community of an unreligious section, which will naturally be critical of this regime.

All this, far from being mere speculation, is confirmed by the experience of Britain, the one Western democracy where the Christian climate is still strong and where the danger of clericalism has been minimized despite the establishment of the Church of England. There is in some writers a tendency to detract from the value for others of the British experience by pointing at the unique political qualities of this people. But the British genius is a historical phenomenon which has not always existed, and there is no reason to suspect in it more mystery than always remains, beyond any understanding or analysis, in every historical phenomenon. Why it arose we can never say; how it arose we can often make intelligible. If Britain has preserved a Christian atmosphere in which to integrate her democracy and has yet minimized clericalism, this is not a mere consequence of her unique genius; her genius has lain precisely in doing this. The continued Catholic tradition of her Church after the Reformation preserved much of the social morality which the churches of the continental reformers sacrificed to religious individualism. The presence of the free churches and the powerful current of secular thought, however, warded off the danger of clericalism —this is the other side of that happy combination. And the happiest part of it is that the powerful opposition, the Labour Party, is composed of approximately the same mixture of elements as is the country at large—High Church, Free Church, and atheist. The religious climate has preserved, and religious dissension has never since the eighteenth century seriously disturbed, the political unity.[2]

2. Since the great Max Weber, fifty years ago, presented England as a Puritan country and therefore a leader in capitalism, this astounding blunder has been faithfully repeated not only by his friend and neighbor Ernst Tröltsch but—as far as I can see—by all German sociologists of religion; even by a man as widely educated and careful as Alfred Müller-Armack (*Das Jahrhundert ohne Gott,* 1948). The assumption obviously is that the Church of England has no life of her own but has been, as a consequence of the Cromwellian revolution, penetrated and absorbed spiritually by Puritanism. Indeed the great influence which diverse Free Churches have exerted on the Church of England several times cannot be denied, but just as little can the original strength of the Anglican tradition and the repeated swing back to the Catholic side be ignored. As a result, the country is indeed half Free Church; but the other half is High Church. The former half has created the individualistic progressive element in English life, including pacifist socialism, and thereby influences the Established Church even today. The latter half, however, has created the conservative, tradition-bound element, not only in the forms of worship service but also in social structure and in the preservation of a vigorous and gradually democratized social ethic on an Anglican or Thomistic foundation. Men like William Temple, J. H. Oldham, and George Bell, or the present-day leading social theorist, V. A. Demant, should really not be counted as Puritans.

One may perhaps venture the contention that, while the Free Church

In the de-Christianized democracies, however, of both the American and continental types, conflict and disorder are rife because autonomous private interests go the limit. Autonomous collectivism offers itself as the logical remedy, but the clash between the two only reveals, in the perverted form appropriate to an atheist world, the essential moral unity of freedom and order. There is no room for a Third Force between the opposites of rationalist individualism and rationalist collectivism; either the individual or the collective appears as the vessel of rationality. If there is or can be a Third Force at all, it must be outside that dialectic, in a different system of thought, on a different plane. The argument from history—that autonomous democracy gradually consumes the moral reserves inherited from the Christian past—and the argument from logic—that the world of pure rationalism leaves no alternative but that between individualism and collectivism—lead to the same result.

The Idea of Social Justice
in the Recent Life of the Churches

Throughout this book it has been shown how modern democracy draws away from the Christian inheritance which had

---

gave rise to English liberalism, the Established Church and the monarchy produced the hesitant attitude toward capitalism and the tendency to place the social cohesion symbolized by the monarchy higher than the particular social stratification. In this sense the monarchy is inclined toward socialism rather than liberalism; social democracy as an expression of the sense of community seems to be its destination. The spirit of this democracy is the counterweight to Free Church liberalism.

Incidentally, it may not be superfluous to mention that the total number of Anglicans in England and the English-speaking countries is estimated as forty millions; and e.g. in the United States the influence in church life of the Episcopalian Church far exceeds the percentage of its three million members. It is Händel's *Messiah* in which Anglicanism has received its great expression in art. Händel's genius was German, his education largely Italian; but he wrote the tremendous work after thirty years of life at the English court, and this is the sociological locus for the understanding of its spirit. In the Anglo-Saxon countries, the *Messiah* has attained a degree of popularity which is unlikely to be equaled by any other great work of music anywhere in the world. But nobody can count it as Puritan.

made it possible. But we have discussed that Christian inheritance itself as if it had been intact, ready to be drawn upon,
except that the very origin of the de-Christianizing tendency in
democracy was traced to medieval clericalism and the religious
wars which filled the sixteenth and seventeenth centuries. In
point of fact, whatever we try to understand as Christian social
ethics—the mutual origin and dignity of the person and the
community; the totality of man's life in the spirit, in the flesh,
and in the institutions which minister to both; the ensuing importance of institutions for man's life in the spirit; and the
Christian possibility of self-transcendence in a new birth "of
the spirit"—the tragic fact is that Christendom, led and represented by Christian churches, swerved from the unmistakable
teachings of its source and reacted to the defection of the modern
world in the bitter resentment which testifies to the sociological
rather than to the spiritual side of Christian life. It would be
utterly erroneous and unfair to blame the tragedy of the modern
world exclusively or fundamentally on the world, as clericalist
self-righteousness and unctuousness continue to do in far too
many cases. If the Church is the appointed guardian of Christian
conscience and custodian of the age-old wisdom of Christian
thought, her greater dignity, maturity, and age make her, rather
than the passing generations of harassed people, responsible for
the tragedy.

The Roman Catholic Church has always, within her own
structure, been strongly authoritarian, but the supranational
character of her spiritual authority has, at the same time, made
her a refuge from the totalitarian ambitions of political authorities. She consistently and successfully resisted the claims to
supremacy of both Byzantine and German emperors, and thus
rescued the most precious of all man's possessions, the supremacy
of spiritual life over political power. This is the real freedom
which the Hebrew prophets had proclaimed in their struggle
against their nation's nationalism, but which the Greeks had
never understood and which Byzantium hence never knew.

But having thus defended "the glorious freedom of the
children of God," the Catholic Church set herself up as its administrator and judge, and provoked first the defection of the

East at the end of the first millennium, then that of the North five hundred years later, and thereafter the ever growing split in all Western societies between the followers and the adversaries of authoritarian control. The generations preceding the Reformation were rife with efforts to reform the internal organization of the Roman Church in the direction of representative government; but all such attempts were beaten down with the argument from the key which the Lord of the Church had entrusted to his vicar, a single person, and which Peter's successor could not share with people outside this line of apostolic succession. Nay, in the battle with defection the militant authoritarian structure of the Church hardened further. Also her sympathy with hierarchical structures in secular society, which seem to complete her own structure and are reminiscent of the age of her uncontested rule, has been preserved through the centuries.

Two qualifications are needed. First, the conservatism of the Church has been strongly paternalistic; it has been social conservatism. That the Indians of South America, after the first years of wholesale massacre by the Spanish conquerors, were spared the fate of their—far less numerous—brethren in Protestant North America was largely due to the influence of the Church. That almost all Roman Catholic countries are conspicuously backward in the art of capitalism is to the discredit of the Church in the judgment of all rationalists and adherents of an economic interpretation of history; but at any rate it proves the efficacy of the Church's paternalism and the insuperable obstacle it has put in the way of that ruthless search for profit through productivity which has degraded man to a mere means.

This leads directly to the second qualification: the Church's effective sponsorship of social legislation in all capitalist countries—though not in those of enduring feudalistic structure such as one finds in southern Italy, Spain, and Hungary. In the struggle against capitalist liberalism, the first incorporation of social rationalism, the Church allied itself with opposition groups on the left and could the more easily do that where her believers were in a minority position as against a Protestant majority and a Protestant ruling class; this was normal in the most conspicuous examples. In Weimar Germany the Catholic Center Party was in a coalition with the Social Democrats in the interlocking governments of the Reich and Prussia for all the fourteen years, and in the United States the Roman Catholic influence was strong in the New Deal administration and continues to be strong in organized labor. The only trouble is that every such case lends itself to a sociological explanation rather than to one in terms of the sublimity of divine justice—else how shall one account for the Church's policies in the citadels of feudalism? There is, however, a considerable degree of national differentiation and a considerable latitude of discussion, and the voice of prophetic justice makes itself strongly heard, particularly in France.[3]

The position of Protestantism in general—the British exception has already been discussed—is still more questionable because the very idea of social justice has been in the discard for a long time. In the western branches of Protestantism, religious individualism allied itself with the social individualism deriving from rationalist philosophy in building up the world of democracy and capitalism, as in the United States. Meanwhile German Lutheranism emerged from its Pietistic phase emphatically conservative for reasons of both its pessimism regarding human nature and its indifference to man's worldly destiny. What matters is spontaneous love, not coercive justice,

3. In New York there is a unique, strictly Catholic monthly, *The Catholic Worker*. Subscription is twenty-five cents per year and it has a circulation of some sixty thousand copies. It is carried by a group of exalted people, among them married couples and families with children, who live together in poverty with unlimited hospitality to the homeless and helpless in a few urban and rural settlements. The founder was a French unskilled worker, Pierre Maurin; since his death the group has been led by an admirable woman, mother and grandmother, Dorothy Day, whose autobiography is highly instructive. The political line is an uncompromising pacifism; it keeps the group separated from communism. The economic and social program is a fairly indistinct "distributism," strongly inclined toward absolute egalitarianism in some members. This is not interesting in itself except as a witness to the width of Catholic discussion. But its social critique and social reporting are often striking, its literary criticism is often instructive, its moral level is sublime throughout. It is raised still higher by the magnificent woodcuts which Fritz Eichenberg often contributes.

which is a matter of "the world." The discussion of institutions was considered godless materialism.

The indirect political importance of the personal ethic deriving from these teachings must not be belittled. Germany's ancient regime was distinguished from those of the other nations by the rigorous, incorruptible, law-abiding reliability and high level of education of its ruling bureaucracy, and Scandinavia was able to use similar qualities in the building of her democracy. But within the social structure the emphasis on personal love was effective only in personal relations. It was clearly meant to penetrate the feudal social unit of lord and serf living under one roof and in daily contact with one another; it could not but be irrelevant when large-scale industrial relations became impersonal and anonymous. Human love, in this highly individualistic interpretation, is limited to the personal circle and cannot be the principle to penetrate and organize, least of all to reorganize, society. The vast and admirable service of Lutheran—as of Catholic—charity agencies is no compensation. Charity works within a system, to mitigate the suffering caused by it; it does not transform the system. That is, the rich remain rich and the poor poor, and nothing in the fundamental relationship is changed. On the contrary, while the material hardships of poverty are mitigated, whatever fundamental injustice in human relations there is becomes accentuated by the one-sidedness of charity. The structure of society, accepted by Lutheran indifference, is positively justified by Puritanism; both in effect renounce the idea of social justice, which the official Roman Catholic doctrine recognizes in a more or less authoritarian context.

The upshot is that the Christian churches have betrayed justice. They have done it in different ways—the Lutheran Church by spiritualizing love and denying the religious nature of justice altogether; the Calvinist churches by identifying justice with their bourgeois order, where individuality is overstressed and the unifying responsible nature of love is minimized; the Roman Catholic Church by identifying justice with the feudal order in which the upper classes held the lower ones in their power and were thus responsible for them. The Chris-

tian churches have thus been discredited in the eyes of many
who have come to feel that the preachers of love are insensitive
to injustice done to others. These critics have drawn the conclusion that the Christian message of love is irrelevant to themselves; and it certainly is not for them to understand the Christian message better than its paid ministers. The churches have
reacted by giving up the infidels, not without trying to persuade
themselves that by praying for them they have discharged their
duty of love. The struggle of the oppressed and degraded for
justice has been denounced as materialistic and godless because,
launched in despair of the freely giving love of the community,
it had programmatically to do not with salvation but with
property. The churches did not even care to preach the Gospel
to them. For this would have required observance of the Pauline
injunction to be a Jew to the Jews and a Greek to the Greeks—
that is, first to establish community with those to be converted
in order to be able to reach them later in their own language
and tell them the profound secret of love once they had come
to experience what love was.[4] But the Christian churches have
never tried to be proletarians to the proletarians. They have
never understood that the very vocabulary in which their message has been handed down to them is inaccessible to the millions of children of a strictly rationalist age and requires translation if it is to be intelligible. The prophetic passion for justice
born of love had evaporated.

That is why the love which Christians betrayed went to the
atheists. A Christian, Walter Dirks, has most succinctly expressed it in the phrase that the great act of love in our age
was performed by Karl Marx, when he, a bourgeois, resolved
to see the world through the eyes of his proletarian brother and
so interpret it to others.[5] Whatever Marxism has become, it is

4. No less a figure than Paul had explicitly referred his audience,
in his speech at Athens, to their philosophical teachings as a starting point
for his own message.

5. *Frankfurter Hefte,* Vol. II, No. 2, February, 1947. This idea is
not new. It underlay the movement of "religious socialism" in Weimar
Germany, which, though very weak in the political arena, has been and
continues to be an influential force spiritually. Its undisputed head at
that time was Paul Tillich, who in his book *Sozialistische Entscheidung*

its original motive—the spark of love for the degraded, the prophetic sense of offended justice—which has persuaded many millions to embrace it when the preachers of love failed to speak the language of love. Karl Marx was not great enough to rise above the pretentious absurdities of his age; this is lamentably true. But the Christian churches did not even rise to their age.

Hence we have the series of impossible antitheses which tear our lives and minds. We are told that Christianity is spiritual while the proletarian struggle is concerned with the body as the only value: idealism versus materialism. But the bodiless spirit has no place in Christianity, which is the doctrine of incarnation. The Lord of the Church took the body seriously and knew no distinction between the body and the soul. The power of His compassion for the misery of the bodies converted the souls. The lesson is unmistakable: He did not accost the soul directly where the misery of the body was too great, and He took this misery as a challenge to the power of love.

(1931) and many preceding writings, several of which may be found in translation in his *The Protestant Era,* penetrated through the rationalistic scientific appearance of the socialist creed to its genuine religious motive, its vision of man and community retrieved from degradation and dehumanization, and thus tried to widen and deepen the spiritual strength of the socialist movement. So far, there is no logical conflict between Tillich's (or Dirks') position and the criticism of Marxism in Chapter VI.

A difficulty does arise, however, when it comes to an evaluation. To characterize Marxism as an essentially although not consciously religious movement poses as many problems as it solves. For there is no such thing as religion in general; there are, at best, rival, mutually exclusive religions. It is as if one said that it makes no essential difference which of several conflicting theories one adopts in some science and its application. Since at best only one of them, if any, can be correct, the adherents of the others are necessarily misled into failure and defeat. Likewise the Marxist pseudo religion, while satisfying the religious urge of the human soul and giving the life of its believers poise and meaning, fails in the more profound objective tests, which Christianity alone can meet because it makes intelligible and bearable the insoluble problems of human life. This is what was pointed out in Chapters V–VII. See my article "Tillich's Religious Socialism," in *The Theology of Paul Tillich,* edited by Kegley and Bretall, New York, 1953. On pseudo religions in general, see *Freedom and Order,* pp. 268–271.

We are told that while this body is mortal the soul is immortal, thus demonstrating its infinite value and superiority. But the Bible knows nothing of the immortality of the soul, while it knows much about the resurrection of the body—which, whatever it be, is something totally different. We are told, on the Bible's authority, that the spirit is willing but the flesh is weak, and that the law of our members wars against the law of our minds. But sin is not the weakness of the body but the corruption of the mind. One may well imagine God's smilingly forgiving the minor sins which come from the weakness of the body; but the sin against the spirit, which does not come from the weakness of the body, is not forgiven. Drunkenness may be bad and the bewilderment of sex may be tragic, but the real sin is lovelessness. Is the lust for power bodily? It is a lust of the mind. The animals, which are only bodies, do not know it but live out their lawful lives. Man's misery lies precisely in the fact that the mind, the instrument of his unique greatness among the creatures of nature, tempts him to abuse his greatness.

We are told that Christianity teaches the infinite value of the individual and that socialism, therefore, is anti-Christian by definition. But first of all socialism has to do with institutions, and institutions cannot be Christian or anti-Christian in themselves but only in the relations they establish between men. In the second and more important place, Christianity is far from teaching the infinite value of the individual. What it does teach is the supreme power of love, which transcends the individual, draws him out of himself, and establishes community, without in the process absorbing the individual. In other words, what follows from the supremacy of love is the equal dignity of the person and the community, the dignity of the community of love, and the dignity of the person confirmed by love. But what shall we say of Christendom which teaches sheer absurdity? Christianity always means the whole existence of man, never an abstract part thereof; it means both body and soul, person and community.

A qualification may seem to be needed regarding the superb achievement of Lutheran Germany, the social insurance legislation of the Bismarckian Empire in the 1880's. The fact that it would never have come off without the dual threat from Marxism and from the economic insecurity triumphantly welcomed by Marxism was discussed in an earlier context; what matters here is the question of the agent responsible for understanding and meeting the threat. Now the matrix of the new idea and of its brilliant technical elaboration was, no doubt, the German universities, at that time still at the height of their reputation and moral authority. The explicit purpose of all the great Christian universities had always been the education of honest, responsible, and competent officials; and in particular Professor Martin Luther, protagonist of monarchical absolutism, was emphatic on the necessity of taming monarchical arbitrariness by the wise counsel of the monarch's aides and their teachers.[6] But the influence of the Christian universities is one thing, the preachings of the Church are quite a different thing, particularly in a setup where the structure of the state and of governmental policy are emphatically considered below the sphere of religious interest and hence outside the Church's concern—matters of "the world." That there should be a ubiquitous long-range and indirect influence of Christian tradition on the history of Christian nations is one thing, that the Church should observe a strictly hands-off attitude toward problems of social justice is quite a different thing. It is quite in line with Lutheran tradition that Bismarck, a devout Lutheran, resented the attempt of a group of conservative churchmen led by a court preacher to organize for participation in social policy and legislation, and a little later an analogous group of liberal churchmen organized with the support of such great scholars as Harnack and Troeltsch remained strictly irrelevant in the life of the Church. What was true in Germany was just as true in other countries. The recog-

6. I am abashed to say that I have overlooked this aspect of Luther's attitude in my book *Freedom and Order*. I owe the correction to Eugen Rosenstock-Huessy and George Wolfgang Forell. The attempt of the latter, however, to approximate Luther's ethics to pragmatism appears to me to go too far; cf. his *Faith Active in Love* (1954), an investigation of the principles underlying Luther's social ethics.

nized political necessity of social legislation did not mitigate the rigor of the asocial interpretation of the Christian message in typical sermons and teachings.

We have the impossible antitheses between the opposite fronts in modern society: justice versus love, democracy versus the Church, ethic versus religion. Each one of these is deprived of its true meaning by the false opposition in which it stands. For in reality justice must be present in love, ethic in religion, democracy in the Church. Love without justice becomes oppressive, religion without ethic degenerates into magic, the Church without the democratic masses into sectarianism. Correspondingly, justice without love is callous and inhuman, ethic dries out if uprooted from religion, democracy dies without a Christian climate. The pernicious antitheses are fundamentally one, and both sides are fundamentally in the wrong. But it remains true that the guilt of the Church weighs heavier than that of the estranged masses of the people, because the Church is older and higher.

The Turn of the Tide

It would be rash to say that the situation has changed completely since the First World War, but it has changed to a considerable extent. There still is the convenient preaching on the wonderful nature of love as a relation between souls, and it is appreciated as an important political position and is defended by much political and financial pressure in church life. But the important thing is that the appeal to Christian justice in behalf of Christian love is no longer a reservation of liberal theologians, who are suspected of laxity on dogma anyway, but has been received in the heart of orthodoxy everywhere, more or less in the terms suggested in Chapter VIII. The effect is profound, both inside the churches—as witnessed by many church pronouncements on national and international affairs, though probably least on the parish level—and in the general public discussion, where the voice of Christianity is heard again, after generations, as contributing something relevant and distinct. It cannot be objected that this would never have happened without the disillusionment and apprehensions after one and two world wars; it is precisely the frustration of secular hopes which figures large in the Christian message and revalidates it against conventional doubts.

Thus it is no accident that after Greece's time of suffering a movement of astonishing vigor and vitality seized the intellectuals of the country and set out to struggle for a new version of the Christian understanding of life and society.[7] Likewise in hard-hit Germany the tremendous Evangelical "Church Days" (with 180,000 participants at Essen, 600,000 at Leipzig) on the one hand, the Evangelical Academies on the other hand, are witnesses to an entirely novel spontaneity among Christian laymen; their effects on church affairs, general spiritual life, and social relations cannot be estimated in advance. Again in Holland, still under the occupation and in the concentration camps, plans sprang up to overcome the petrified division of noncommunicating church parties by a new final link in theological education and a systematic training for Christian social and youth work.[8] The World Union of Churches, conceived decades ago with full consciousness of its significance in church history and built up step by step, became a reality with a minimal apparatus and an immediately tremendous echo; the unity of all Christian endeavor beyond all ecclesiastical and theological demarcations tends to assert itself here (with the Roman Catholic Church and the Orthodox churches in Soviet countries remaining aloof indeed, if not unsympathetic).

It would be foolish to exaggerate the success and ignore the dangers that beset us on all sides. Whatever weird methods the Hungarian Communists may have used to break Cardinal Mindszenty's strong spirit and will, his conflict with them had come into the open over the land reform, which he vehemently denounced because of ruthless and vindictive measures used in

7. The Christian Union of Professional Men of Greece published even in English translation their remarkably comprehensive book *Towards a Christian Civilization* (Athens, 1950) written by Professor A. N. Tsirintanes.

8. This reference to Holland, unfortunately, is not found in the German version of this book.

the expropriation of the feudal estates; his uncompromising stand thus amounted to a defense of gravest ancient wrong. This again did not prevent the Supreme Pontiff in a public exhortation from proclaiming that the issue had now been joined between the good and the wicked, and Roman Catholic self-righteousness, which always appears shockingly un-Christian to Protestants, reached a new high in precisely this case, where the political record was anything but clear.

Nothing similar had happened in Protestantism, and the World Council of Churches in its Amsterdam Assembly took full account of those moral failures of Christians which had made the victims receptive to Communist remedies for their plight. But in theology itself the hardly won new position has been endangered again by a Biblical literalism which identifies present-day Christendom far too directly with the persecuted members of the primitive church. Karl Barth himself in his opening address at Amsterdam unqualifiedly warned against the presumption that man was responsible for God's business in directing the course of history. And the World Council gave prominence to an impressive statement [9] in which the British historian Martin Wight epitomizes the new eschatology in the phrase that the real history of the world ended in the year 33 and everything ever since is only an epilogue which does not really matter. The only thing that matters is the Second Coming of Christ, and Christians should welcome the increasing terror and atrociousness of worldly affairs as the appointed signs "that their salvation draws near." However admirable the serenity thus gained amidst the anxieties of present earthly life, it is bought at the price of sacrificing Christian ethic and disclaiming responsibility. The man on Patmos, to whom the doom of the Beasts, the great powers, was revealed, was obviously without responsibility for them because he was in their chains. But can as much be said of modern Christians in comfortable positions of authority in the democratic world? Can they disclaim responsibility for the bomb over Hiroshima? And would it then not be much more pertinent for literalists to apply to themselves the tenth chapter of the Epistle to the Hebrews, according to which

9. *Ecumenical Review,* Vol. I, No. 1.

the renewed sin of the already redeemed cannot be forgiven? "It is a fearful thing to fall into the hands of the living God."

As in church life, so in public life the situation is confused at the moment of this writing. There was, immediately upon the end of the Second World War with its rich lessons of priests and atheists fraternally sharing dangers and sufferings in the underground struggle, a hopeful surge of democratic sentiment among Christians, in Germany and Italy no less than in England, Holland, and Scandinavia, but most conspicuously in France. The movement was clearly defined by its emphasis on social democracy as a combination of personal liberty and social justice. Upon the spectacular rise of the French Catholic Democratic party there has followed a rapid decline, the principal cause of France's weakness and the gravest disappointment in European postwar history. The most significant example of Christian and left-wing forces wedded in the same cause, then, was not new in itself, namely, the British Labour Party; what was new was its temporary rise to power and responsibility. Nevertheless the importance of the new continental parties remains great. It need not be sheer accident that the French Catholic Democratic party has proved eminently productive of minds and ideas in European postwar history. But the significance of these parties is primarily one of principle, as a breach with the age-old antidemocratic tradition. What they signify is that Christian justice requires new forms of life today and that such new forms can be vessels of social health only in a Christian atmosphere.

This program must be guarded against two misunderstandings. The existence of a Christian party would not be desirable at all if this were not a de-Christianized world; the ringing proclamation of the relevance of Christian principles to public life is good only because it is needed, just as a medicine is not good in itself but only upon indication. This implies, second, that there is not and must never be a left-wing monopoly on Christianity. Once more, that there should be Christian left-wing parties can be justified only against the background of Christianity having long been identified with right-wing parties exclusively; not to erect a new monopoly but to break the existing monopoly is the meaning of a Christian left-wing party. Had there been in the past a left-wing monopoly of Christian representation, the emergence of right-wing Christian parties would be a sign of returning health. In the light of these considerations, the desirability of an officially Christian party in post-Hitler Germany is much more questionable than that of the new parties in Italy and France, although it can be argued in the German case that the immediately preceding overtly and anti-Christian past had to be washed off by a confession of faith even in the name of the new party. And the spectacularly European course in the international policy of the party might not have been possible without the appeal to the highest authority to overcome the traditional nationalism.

In principle, Christianity must be free from political entanglement. It must be demonstrated that both conservative and progressive political programs may be derived from Christian ethics, as both the priestly type who hallows life and makes hardships bearable if they cannot be removed, and the prophetic type who preaches a life in greater fullness and justice, are authentic and necessary figures in the tradition of the Church. But this implies, on the other hand, that neither conservatism nor progressivism can claim strict logical derivation from Christian principles, because the political application is separated from the general principle by the wide zone of factual material and technical functions which are essential in any program of policy but cannot be judged and selected on merely moral grounds. Preachers are as apt to brush them aside in their moral exhortations as experts are apt to substitute them for moral principles. This technical factor will be judged differently by different experts, Christian or not, and its presence in the world of political and social institutions definitely precludes the possibility of one "Christian policy." William Temple and John C. Bennett have forcefully made this point. What remains is the possibility and necessity of having opposite political programs under the one roof of Christianity, which is precisely what the transformation and Christian reintegration of democracy require. There are many mansions in our Father's house, and Christianity is the foundation of social life precisely because it is not a political program, and different political programs only follow from its inspiration and are thereby held together.[10]

The "Third Force"

As Christendom had to be retold and is at last being retold the full dimension and profundity of the principle of love, which includes justice, so the democratic world had gradually to learn again the full dimension and profundity of liberty, its supreme principle. This is far more than an accidental parallelism; there is an essential convergence between the new trend of Christian thought and the new trend in Western public and international life. It is the reawakened sense of social responsibility and justice which causes the democracies to rise above their traditional narrow and selfish interpretation of their liberty to a level where they try to enhance liberty by restraining its abuses, widening its scope, and expanding its benefits. They enhance liberty by subjecting it to criteria of social responsibility and justice. In the terms used in Chapter VIII, they rise to a creative use of liberty in the attempt to make life richer and justice fuller in the world. They set a new beginning by rising above the level of mere logical necessity, the level of the economic interpretation of history, where existent tendencies are elongated into the future but cannot be reversed or amended because the premises are fixed.

The economic interpretation of history was shown to be

10. The political prejudice in which the great Karl Barth indulges can be seen from the fact that the possibility of a Christian conservative attitude never occurs in his study "Christian Community and Civil Community" (translated in *Against the Stream* from the German *Christengemeinde und Buergergemeinde,* 1946). Even the word "conservative" is never used, only occasionally the word "reactionary." A Christian is to be a democrat or a socialist, period. The often wiser Hellmut Gollwitzer, whose report on his five years of captivity in Russia, *Unwilling Journey,* is the most moving document of a personal encounter with communism, arrives at the possibility of a Christian conservatism ten lines before the end of his parallel study *Die Christliche Gemeinde in der Politischen Welt,* 1954.

plausible only because, and insofar as, man does not use his creative freedom to break through the law of economic necessity but merely adapts himself to its rule. But that he did not in modern times use his liberty is a historical fact, and it seemed triumphantly to vindicate that somber doctrine of rational necessity driving to its appointed end. The question that had remained open in those earlier discussions thus is not one of principle but one of fact. Is creative freedom practiced by us? Are we still capable of creating a new start of history—that is, of re-creating ourselves? Are there creative solutions to be found for urgent problems of our day?

In a way the answer is implied in what was said on the recent social dialectic. Rather than driving from individualism to collectivism and stopping there, it rises above the thesis of individualism and the antithesis of collectivism to the higher level of what is improperly called a mere synthesis, in a constitutional democracy. The word "synthesis" suggests the constant misunderstanding of a halfway station, a "mixed economy," while the important thing is that new criteria are found outside and above the dialectic of individualism and collectivism and cannot be deduced from them. Nor is the reference to pragmatism sufficient for the understanding of this real dialectic. It can work within a structure which is intact as a whole and tacitly accepted as the framework of life; it cannot serve as a criterion in the contest between different structures and beliefs, each of which might be workable in itself and none of which is tacitly accepted.

In describing this dialectic of modern history, we must, however, guard against any confusion with Hegelian or Marxist dialectics, both of which are laws of a more or less—less in Hegel's case—rigid development, and both of which for this reason include predictability—the test of their being laws. We do not say that history must choose this way but only that it has chosen it in this particular instance; we explain nothing, we only describe. We describe human action because we understand it; but understanding is altogether different from explanation. Understanding as the tool of description is not likely to be accepted by modern positivism, but the insistence that there is no explanation in description is certainly due to positivism.

These considerations are anything but purely academic. We have made little use of the passion-charged word "dialectic" because we do not need it. We have described the form which events have taken and have called it dialectical, but this description would be valid and intelligible without that name as well. The reason, once more, is that "dialectic" to us is the name of certain structures in reality—the relationship between freedom and order pre-eminently—but not a law about a necessary sequence of structures. We describe dialectical forms and sequences where we find them, but we are far from expecting to find them everywhere, least of all everywhere in the sequence of structures. We cannot do any of these things because "dialectic" in the sequence of events is that creative rise over (dialectical or undialectical) necessities of Marxist or any other scientific type which is linked to freedom and defined in opposition to any "law." We do not say that constitutional democracy *had* to follow upon the thesis of dogmatic individualism and the antithesis of dogmatic collectivism; we only say that it *did* follow, although there was, according to the Marxist dialectical law, every reason not to expect this—the test of freedom.

Hence also we do not expect any necessity, dialectical or other, for Western mankind to emerge victoriously from the troubles which beset it at this hour. The necessity is rather on the negative side, and our quest is for the—never assured—possibility of a creative solution. Constitutional democracy has proved to be the answer to the challenge on the national level by tearing the dialectic from Marxist collectivism, allegedly its last word, and thus immunizing Western society against Marxist collectivism. Meanwhile, however, Marxism, barred from the countries of its origin, has turned to the non-Western societies, to Russia and China, the "underdeveloped countries," and is engaged in the attempt at southward expansion from there.[11] In addition, the Second World War reduced the European heart

11. "Marxism and Underdeveloped Countries," *Social Research,* June, 1952.

countries of Western society to a misery unknown for generations and rent the established fabrics of life so as to approach
the pulverization which is the logical preparation to mechanical
reaggregation by communism. Both developments, in Asia and
Europe, posed a new challenge to Western creativity on the international level. On the one hand, the colonialism which was
largely responsible for the backward condition of ancient
civilized nations had to be liquidated and a helping hand had
to be extended to the former victims to put them on their feet,
lest they seek their emancipation by calling in communism. On
the other hand, economic reconstruction and social stabilization
in East and West require huge funds, and the only available
source for them is the intact wealth of the United States. Thus
the contest, lost by communism on the national level in peace-
time conditions, is reopened on the international level. There is
no reason to doubt the possibility in principle of creative solutions—they exist almost always—but the problem again is that
of finding such solutions in the quite concrete, material, and
technical terms which alone define historical creativity.

The Marshall Plan

If examples of such creative use of freedom in recent years
are to be given here, this can be done only with fear and trembling. What will be described is a beginning, it is not a finished
work. The more we boast of the beginning as if it were a finished
work, the graver is the danger of our relaxing into the complacency which is the undoing of creative freedom. The beginning
which has been made has been achieved by a great moral and
intellectual effort; it cannot be continued and completed without more such effort. In point of fact, such complacent relaxation has long set in and threatens to destroy everything that has
been achieved, and more. On the other hand, the significance
and principle of that beginning are far-reaching indeed. It
proves both the possibility of creative freedom in this age, and
the presence in skeptical modern man of that imagination and
power which were too long denied by scientists in search of the
causal necessities governing social life. If we cannot succeed

without the humility that comes from fear and trembling, we cannot succeed either without the confidence and courage which feed on the beginning already achieved; we have already tested our strength and have not found it wanting.

The first example of creative freedom in dealing with our emergency is the Marshall Plan. Through it America has made use of her creative freedom to transcend her own traditional narrow understanding of freedom. To transcend oneself is the very mark of freedom. It is the regeneration of which the Bible speaks, the new birth of freedom demanded by the Gettysburg Address. The Marshall Plan has transcended the fatal schism between the liberal and the socialist versions of liberty which had all but wrecked Europe. On the basis of the common belief in liberty, the Marshall Plan has built an international community whose national members are permitted to disagree on matters of application of the supreme principle, thus giving evidence of their respect for one another's freedom.

The idea behind the plan was a conception of foreign policy. Its original motive was the defense of the United States against both communism and the danger of war by a constructive fight against poverty rather than by mere armament. Clearly Western Europe—that is, Britain, France, Germany, Italy, and six extremely able smaller nations—even after the loss of much equipment and most foreign investments, was and remained a source of so much intellectual strength and organizational experience that it could be made, by unified reconstruction, a "Third Power" side by side with the two giant states. Through the Marshall Plan, America undertook to finance that reconstruction. That is, America offered to reduce her own position as one of two effective powers to that of one of three powers. Speaking by way of oversimplification, she offered to reduce her position of 50 per cent of effective power to that of 33 per cent. Naturally, this spectacular offer was not unselfish. A statesman is not permitted to sacrifice the interests of his nation to any ideal of purely unselfish generosity; the distinction of constructive statesmanship lies in that farsighted wisdom which easily blends with practical generosity. The offer was made in the hope that, should the array of potential power not prevent

armed conflict, America would find herself not with 33 per cent
nor with 50 per cent of the total power but with 67 per cent;
and this very prospect might well secure the preservation of the
peace, if atomic and superatomic weapons should prove more
and more unusable. It is true that in 1948 the rapid rise of the
military power of China had not yet been taken into account;
it became surprisingly visible only a brief while later, in the
Korean War. This qualification diminishes all percentages in
the estimate just given but in no way invalidates the argument
in principle.

Much has been made of America's alleged interest in exports
under the Marshall Plan as an insurance against an economic
depression. The idea is easily linked with the idea of economic
imperialism as being the only remedy to depression under
capitalism: the Marshall Plan would then be a disguised form
of economic imperialism, forcing on the recipient countries
American goods unsalable in free markets at home or abroad.
But as a measure of business-cycle policy the Marshall Plan
would be quite inadequate because a serious depression would
not effectively be met by exports of three or four billion dollars
a year (even though multiplied by two or three in the circulation of incomes); several times that amount would be needed.
Much more important, however, is that everything in business-
cycle policy depends on timing, and the Marshall exports, being
fixed in time, could aggravate the danger of inflation if they
coincided with a domestic boom just as easily as they could serve
as a cushion in a depression. They did reinforce the inflationary
boom, in point of fact. The public debate had made this
ambivalent and hazardous character of the Plan quite clear in
advance. So much the more, then, does the international, and
in this sense political, motive of the Plan stand out in great
clarity.

What had thus started as a proposition in foreign policy became a new social principle when it came, as it immediately
must, to be translated into terms of the domestic policies of the
nations concerned. The naïve expectation held by many in the
United States that the Marshall funds would make the recipient
countries safe for the American conception of democratic

liberty incorporated in the freedom of enterprise was rudely shattered when these countries made it clear that they would not sacrifice their integrity for credits. They could afford to use this language because the whole conception of the Plan implied that America needed them as much as they needed America. This initial effect was the most startling of all the results of the plan; it was the birth of a new social and moral principle in Western history. Or rather, the new idea was born when the American statesmen—Marshall, Acheson, and Vandenberg—accepted this interpretation of the Plan and steered it safely through Congress. For what that meant was that America rose over her traditional conception of liberty and her vested interest in it to a higher understanding. America's love of liberty was tested and proved when she preferred the liberty of others to deviate from her own form of liberty to her own ideological and material stake in that form; differences in the conception of liberty were secondary to the common belief in liberty.

To repeat, America did not achieve this for ideological or idealistic reasons, but as a practicable way out of a dire impasse. Nor must it be forgotten that, even so, success would have been extremely doubtful without the exasperated denunciation of the Plan by the Soviet. After all, there is nothing wondrous about the fact that it took a unique concatenation of conditions to have American capitalism finance British socialism—for this is what it was. It runs counter to all theories and all textbooks; it is contrary to the logic of capitalism and to the logic of socialism; it is an act of creative freedom. It brought into the open the kinship between American constitutional democracy and European libertarian socialism, which are not identical—else there would be nothing spectacular in the Marshall Plan—but are not too far apart to make the Marshall Plan possible, and thus to establish the Western community of nations on a firmer foundation precisely because of the wider margin of freedom within that community. That the donor respects the spiritual and social integrity of the recipient can be seen only when there are differences between them; defense of the recipient's integrity despite financial dependence on the donor was the moral condition of the Marshall Plan's success. Nobody has understood this better than the first administrator of the Plan, Paul Hoffman, a good American businessman if there are any.

The unique generosity of this program flows from the greatest of American virtues. It is without precedent in history for domination of the world to devolve on a nation which does not want it. America does not want to rule the world, but the Western world cannot survive without some form of American rule. This strange concatenation is not without serious drawbacks: America must rule without being in any way power-wise. America's reluctance to assume the position in which she is cast by history traditionally expresses itself in isolationism, and so deserves to be criticized as an escape from responsibility and ultimately as callousness. But even in isolationism America's love of liberty, her respect for other people's independence, is discernible. America's conception of liberty has been badly unbalanced by the confusion of liberty with private contract; all the urgent social and economic problems and dangers of American life stem from this root. But America's unique virtue is in taking her political libertarianism seriously and applying it in the international field, so as to preclude her own supremacy. The Marshall Plan may thus be characterized as the acceptance of responsibility without control. Again, this does not by any means imply complete unselfishness of motives, and the conception continues to be menaced from many quarters and to recede more and more under the surging wave of nationalist impatience, where the experience of power too easily engenders the enjoyment of power. But this is no reason to belittle the greatness of the original idea of the Marshall Plan and the brilliancy of its execution.

The End of Colonial Imperialism

The significance of the Marshall Plan, however great, is possibly surpassed by that of Britain's achievement in lending a helping hand to the rise of India to statehood and independence. America recognizes versions of liberty different from her own; Britain helps build the political liberty of her colonial subjects.

Both use their creative freedom in such a manner as significantly to expand the extent of freedom in the world.

This appraisal of India's emancipation can as easily be mocked as that of the Marshall Plan. For there can be no doubt of the large element of self-interest in Britain's recent policy in India. Less than the United States in the case of the Marshall Plan did Britain act spontaneously in leaving India; she had to go if she did not want to risk an uprising, which might have thrown India into the arms of communism. But once more, unselfishness is not among the logical possibilities or virtues of statecraft; no statesman would be morally justified in sacrificing the vital interests of the community. The difference is not between selfishness and unselfishness but between traditional oppression and a farsighted pursuit of interests in such a manner as to reconcile them with the interests of others and make a former colonial subject and potential rebel into a friend. A truly great man, Winston Churchill, bears unwilling witness to this distinction in his indignant refusal, a few years earlier, "to preside over the dissolution of the British Empire." He could have been headed for the Empire's collapse; Sir Stafford Cripps, Field Marshall Wavell, and, with the decisive contribution, Viceroy Lord Mountbatten engaged in the attempt to transform the untenable Empire into a Commonwealth.

If anyone doubts that their action and that of their country is an act of creative freedom, based though it is on self-interest, he need only ask himself why there is no room for this solution in the Marxist picture of imperialism, which assumes the necessity of final catastrophe. And if anyone rightly claims that the founders of India's independence are not those Britishers, but Gandhi and Nehru, he need only ask himself whether and how without the cooperation of their adversary they could have succeeded in setting up an independent India at peace with the Moslem population within and without its borders. Further criteria for a sound appraisal of events in India are afforded by their sequel in Indonesia, where the Dutch did grudgingly what they would hardly have done without the moral pressure coming from the Indian precedent, and in Indochina where con-

ditions admittedly are even more complicated than in India, but
where the French have failed the creative task of reconciliation
and delimitation which the British discharged in India; this
could not but result in gravest peril to the French and to the
entire Western community.[12] For the emergence of a free India
with the active support of her former rulers clearly marks the
end of Western imperialism everywhere.

One can say that both the Marshall Plan and Britain's help
in setting up an independent India—and Burma—are inspired
by the idea of universalizing liberty, after liberty had too long
been used by the strong to subdue and hold down the weak. Or
one can express the same thing by saying that liberty and equality are here reconciled, equal political liberty being sought for
nations of different strength. Or one may, finally, say that liberty
is here saved and tempered by justice—precisely that justice
which demands equality for the weak with the strong. Which-
ever of these wordings is preferred, the important thing is the
recognition that the West, after several generations of mere lip
service, now makes a sincere effort to live up to its own high
principles.[13]

President Truman's Point Four Program and its more concrete British counterpart, the Colombo Plan, were designed to
round out the picture. If the weak are to be emancipated from

12. It should be added that De Gaulle had proclaimed the imperative
necessity of radically transforming the French Empire ever since he first
assumed leadership in 1940. Cf. "DeGaulle and Democracy," *Christianity
and Crisis,* May 25, 1959.

13. This assertion is not refuted by reference to the uprising of the
Mau-Mau in Kenya, just as that which was above said about America is
not refuted by the counterrevolution in Guatemala in the same year 1953.
These events prove a lack of consequence which is not excused but becomes intelligible if we remember that the problem is not that of a logical
operation but of subduing local interests at quite different points of a
highly complicated international situation. The attention of the nation
and its public opinion are fully absorbed by the great political issues, and
thus in a local problem of a politically remote phase the local interests
have the field all to themselves. This proves that a great people is sorely
imperfect even in its great moral achievements. But it remains true that
Europe was more important politically than Guatemala and India more
important than Kenya.

political control by the strong, they must be strengthened economically too. In a sense these plans burn the ships behind the new venture of the West by setting up a program whose realization would make a return to imperialism more or less impossible. While this is only a negative merit, the positive promise to the hundreds of millions of people living in abject misery is immense. For the fast-moving dynamics of present-day history it will be of greatest importance to be able to point at some tangible and concrete building projects to give substance to the program and to stir the imagination. For if planned progress in welfare is the program of the Communist rival, it does not suffice to oppose to it political independence and social liberty, whatever its meaning under Asian conditions; the contest can never be won without some substantiated promise of welfare too.

Now Western technology has grown in a specifically Western cultural pattern; Max Weber and Arnold Toynbee [14] have shown that it could not have grown anywhere else. That implies that Western technology conflicts with value systems of non-Western countries where it now is to be introduced, as it had originally conflicted with the value systems of the very Western nations, thus giving rise to the economic interpretation of history. The only major community so far where Western technology has been introduced in such a manner as not to disrupt the social and cultural pattern is Japan; but in view of the diversities of cultures, her model can be studied only for its wisdom, not for the methods employed. And one overpowering cultural problem even Japan did not tackle at all: the problem of birth control at a time of rising productivity so as to meet the Malthusian threat. These are no arguments against the Point Four and Colombo Plans; only the immense scope of the problem and behind it the required change in moral climate must be emphasized.

Now the example of Japan suggests a further grave problem in economic and technological modernization: the political problem. Japan's was a strictly authoritarian social and political structure, and this made it possible to guide the modernization effectively and safely through the two opposite dangers of in-

14. Cf. Toynbee's *The World and the West,* 1953.

effectiveness and social disruption—both of which would lead
to communism. This is not to say that, after a rather long experience in modern methods, Japan would not now be ripe for
less authoritarian control than she still retains. But the point is
that there can be no greater and more pernicious error than the
widespread belief that business and industrialism are inherent
in human nature and will spring into action as soon as they are
given a chance by a relaxation of authoritarianism. What may
be said to be inherent in human nature is a desire for welfare
and maybe, to a certain extent, for wealth; but the rational
disciplines required for industry are quite foreign to village life
in India or Japan and are not easily acquired in exchange for
the ancient disciplines of the village. In other words, business
and industry presuppose re-education, and this is not merely a
general anthropological problem as suggested above but an
eminently political problem. Let anyone who doubts this ponder
the fact that in Western society itself business and industry
were the products not of liberalism but of the absolute state
and its authoritarian economic policy called mercantilism; the
father of American industrialism, Alexander Hamilton, was a
statesman in the mercantilist tradition.[15] It is very true, of
course, that at that time industrialism was unknown in the
West, while it is known and desired in Asia today; this must
give democracy a far better chance than it would have had
around 1800. But the point is that even so democracy, if it relies
on laissez-faire, would be sure to lose out to Communist planned
progress in welfare. For democracy in Asia to be a real alternative to the European absolute state, Japanese authoritarianism,
and Communist dictatorship, what is required is vigorous and
inspiring leadership on the village level.

This, however, brings us back to the more strictly economic
problem. Point Four and Colombo—even if multiplied in
amounts instead of being cut down, because we can no longer
"afford" them—can never suffice, for the problem is not only
one of national structures to be reorganized but of an eminently
international structure geared wrongly. This rounds out our

15. Cf. "Comparative Economic Systems," in A. Dudley Ward (ed.),
Goals of Economic Life, 1952.

discussion in the preceding chapter, where it was argued that the free market of liberalism, far from being the economic form of the principle of free choice, has created in America a rigid physical structure whose smooth operation demands industrial expansion at an undiminished rate, while the moral and international problems of such expansion are rapidly worsening. We look now at the reverse side of the medal: What has the same free market done to the Asian economies?

In an economic body integrated by national history there is a certain distribution of incomes, which may be uneven and unfair but must in the long run provide for the minimum livelihood on the lowest layers of the income pyramid.[16] Even more important, experience proves that growing national income remains by and large distributed proportionately (and becomes flatter more recently), so the income pyramid does not change its shape, as all layers benefit proportionately and the base and the top rise equally—provided market principles are unaffected by deliberate discrimination, e.g. on feudal or racial grounds. But there is no cultural or other proportionality in the distribution of purchasing power in the world market. The preponderance of the United States economy—50 per cent of the industrial output of the world comes from a country inhabited by 6 per cent of the world's population, which country is also an exporter of food—is such that it can adequately be described as an autonomous system, disregarding its international economic relations. But the Asian countries, unable to compete for even the most vitally needed goods if America chooses to buy them, can get only what America does not care to have. In the domestic

16. The economic argument runs that if the minimum is not covered the ensuing famine would reduce the supply of menial services and thus raise their wages until the minimum is reached. It is more realistic to say that growing wealth of the upper stratum spreads downward by being spent, either on personal services by the poor or as capital for their productive employment. But in the colonial countries the wealth of the native upper class is all too often spent for luxury or investment in the imperial countries. A grotesque example is offered by the operetta emperor whom the French to their shame installed in Indochina a few years before their catastrophe: he preferred to spend his French subventions on the French Riviera.

American economy, while the rich buy very much, there is enough of everything for the relatively poor; but nothing of the sort obtains in the world market. To use a spectacular example, as America buys paper all over the world to feed it to her advertisements and her so-called comics, the British find it difficult to print serious books, and India lies open to the millions of twenty-cent editions, in many Indian languages, of the Communist classics and cannot afford enough American books at five dollars apiece to counter the propaganda—not even if there were such books. To attribute to the free market the optimum distribution of goods, the maximum degree of efficiency, and the sole guarantee of personal and political liberty is a bold enterprise.

Imperialism and colonialism mean dependence on foreign rule, foreign necessities, foreign whims. America, former colony herself, is dead set against any form of colonialism; Britain has honorably liquidated her colonial rule in India, Ceylon, Burma. Yet the Asians, and not only propagandists but the most brilliant and morally ambitious statesmen, continue to suspect our every step of imperialist motives. We resent that and try to forgive it by explaining it to ourselves as a kind of cultural lag, the persistence of a formed habit. But the Asians are right: Western colonialism is not dead, since Western necessities and Western whims continue to determine their lives and keep them in defenseless and helpless dependence—the very mark of colonialism. Political rule is gone, but their economies are integrated into the rigid structure of a world market formed under conditions of political colonialism without social balance and perpetuating the results. The Asian economies—and similarly situated economies elsewhere—are appended to a structure controlled by American (and European) purchasing power and dominated by its autonomous cyclical fluctuations. For the Asian economies, far from being developed by the colonial rulers, were organized by them to provide Western industries with raw materials, which sell in periods of prosperity and rot in adverse conditions and bring the producers an income or no income depending on whether there are a few per cent more or less of purchasing power spent in that market by America. Such is the unbalance. Every change in Western tastes or economic policies or military plans throws the national economies of allegedly sovereign nations in all parts of the world out of gear. So long as they must remain spectators—and possibly victims—as America takes counsel with herself which course of economic policy to choose in the interest of America, the much vaunted partnership of free nations is a mockery.

These facts are quite well known in themselves. But they are not usually interpreted in the light of the principle from which they derive—that of letting things economic take their course without direction, of even denying that there is in them an inherent direction, these being purely private decisions made in freedom, and of letting everybody make his further decisions in equal freedom. Karl Marx uncovered the hidden power structure disguised as private freedom, but he was not the first to do it and not the most successful because of the narrowness of his concept of social class. As early as the 1830's, Frederick List, pupil of Alexander Hamilton and champion in public discussion of American and German industrial emancipation from British supremacy, made exactly the point that the Asians make against us today with still more right. In an unbalanced international system, the free market produces the unbreakable preponderance of the developed and strong nations over the undeveloped and weak. In the case of America and Germany the simple answer to the problem was tariff protection to secure for the infant industries their domestic market; nothing more was needed because the intellectual, social, governmental, and financial prerequisites of industrialization were given or could easily be had. Meanwhile industrialism has achieved a fantastic advance, and the Asian nations, on the other hand, are not only relatively but absolutely far below the industrial qualifications attained by America and Germany in the early nineteenth century. Hence Hamilton's and List's solution is far too simple for our present problem: no Asian tariffs, however necessary in themselves, would secure or steady the export markets of Asian raw materials in America and Europe. This clearly demands partnership and mutuality rather than the dictation which is not even aware of dictating anything.[17]

In other words, the reawakening of social responsibility and justice has not yet arrived at the most difficult part of its present assignment. The undisputed merits of the free market—discussed in Chapter IX—presuppose a balanced social structure and a somewhat even distribution of industries, each sustaining the other in the national division of labor. But no social and economic balance exists in the international economic system, and its Asian sections have no national economic system of their own but live as mere appendages of the balanced national sections in America and Europe. Nay, the free market, which has created this structure, has frozen it and can do nothing but perpetuate it. Social responsibility must set deliberate goals as a framework within which economic activities can move, and statesmanlike wisdom should recognize the catastrophic explosion that must be the logical end unless it be transcended in that act of creative freedom for which the nations of the world are desperately hoping.

Second Note on the World Congress of Churches at Evanston

William Adams Brown, Jr., in "Some International Implications of Christian Economic Ethics" (in the above-mentioned volume *Christian Values and Economic Life*, New York, 1954) gives a survey of this complicated moral problem which the

17. Once more we wish to refer to Edgar Salin's fundamental critique of neo-liberalism. It is no accident that in economic policy he derives from List and is thereby superior to the critics deriving from Marx. The latter argue in terms of economic classes and are forced, in world economic discussion, to consider the underdeveloped countries as proletarians of white capitalism, which is incorrect in the first place (cf. *Economic Systems and Social Systems,* Chapter VII) and in the second place casts a strange light on Indian nabobs and Western proletarians. List and Salin, however, think in terms of political units, which as such are subjects or objects of a political will. The failure to understand the political element—reducing it to the social and economic element—blinds Marxism again to the political problems of its own setup—i.e., to the abuse of power.

rich and powerful United States has to solve in its commercial and financial deals with weaker countries, but almost more in its plans for aid and subventions to them. The essay is excellent in presentation, conscientious in evaluation, and frank in utterance. The sole objection concerns the title, which does not provide what it promises; the author himself says this toward the end in so many words. What he gives is an analysis of American business policy within the framework of the existing international structure—which does not preclude the possibility that many of the measures discussed will tend to rebuild this structure piecemeal. But what he does not give, and does not intend to give, is a fundamental analysis of the structure as a whole and of the necessity of a planned reconstruction. Nothing would warrant the assumption that the author would be disinclined to a fundamental discussion of the world economy and its long-range requirements. But so far anyway the gap is wide open; in this entire series consisting of six volumes (series on the *Ethics and Economics of Society,* edited by the National Council of Churches of Christ in America) one will not find a single reference to it.

Still more surprising, however, is the same gap in the decisions of the World Congress of Churches in Evanston, in August, 1954. In addition to the decision on the responsible society, discussed in the preceding chapter, the decision on international relations would have offered an urgent opportunity for a statement. There were in attendance in Evanston more than 1200 official delegates and representatives of 132 Protestant and Orthodox church communities from 60 countries assembled in serious work during seventeen days in order to emphasize, across and above political and ecclesiastical boundaries, the unity of their faith and the community of their resulting responsibility. Among them there were for the first time a large number of representatives of Asian and African churches, and they were prominent participants in the discussion.

The report on international relations, for all its intelligent and thoughtful remarks, holds too narrowly to the framework of problems dealt with by the United Nations to be able to advance beyond them. The report recommends a multiplication

of technical aid programs and facilitation of international com-
modity exchange—that is all. The report on "The Responsible
Society in World Perspective"—already characterized—says
that "Christians have the duty of calling the attention of governments to the fact that national economic policy affects the
life and welfare of other nations. . . . Excessive impediments
to commerce may produce economic crises elsewhere. The
greater the economic power, the greater the responsibility in this
field. In particular the richest countries should be aware that
one of the tests for the judgment on their policy will be the
effect on the underdeveloped areas." Furthermore, one of the
principal sections bears the title "The Problem in the Underdeveloped Areas"—*nota bene,* "in" these areas, not between
them and the developed areas. This section limits itself to sum-
marizing the valuable results of a study conference in Lucknow,
India, in December, 1953, which had recommended "to regard
certain problems as world problems," namely, "the development
of political institutions"—i.e., of efficient and humane-minded
governments; also agrarian reform and rural development, industrial development, population, political independence, and
finally the responsibility of interdependence. Under this last
heading it is said: "A number of countries have achieved national freedom and full sovereignty after a colonial period. But
they find it difficult to adjust themselves to an international
situation where the political and economic sovereignty particularly of the weaker nations is necessarily limited by the
facts of mutual dependence." This proposition is the opposite
of the truth. The problem is their one-sided dependence, the
complete absence of economic sovereignty. And nothing else is
being said.

Why do we subject only the utterances of the World Congress of Churches to such a detailed critique? Because it is the
sole agency of which a far-ringing message of hope and leadership could have been expected. For here alone is there a body
which can organize tremendous international manifestations
and which, by virtue of the combination of its international
composition with its supranational objective, commands the
necessary scope and can keep the necessary distance from politi-

cal and financial interests. In this Congress alone a person speaks, in the first instance, not as a representative of limited interests but as one who wrestles with his responsibility before God. Had the World Christian Congress made the reconstruction of the world economy its own cause, as it had earlier made social reform its own cause, its authority would have increased and the overdue reconstruction of the world economy would have come a little nearer. So far, nobody else has done this. That is why the frustration of this hope is a great calamity.

Naturally the World Council of Churches would not be, or would no longer be, the most fitting agency for such an initiative if the problem already permitted concrete attempts at a solution. But so far nobody can say anything concrete because everything is still obscure. The first task is to create a climate in which it becomes possible to understand the problem which even the World Council has misunderstood, so that the world conscience can be mobilized. For without a powerful word of the world conscience a concrete discussion urging a solution certainly cannot take place, nor can a practicable solution be found. Discussion, first of all, ascertains what is possible and what is not. "Possibility" in this context does not mean technical possibility; there is no possibility in this sense for the time being because the "necessities" of our terminology crush them. "Possibility" is creative possibility, and it arises under the pressure of the world conscience, just as England's friendly withdrawal from India after three hundred years of "impossibility" became possible and real under the pressure of the British—and the world—conscience, and exactly as the gradual emancipation of the Negroes in the United States became possible in a corresponding way.

The Schuman Plan

France's contribution to the change of climate in Western life is the Schuman Plan, brilliantly conceived and forcefully inaugurated by Jean Monnet, and rightly named for Robert Schuman, whose moral authority steered it safely through the cliffs of French and international politics. The plan gave rise to a strong organizational nucleus of common material interests in Europe, in defiance of all time-honored notions of national sovereignty and national interests, under the management of a group of men who, according to the constitution, owe responsibility exclusively to "Europe," but in no wise to the diverse national governments of their respective countries. The United States could not have suggested this, and Great Britain felt too much bound to the world-wide Commonwealth to join an organization "European" in a higher sense. But it is in the interest of all believers in the "Third Force" to have at their disposal a nucleus for further growth, in precise parallel to the stimulus applied by the Marshall Plan.

The Schuman Plan belongs in the general picture of Western renewal because it positively overcomes the time-honored idea of international unification by imperial power and replaces it by evenly cutting all rights of national sovereignty in favor of a nucleus of supranational power. The fact that the partners in this new enterprise had been adversaries in the most terrible war and that the offer came from the finally victorious side gives the Schuman Plan the character of that farsighted wisdom which aims at reconciliation. More encouraging than the plan itself is the European enthusiasm, the European patriotism from which it springs, which it helps to strengthen, and which has kindled the imagination of vigorous youth groups in Germany as well as in France and has captivated some of the strongest minds in European public life.[18]

18. This momentum of pro-European enthusiasm has asserted itself, since the publication of the German edition of this book in 1955, in surprising and increasingly important innovations and has thus more than made up for the setbacks of the movement, which were discussed at some length in the German edition in connection with France's political and international weakness.

Conclusion

TRULY, the West in these days does not lack fertile ideas and courageous projects by which long-cherished prejudices and deep-rooted wrongs may be undone. But it does not follow that the preservation of the West through its renewal is secure. That deep-rooted wrong has been tolerated long enough to make the critic, communism, the terrible menace that it is. Its Messianic faith in human rationality cannot permit itself any inhibitions or laxities in the attempt to undermine the West's life. The most general problem of Western strategy concerns the necessary volume and the necessary limitations of the armaments designed to preclude war. Particularly at a time when industrial progress is the most important weapon, there cannot be absolute security, and therefore the responsible experts will always strive for a maximum. But the greater the advantage, the greater also the temptations of a moral and political nature. During several precious years America has concentrated the main weight of its expenses and attention on armaments and on military alliances, and has thereby bared the international social and spiritual front to the attack. The author is not competent to judge how the minimum requirements of the two fronts are to be reconciled. The subject matter of this book is the spiritual and social requirements.

The spiritual weakness of the West was the main subject of our analysis, and we developed it backward from the ensuing social weakness. The spiritual weakness is not, to any appreciable extent, a weakness of individual morality; it is, to a perilously large extent, a misguidance of spiritual efforts. The same claim to rational autonomy which finds its most radical culmination in Marxism has fearfully weakened the fertility of Western academic life—for centuries the source of ever new creative ideas—because, strictly speaking, "creative ideas" are considered in that system of thought unscientific, logically impossible. It is not the concrete material of the unique situation which is being studied, but the ascertained regularity or the various combinations of the same regularities. If this is taken as the heart of the matter, it follows either that one keeps strictly to the position and leaves it at that—this is the proper logical inference—or that one adds to the driving factors in such a way as to direct the regular processes to a desired end. Liberty alone cannot be that desired end, because the end is to be attained by control of human behavior and is the easier to attain the less people think of their liberty.

The natural end of aspirations based on regularity and homogeneity can be, at the very best, a universally valid end but no concrete solution of concrete problems: not the Marshall or Schuman Plan or organization of Indian liberty or reconstruction of the world market—ends far too small for scientific ambition—but eternal peace and peace of mind. For once these are achieved, there is no more necessity for those and their like. We do not say that all those who use those methods think this way; we say that if they do not think this way they are not logical. And that the Messianic ambition of those methods necessarily misses that which is possible and necessary here and now because it can understand it only as part of the general but has no access to the concrete, individual, and singular. Social security, of which the West boasts, has been conceived and worked out in the last century in the cooperation of many professors from different fields, at a time when the social and cultural sciences still preserved the Christian inheritance of the university and in addition were under the spell of the historical method, which—whatever its shortcoming—impressed them with the sense of the uniqueness of the historical situation and of the belonging together of the single researches. Contrariwise, not a single professor has left his mark on the great international ideas and decisions of the last years. This should put the social sciences to shame—the empirical proof of their barrenness should suffice.

It is the theologians—in the widest sense, including the Christian historians—from whom the great impulses flow into this time, as they receive their impulses from the time. One cannot prove this influence in the individual case; there are no direct connections, they did not personally contribute toward the great decisions, they are no experts. But the change of spiritual climate needs no proof. The great achievement of the Christian thinkers lies in having made inspiration possible once more by unfolding the width of the Christian doctrine and sounding its depth—that is, they have unfolded the width and depth of life and have appealed to the power of renewal. The more all the new ideas in public and international life run counter to scientific regularities, the more they bear witness to the newly retrieved Christian freedom of responsible decision.

The responsible decision is that for the "Third Force," as it first grew up in the more recent political and social contributions of the Western countries and then, under the dual threat of the totalitarian systems, sprang over to international relations. Its principles are personal freedom and social justice, where freedom represents the dignity of the person and justice the dignity of the community. The mere side-by-side position of the two is inadequate, naturally; they overlap because justice owes the person, among other things, his freedom, and freedom frustrates itself unless it is curbed and limited by justice so as to be general personal freedom. If the relationship is construed in this manner, then justice, in other words, presents itself as the supreme social and international principle (and has thus been described in *Freedom and Order*).

Now justice is a Christian principle, contained in love because love is love between persons who for the sake of love want to be fair to each other; without love, justice can indeed institute delimitation but not reconciliation, harmony, and life. On a social scale, justice has an institutional dimension, since it has become clear again that the individual soul, far from being the only determining force in society, is in turn largely formed (or deformed) by the forces and institutions of society. Christian justice must be realized, ever and ever anew, in the institutions of society.

At the same time democracy has begun to understand that the freedom of the person can never be an automatic by-product of private property or of class war; that it never can be secured by social forces or institutions; that likewise progress cannot be counted upon if it is to mean more than material growth, namely moral growth; and that, hence, a spiritual effort is required to lift liberty above the vicissitudes of institutional changes to a higher plane and anchor it in this plane. In other words, it becomes more and more clear that the liberty and dignity of the person are secure only in a Christian atmosphere, where they flow straight from the supreme principle; and that, on the other hand, justice can be realized only by institutions of social democracy in the centers of modern industrial life. It is this merger of the two elements which we have called the Third Force because it is not located as a mediator halfway between other institutional systems but has a higher spiritual principle.

The two original forces joined therein supplement each other but do not stand on the same plane. Christianity and social democracy do not stand side by side. Christianity stands higher and is, for this very reason, in constant danger of not penetrating to the lower, material, institutional strata in which the supreme principles must be incorporated if they are to become reality. Social democracy on its plane, the material-institutional one, is in danger of losing sight of the spiritual necessities which alone can justify institutional changes. The merger of liberty and justice is not a merger of Christianity and democracy; it is the reconstruction of human life on the two planes of spirituality and materiality, after a period of bodiless spirituality and soulless materiality. For man lives on both planes, and democracy too must live on both.

Indexes

Subject Index

Index of Persons

Epicurus, 21
Eucken, W., 253

Fetscher, I., 143
Feuerbach, L., 154
Finer, H., 256
Flitner, W., 68
Forell, G. W., 297
Freud, S., viii, 75
Friedrich, C. J., 234, 270

Galbraith, J. K., 261, 263
Ghandi, M., 311
Goethe, J. W., 161
Gollwitzer, H., 224, 303
Gregory I, 13
Gregory VII, 13, 179
Gumplovicz, L., 40

Hahn, O., 57
Hamilton, A., 188, 218–219, 317
Handel, G. F., 289
Harnack, A., 297
Harrington, J., 126, 280
Hayek, F. A., 28, 32, 120, 253, 256, 257
Hegel, G. W. F., 29, 43, 66, 67, 98, 104, 108, 120, 121, 125, 129, 135, 147, 157, 159, 162, 189, 201, 203, 204, 304
Heisenberg, W., 69
Hildebrand, *see* Gregory VII
Hilferding, R., 150, 161
Hitler, A., 171, 256, 276, 277
Hobbes, T., 21
Hocking, W. E., 68
Hoffmann, P., 300
Hook, S., 205
Hromadka, J. L., 169, 224
Hume, D., 215
Hutcheson, F., 216
Hutchison, J. A., 125
Huxley, J., 71

Innocent III, 179
Isaiah, 222
Ivan IV, 183
Iwand, H. J., 211

DATE DUE

Lewis and Clark College - Watzek Library
HX536 .H39   wmain
Heimann, Eduard/Reason and faith in mode

3 5209 00423 4254